Economics for Hot
Catering Students

The English Language Book Society is funded by the Overseas Development Administration of the British Government. It makes available low-priced, unabridged editions of British publishers' textbooks to students in developing countries. Below is a list of some other books on hotels, catering and tourism published under the ELBS imprint.

Branson and Lennox
Hotel, Hostel and Hospital Housekeeping
Edward Arnold

Burkart and Medlik
Tourism: Past, Present and Future
Heinemann Professional

Davis and Stone
Food and Beverage Management
Heinemann Professional

Kinton and Ceserani
The Theory of Catering
Edward Arnold

Lillicrap
Food and Beverage Service
Edward Arnold

Paige and Paige
The Hotel Receptionist
Cassell

Sutton
Financial Management in Hotel and Catering Operations
Heinemann Professional

Venison
Managing Hotels
Heinemann Professional

Economics for Hotel and Catering Students

HOWARD L. HUGHES

Principal Lecturer in Economics, Department of Hotel, Catering and Institutional Management, Manchester Polytechnic

ELBS

English Language Book Society/Hutchinson

Hutchinson & Co. (Publishers) Ltd
62–65 Chandos Place, London WC2N 4NW

First published 1986

ELBS edition first published 1988

ISBN 0 09 172906 8

Printed and bound in Great Britain by
Courier International Ltd, Tiptree, Essex

Contents

Preface

Many economics textbooks start with a reference to the inadequacy of existing textbooks for the author's purposes. I make no apology for offering exactly the same reason for writing this one. Over several years of lecturing to students on hotel and catering management courses, I have felt that current books are not appropriate. What is the starting-point for this belief?

Students on hotel and catering management courses are usually highly motivated towards a career in that industry; they often see their courses as vocational and not always as educational experiences. They have not come on such a course with the primary intention of studying economics and may regard it as a 'necessary burden'. They may not always see it as being as relevant to their future careers as, say, law or accountancy. In the process of attempting to demonstrate relevance and stimulate interest, a lecturer may find that the economics input becomes 'watered down'.

It is not an easy task to develop an economics input which combines the essential strengths of economics and the unity of the subject with meeting the demands of students. At the heart of the problem is the need to provide a meaningful and significant economics input on a highly vocational course.

I am certain that economics should be an input to such courses since it can:

- Create an awareness and understanding of the economic environment within which all organizations operate.
- Create an awareness and understanding of the interactions between that environment and the organization.
- Introduce the methodology and those concepts of economics that may be pertinent for problem-solving and decision-making in organizations.

The traditional economics course is not particularly appropriate, however, for the education of future managers (regardless of the perceptions of the students themselves). Much of a conventional economics course is fascinating and intellectually stimulating in its own right and is valuable in developing certain 'higher-order' abilities. It may, though, be too abstract, theoretical or remote to be of much direct managerial use.

Industrial economics has some attractions in that it discards much traditional model-building, and emphasizes observation of reality. It is more likely to deal with 'what is' rather than 'what ought to be' and therefore might be appropriate for such vocational courses. But a 'pure' industrial economics course is not necessarily any more appropriate than is a 'pure' conventional course because much of the empirical work undertaken may not be of direct relevance to potential management either.

Another possibility is to move towards an economic study of the hotel and catering industry. A major difficulty is that the industry has not been subject to economic analysis of a nature or on a scale sufficient to write about 'the economics of the hotel and catering industry'. Such an input could therefore become descriptive and a catalogue of technical factors to the exclusion of economics.

If it were possible to present an input of 'the economics of the hotel and catering industry', it is arguable whether even that could provide an adequate economics education. It could, in isolation, present a distorted view; it would be easy to lose sight of the 'whole' economic picture and to fail to view the industry in context.

The industry should, however, form some part of the economics input. A study of the industry should generate interest in the student and demonstrate relevance.

It would seem that the best way forward, at present, is to adopt an amalgam of conventional micro-economics, industrial economics and the hotel and catering industry. The hotel and catering industry will not be the main focus of study but should be introduced as and when appropriate. This is the basis of this book.

There has been here at the polytechnic, and at other centres of hotel and catering studies, a continuous examination of economics, and of its structure, content and approach. It would be a foolish person who could claim that this process could now cease; this book represents only the latest stage of my thinking and I have no doubt that within a year or two I would have written something different.

I have, in this book, been selective in what I have included. Generally I have used the 'need to know' criterion in deciding what to include; I have interpreted that 'need to know' in a sense that goes beyond the immediate 'demands' of hotel and catering students to those wider issues which might be desirable in the *education* of future policy-makers. The selectivity may give rise to some lack of cohesiveness but I hope the benefits will outweigh any problems.

There are omissions compared with a conventional economics textbook (e.g. indifference curves, isoquants, etc.) and there are some concepts and theories which are only lightly touched on. Conversely, there are certain parts of this book which may not be touched on in conventional books (e.g. development of tertiary sectors) and parts which expand on what might be found in conventional books.

I have tried to avoid theories for their own sake, unnecessary jargon and complex model-building. I believe economists have often succeeded in surrounding the subject with a mystique that needs to be stripped away. There is always a temptation to avoid economic theory completely but it is important that students appreciate the theoretical underpinnings of 'the real world'. It is impossible to fully comprehend the complexities of reality without recourse to a theoretical framework.

I have also kept away from descriptive detail in the belief that principles and theories can be enduring whereas description is not. This book is certainly not a description of the hotel and catering industry. The book may appear to some to be too theoretical but students should find it less abstract than many conventional economics textbooks and at the same time more applicable to their industry.

Where the hotel and catering industry has been introduced in the text, I have usually confined my consideration to the 'commercial' sector and within that to accommodation and catering. Welfare and industrial catering and pubs and clubs are covered only briefly in this book.

The economics framework adopted is one that can be applied to other industries and this should facilitate interindustry comparison and set the industry in context. As noted earlier, there is a dearth of economic studies of the industry and the book is, in this sense, clearly not complete. Many of the relationships and activities identified here could form the basis for future empirical work within the industry. At this stage, however, in several parts of this book, it cannot be claimed that there is more than a juxtaposition of theory and conjecture about what happens in the hotel and catering industry. Much more needs to be done if the industry is to be analysed from an economic perspective.

The book, then, is not a book about the hotel and catering industry or its economic aspects, nor is it a conventional economics textbook. It is an economics book for students on hotel and catering management courses.

In particular, it should meet the needs of students on BTEC higher national diploma courses (Structure and Resources units), those studying for 'the Industry' paper of the HCIMA, students on hotel and catering degree courses and those on post-graduate hotel and catering courses. The input of economics is relatively minor on such courses and it is envisaged that the book would be the basis of a 60–90 hour module. With some judicious selection, the book could also be useful to students on diploma courses.

No prior economic knowledge is assumed, though a lecturer is entitled to expect that such students will have some degree of familiarity with current economic events. I have deliberately avoided recourse to mathematical representations of economic relationships as I have never been convinced that it assists the average student to understand economics.

This book has tried to steer clear of those aspects of hotel and catering which are rightly the concern of others – such as marketing, operational research or accountancy. I have tried to concentrate only on the contribution that economics can make. If students succeed in recognizing that other subjects they study have equal or more important contributions to make to particular topics, so much the better.

I have not, either, considered macro-economics at any length. This is not because I believe that it is of little significance but because I believe there is 'no need to know' the fine detail. A detailed study of macro-economics, even at the level encountered in most basic economics textbooks, may be more than is necessary. If lecturers feel otherwise, there are many fine textbooks that can serve.

H. L. Hughes

Preface to revised edition

This revision is no more than an update of statistical information and government policies. Not all of the data in the 1986 edition could be updated, in fact, and most of the revisions relate to general economic matters rather than to the hotel and catering industry. Additionally, some information has had to be obtained from sources other than those used for the 1986 edition; there is often, therefore, some inconsistency between that earlier information and that presented here. There are occasional inconsistencies even where the same sources have been available, usually because of subsequent revisions to data.

No attempt has been made to alter the basic concept of the book nor to incorporate any recent related research.

H. L. Hughes

Acknowledgements

The book is an eclectic one and I must acknowledge my debt to many authors. The sources cited in footnotes and elsewhere will indicate the extent of this debt.

In particular, I must acknowledge that *Profile of the Hotel and Catering Industry* by S. Medlik (with D. W. Airey) has been a starting-point for much of what I have written. On the economics side, my greatest debt is to R. G. Lipsey's *An Introduction to Positive Economics* and to A. R. Prest and D. J. Coppock's *The UK Economy: A Manual of Applied Economics*; both were in their first edition when I was an undergraduate and I am very much their product. The contribution of *An Introduction to Industrial Economics* by P. J. Devine *et al.* has been significant more recently.

On a more personal level I gladly recognize the contribution made to this work by my colleagues – Gary Akehurst, Stuart Horsburgh, Anne Minter, Graham Stone and the late Jack Clare. They have all helped me in many ways, especially by discussing the different approaches to hotel and catering economics.

Students who have endured my experimentation in approach and content over the years deserve a special commendation. They have patiently tolerated and humoured me and even, on occasion, allowed me to believe I was making a valuable contribution to their education.

The library staff at the Hollings site of the polytechnic have been invaluable. Led by Lynn Elliott, they have always been courteous and co-operative; without their willing and cheerful assistance the work would have taken a great deal longer to complete.

My special thanks to Madeleine Barry for turning the most appalling scrawl into her usual impeccable typescript.

Finally, in the true tradition of authors, I reserve most thanks for my wife, Marion, and children, Andrew and Claire, each of whom would like to become more regular customers of the hotel and catering industry. They have inspired and encouraged throughout, as well as served to remind me that there is more to life than economics.

All errors, omissions and misjudgements in the book are, of course, my responsibility entirely. I hope that students and lecturers will not hesitate to bring them to my notice at the earliest opportunity.

CHAPTER 1

Industry

Services

Economics is often considered to be concerned with a study of the way in which individuals, organizations and countries seek to overcome the problem of 'scarcity'.[1*] There are not enough resources available to satisfy the wants of everyone, whether that availability is judged at the level of the individual or of the world as a whole. Those resources which are available to be used in satisfying wants are generally classified as:

1 *Land:* all of the natural resources such as coal, iron ore, fish, water, as well as the land itself and all that grows on it.

2 *Labour:* all human resources, whether skilled or unskilled.

3 *Capital:* all man-made resources in the form of physical assets such as factories, shops, hotels, restaurants, machines, tools, etc.

In addition, a fourth category is sometimes identified, namely 'enterprise'; this is the resource that is considered to take the initiative in bringing together the other resources. It may usefully be included under 'labour'.

However classified, such resources are required in varying forms and proportions if wants are to be satisfied; collectively they are known as 'factors of production'. There is at any one time a fixed quantity of these factors which can be used to satisfy wants, but there are an apparently unlimited number of demands upon these factors. Somehow these unlimited wants and the limited factors have to be reconciled. The economic problem is thus basically one of allocating the scarce resources between competing demands. All wants cannot be satisfied at the same time and choice is necessary:

1 Which goods and services are to be produced and thus which wants satisfied?
2 How are these goods and services to be produced, out of the wide range of technically possible means of production?
3 Who is to receive the goods and services once they are produced?

* References and notes are collected in a section beginning on page 222.

Since resources are so scarce, it is essential that the best possible use is made of them so that maximum satisfaction is obtained; i.e. the allocation of resources needs to be 'optimal'.[2] (See also Chapter 2.)

Basically there are two ways in which an economy might seek to attain this 'optimal resource allocation'. It may operate as a 'market' or 'free enterprise' economy where the unrestricted operation of the price mechanism allocates resources, or it may be characterized by rather more intervention and operate as a 'command' or 'planned' economy, such that some central body allocates the resources. Neither alternative exists in an extreme form in any economy and each economy is a mixture of both systems. Which one is better in terms of achieving an optimal allocation is largely a matter of personal judgement.

All economies, however, are characterized by an output of goods and services to meet wants. Ultimately production, i.e. the transformation of factors into an output, takes place to provide for the wants of the population. These wants may be satisfied by an output of goods or by an output of services. The basic difference between the two is that goods have a physical dimension and are tangible, whereas services do not have such characteristics and are 'invisible'.[3] (In practice, the distinction is not so clear-cut.)

Both goods and services can satisfy wants and they are both capable of being bought and sold. Both thus contribute to the generation of employment and of income in an economy. The fact that services are not reflected in some physical object does not detract from their 'economic worth' in any economy. There is sometimes a tendency to dismiss service producers as being 'unproductive' with the 'real' wealth being generated by the producers of goods. In economic terms, as has been seen, this is not so. Economic activity occurs through the production of goods and/or services. Wants can be met by goods and/or services and it is the fulfilment of such wants that is the objective of economic mechanisms.

Such a view does not imply any judgement about whether services are 'desirable' or 'useful' since these are matters for the individual's value judgements. For instance, the provision of luxury hotels in tourist resorts in some of the poorer countries of the world may be considered undesirable by some, though it remains an economic activity. It may be that some services are considered by some to be more 'useful' than others. Banking and insurance, transport and communications may be vital if manufacturing is to function effectively, whereas other services such as restaurants or entertainment may be less vital and rather more 'frivolous' activities. This will be returned to later when some evaluation of the 'usefulness' of hotel and catering activities in particular will be made. (See Chapter 9.)

The service economy

If any economy is examined it is apparent that its output is a mixture of both goods and services. Table 1 refers to gross domestic product (GDP) which, put simply, is a measure of the economy's output in a year. (See Chapter 8 for further discussion of this.)

Table 1 *Gross domestic product (GDP) by industry, UK, 1986*

		% of GDP at factor cost	
(a)	Agriculture, forestry and fishing	1.8	
(b)	Energy and water supply	7.5	
(c)	Manufacturing	24.3	
(d)	Construction	6.2	
(e)	Distribution, hotels and catering; repairs	14.0	60.2
(f)	Transport	4.5	
(g)	Communications	2.7	
(h)	Banking, finance, insurance, business services and leasing	15.8	
(i)	Ownership of dwellings	5.8	
(j)	Public administration, national defence and compulsory social security	7.2	
(k)	Education and health services	9.1	
(l)	Other services	6.4	
	Adjustment for financial services	−5.3	

Source: Central Statistical Office, *UK National Accounts, 1987 Edition* (HMSO 1987).

The forms of economic activity that are found in an economy can be grouped into three categories:[4]

1 Primary sector, i.e. mostly made up of agriculture, forestry, fishing.

2 Secondary sector, mostly made up of manufacturing.

3 Tertiary sector, i.e. services (categories (e)–(l) in Table 1).

The tertiary sector includes among others, transport and communications; banking and insurance; education and health; retailing and wholesaling; public administration and defence; as well as the various elements of hotels and catering.

Different studies of economies have included different activities in each of the sectors: construction is sometimes included in services, for instance, and transport and communication sometimes excluded.[5] Some of the services have been separated out into 'quaternary' and 'quinary' sectors but these terms are not widely used and all services will here be designated tertiary activities.[6]

Economies in the 'developed' world have passed through stages when different forms of economic activity have been dominant. For instance, the UK was a 'primary' economy before the Industrial Revolution of the late eighteenth and early nineteenth centuries and was dependent upon the

Table 2 *UK employees in employment by sector*

	1961	*1986*
	(% of all employees)	
Agriculture, forestry and fishing	3.2	1.5
Manufacturing	38.4	24.3
Services	46.6	67.1

Sources: Central Statistical Office, *Social Trends*, No. 14 (HMSO 1983) and *Social Trends*, No. 18 (HMSO 1988).

Table 3 *Relative importance of services and manufacturing in total output 1960–85*

	1960	*1985*
	(% of current price GDP)	
Manufacturing	36.5	25.1
Services	47.7	61.3

Source: T. Barker and P. Dunne (Eds.), *The British Economy After Oil: Manufacturing or Services*? (Croom Helm 1988).

'secondary' sector after the Industrial Revolution until it may now be considered a 'service' or tertiary economy. (The phrase 'post-industrial' society[7] is slightly misleading in the economic context, but refers to a similar emergence and dominance of services.) Currently, most developed economies are characterized by a very large proportion (if not the majority) of the labour force being employed in the tertiary sector. Well over half of the UK working population is currently employed within this sector (see Table 2). It also accounts for a very large and growing proportion of the output (GDP) of the country: 61.3 per cent of GDP in 1985 (see Table 3).

What has caused this emergence of the tertiary or service economy?

Influences on the service economy

At any one time the proportions of employment and output accounted for by the tertiary (or any other) sector in different countries will differ according to the individual characteristics of each country, but there seem to be a number of common influences that have served to bring about the service economy.

1 There is a tendency for consumer expenditure to alter in structure as changes occur in consumer incomes (in particular, real disposable income of consumers, i.e. income after deduction of income tax and national insurance and after allowance for inflation).

Table 4 shows how the relative importance of various forms of expenditure

Table 4 *Pattern of household expenditure 1960–86*

	1960	*1970*	*1980*	*1986*
	(each category as % of total expenditure)			
Housing	9.3	12.6	15.0	16.8
Fuel, light and power	5.9	6.3	5.6	5.9
Food	30.5	25.7	22.7	19.6
Alcoholic drink	3.2	4.5	4.8	4.6
Tobacco	5.9	4.8	3.0	2.6
Clothing and footwear	10.3	9.2	8.1	7.5
Durable household goods	6.3	6.5	7.0	7.8
Other goods	7.1	7.4	7.9	7.8
Transport and vehicles	12.2	13.7	14.6	14.3
Services	8.9	9.0	10.8	12.7
Miscellaneous	0.4	0.3	0.5	0.4
	100.0	100.0	100.0	100.0

Source: Department of Employment, *Family Expenditure Survey 1986* (revised) (HMSO 1988).

has changed over a twenty-two-year period. Housing, durable household goods (TVs, cameras, washing machines, etc.), transport and vehicles, and services, in particular, have risen in importance, whereas food, tobacco and clothing and footwear have shown a particular fall in importance. This does not mean that consumers have spent less on these categories but rather that the rate of growth of expenditure on them has not kept up with the growth of expenditure on other items – and therefore their relative importance falls.

As consumers become better off and able to purchase more goods and services, the pattern of consumer expenditure usually alters. The proportion of expenditure or income spent on food, for instance, usually diminishes (from 30.5 per cent in 1960 to 19.6 per cent in 1986, see Table 4) and gradually services begin to emerge as significant items of expenditure. New, higher-level wants, perhaps non-essential, can be satisfied. The consumer is no longer preoccupied with basic nourishment and shelter and new demands emerge. (Whether these new demands arise 'naturally' within the individual or are originated by the producers themselves is arguable.)

It is noticeable though, in most studies of the industrial structure of economies,[8] measured in terms of contribution to output, that there is a common tendency towards a reduction in the importance of the primary sector, a rise in the relative size of secondary activities and an initial but *not continuing*, rise in the importance of the tertiary sector. There seems eventually to be a flattening-out of the share of tertiary activities in total output.

Consumer expenditure, after a certain point, shows a continuing and similar rate of increase in the demand for *both* goods and services, without the demand for the former falling relative to the demand for services. In developed economies there is a continuing growth of demand for goods of all sorts (especially 'durable goods' and 'transport and vehicles') and the demand overall does not seem satiable. Some goods and services are in joint demand, e.g. the demand for holidays and the demand for buckets and spades. In addition, many goods and services are still, in effect, substitutes for each other, and as incomes rise it is quite possible that consumers will switch between goods and services as, for instance, their relative prices change. If services generally become relatively expensive because of their high labour content there may be a shift to relatively cheaper goods to satisfy consumer wants. New goods may appear which can satisfy these consumer wants previously satisfied by services, e.g. television to replace cinema.

Although increases in income have undoubtedly led to changes in the pattern of output, there is little to suggest that there is, in terms of output of the economy at least, a *continuing* shift away from the secondary sector towards the tertiary sectors.

Many services are not purchased directly by consumers but are provided for manufacturing and other firms, and most service firms use or distribute the products of manufacturing. Because of this interdependence and the continuing demand for manufactured goods, there is no reason to expect growth of service sector output at the expense of manufacturing.[9]

2 The growth of service employment is further explained by this interdependence with manufacturing. As the production and consumption of goods has increased, so, too, has the need to expand the services of public utilities (gas, electricity and water), transport, distribution (shops and wholesalers) and the like. These 'producer' services were probably earlier and more important sources of service employment than were the 'consumer' services (especially recreation and leisure) that are demanded as incomes grow. Most service industries provide services to both producers and consumers; over half the people employed in service occupations provide services not to consumers but to other industries.

Because many service jobs are in the manufacturing sector, reference to service *industries* will understate the full extent of service *employment*.

Apart from those people employed in service occupations within manufacturing, manufacturing also uses the services of people employed in separate service firms. These would obviously be identifiable as 'services', whether industries or employment was taken as the reference point.

Over time, it is likely that those 'separate' firms serving the needs of manufacturing and other industries will increase in relative importance. As economies grow, it becomes economical for separate organizations to develop in order to perform functions previously performed by producers (and consumers) themselves, e.g. legal and financial firms; hairdressers and cleaners. At the early stages of economic development there would not be sufficient work for 'external' and separate service specialists to perform. Specialist service firms may be able to provide a more effective and cheaper service to a number of organizations or individuals than each organization or individual could provide for itself.

Many of these services may be provided for manufacturing firms which 'buy in' the specialist knowledge and expertise. Additionally, the very complexity of modern life has encouraged the growth of such specialists. The depth and breadth of knowledge is so great that no one organization or individual can possess it all. Thus specialist service firms are at an advantage in being able to provide expertise not normally available to others.

3 A further important influence upon the development of the service economy may be the opportunity to improve 'productivity'. (This may be taken to refer to the value of the output per person employed.) In the case of the primary sector, much of the increased demand for the products has been met without the need for a proportionate increase in employment of manpower; the output per person employed, or productivity, has increased largely because of the substitution of capital for labour. A similar situation has existed in the secondary sector.

In the tertiary sector, however, it may be rather more difficult, because of the nature of services, to increase labour productivity.[10] Services tend to be labour-intensive and in many cases labour is difficult to replace by capital. This is not true of all services, of course, e.g. the replacement of some hotel room services by room drink dispensers. Technology is being increasingly applied to service occupations.

Thus there has been a 'displacement' of labour from the primary and secondary sectors, whereas the growth of the tertiary sector may only be possible through a growth in employment in services. Productivity may tend to grow faster in manufacturing and agriculture than in services; thus even without differences in the growth of demand for goods and services, there would be differences in the growth of employment in each sector. There is a tendency for the share of tertiary employment to rise in most advanced economies, at the expense of the employment share accounted for by the primary and secondary sectors. (Compare this with the relative shares of each in total output.)

4 Other influences have included the awareness and demands of developed economies for the provision of health and educational services for the population. Such economies are usually also wealthy enough to provide these services. Changes in the size and age structure of the population have also had an impact.

The complex workings of developed economies may also have given rise to a need for local and central government in order to manage those complexities.

Political decisions about the role of government in the economy and society will influence the size of the public service sector. A large part of the growth in service sector employment during the 1960s and early 1970s was in the public sector.[11]

5 The process of 'de-industrialization' may provide some short-term explanation. Since the mid-1970s, concern has been expressed in the UK about a contraction of the manufacturing sector, especially in terms of the fall of employment in manufacturing.[12] This is rather different from the situation discussed so far, which was an increase in both manufacturing and services employment, though the growth occurred at different rates so that the relative importance of each altered. If, however, manufacturing employment falls in absolute terms, but service employment does not, then the relative importance of services will also rise. This 'de-industrialization' may be a reflection of, for instance, the failure of British manufacturing to compete internationally, or of an increased government demand for available resources.

The five influences above have probably been the most important in the emergence of the service economy, though other factors such as leisure time, transport developments, and technological breakthroughs have also had an effect.

Economic development[13]

Economies are constantly changing and developing their patterns of production to meet consumer wants. The pattern of production of any one economy is unlikely to be the same from one year to the next, and at any one point of time, no two countries are likely to have the same pattern of production. In addition, no two countries are likely to develop in identical ways.

A dominant service sector is, however, characteristic of the later stages of development of economies. The less developed economies of the world do not usually have a large proportion of employment in, or output derived from, the tertiary sector. (See Table 5 and also the changes apparent in the UK, indicated in Tables 2 and 3.)

The stage and rate of development of a country are the results of many complex influences. Certain of these influences may be identified separately, but it is, in practice, difficult to isolate the influence of each upon an economy. Each is closely interrelated and interacts with the others to determine the long-term growth or development of any economy.

Growth of output will be the net effect of two broadly-defined changes:

1 Changes in the productive capacity of the economy.
2 Changes in the utilization of that productive capacity.

In the long term, the first influence has a decisive effect upon growth. The ability of an economy to produce goods and services is limited by its 'productive capacity' which in turn is determined by both the quantity and quality of the resources, land, labour and capital, it has available. The productive capacity may thus be raised by increases in the availability of such resources. In addition, education and training programmes may serve to raise the 'efficiency' of labour, technological advances may improve the efficiency of machinery,

Table 5 *Variation in industrial structures with level of development*

	Predicted values at different levels of output (GNP) per head			
Sector	*Under $100*	*$500*	*$1000*	*Over $1000*
Production (% share)				
Primary	52	20	14	13
Secondary	13	29	35	38
Tertiary	35	51	51	49
Total	100	100	100	100
Employment (% share)				
Primary	71	39	25	16
Secondary	8	26	33	37
Tertiary*	21	35	42	47
Total	100	100	100	100

*Includes public utilities.

Source: H. Chenery and M. Syrquin, *Patterns of Development, 1950–1970* (OUP 1975).

and so on, and enable an economy to produce more from its existing resources. Those economies that are not able to obtain sufficient amounts of resources or that have a stock of resources of 'low quality', are unlikely to develop as rapidly as those economies well endowed with resources of high efficiency. There will be many other influences upon productive capacity, including various governmental policies, the organization of production and the extent of international trade.

Given the supply limits imposed by the productive capacity, then the level of demand within an economy will influence the actual level of economic activity, i.e. point 2 above. (See Chapter 8.)

Industry

The discussion of the service economy is based on an ability to group together economic activities into the three sectors of primary, secondary and tertiary. Such a classification is usually undertaken by identifying industries. The hotel and catering industry and other service industries are within the tertiary sector, but what exactly is an industry?

Consider first, the firm. The production of goods and services to meet wants is usually undertaken by firms. In economic terms these are the units of ownership and control and may take several legal forms, such as sole trader, partnership, private or public companies, etc. Each firm will, in turn, be made

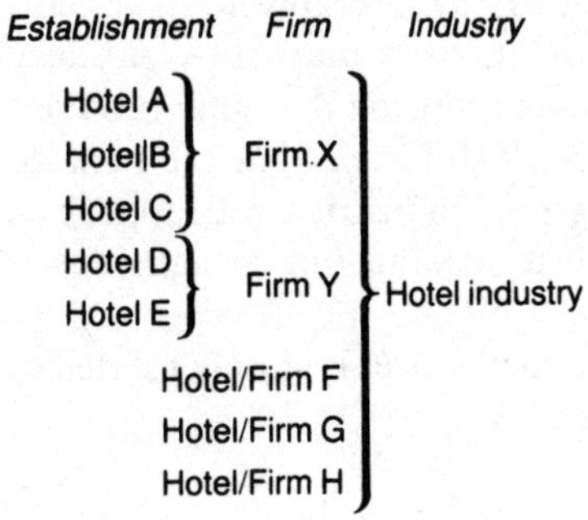

Figure 1

up of one or several establishments (or units), i.e. the unit of production – the factory, shop, hotel, café. The establishments of any one firm may be located in close proximity to each other or may be widely dispersed geographically, but will be identified as separate establishments by being located at different addresses.[14] The establishments of any one firm may also produce the same or differing goods and services. A firm may thus be a one-establishment operation producing one particular good or service, or at the other extreme, may be a multi-establishment operation producing a different good or service in each.

Firms themselves can be grouped into industries; firms which produce the same good or service may be classified as belonging to the same industry (see Figure 1).

However, because many firms produce several different goods or services, identification of an industry is difficult in practice. If a firm owns hotels and hi-fi stores, and manufactures frozen foods, to which industry is that firm to be allocated – hotels and catering, or retail distribution, or food processing?

Firms may also alter the composition of their production, moving from the production of one good or service or set of goods or services to another over time. New goods and services appear creating new industries or modifying the structure of existing ones, e.g. fast food and take-aways. A further problem arises when deciding whether two firms do, in fact, produce the same product. Is a five-star hotel in a city centre run by one firm the same product as an unclassified guest house at the seaside run by another? Is a Wimpy Bar the same product as 'Joe's Burger Joint'? Are the two in the same industry?

Governments, in their classifications of industries, tend to approach it from a wider perspective. The standard industrial classification (SIC) of the UK Government takes the establishment (unit) as the unit of analysis and classifies industries not only by reference to the similarity of the finished product (as suggested above), but also by considering the similarity of the production process and/or the raw material inputs.[15] Thus SIC industries (the basis for official published data such as Table 1) are classified by several criteria.

An establishment will be assigned to an industry by reference to its 'major' output or input. Establishments in any one SIC industry may, thus, produce many quite different products[16]; establishments producing the same products may be placed in different industries because of differences in their major activity. A firm with establishments in differrent industries will appear in several industries except where it is not possible to separate out the activities of each establishment.

The term 'industry', as used in the 'same product' sense, is closely related to the more rigorous economic concept of 'market'.

Market

A market exists, in economic terminology, where buyers and sellers of a single product are in contact with each other; a market is a grouping of *outputs* which are identical, no matter by which firm they are produced. Compare this with the discussion of industry which is concerned with grouping firms rather than grouping outputs (see Figure 2).

In Figure 2, firms A, B and C own hotels and are active in the hotel market, whereas firm A is also a paper producer and is a supplier to the paper market. Firms F, G and H assemble cars, but firm F also owns hotels and is thus in the hotel as well as the car market. Firm E from the paper industry also operates in the hotel market.

Each industry, and each firm within that industry, may thus be concerned with several markets. Originally, economists envisaged each firm as producing only one product and much economic theory is based on that assumption – and markets would therefore be identical with industries. Later discussion of the

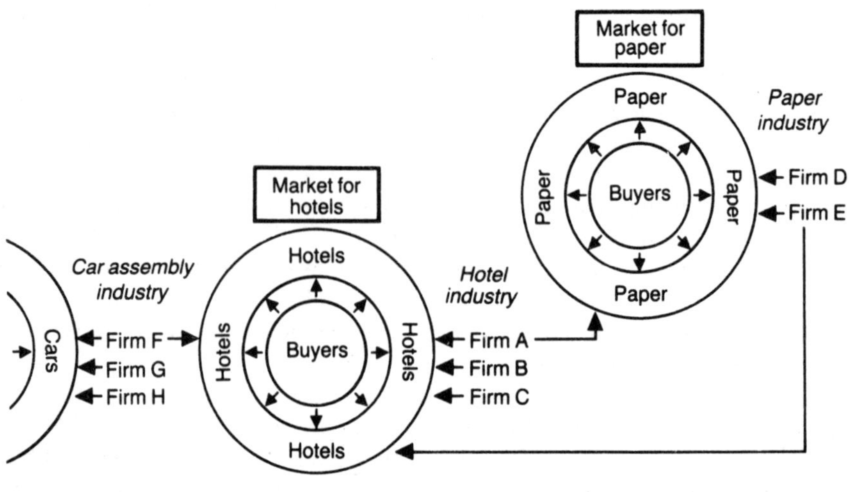

Figure 2

firm (Chapters 3 and 4) will confirm that this is not necessarily a correct assumption. Many problems identified and analysed by economists are concerned with 'markets'. In particular, a large part of economics deals with the nature of the competitive structure of a market and the consequences of that structure for the achievement of 'optimal resource allocation'. However, data is more readily available for 'industries' than for markets and these classifications need not coincide.

As with the term industry, the concept of the market is based upon an ability to identify a single product. In practice, it is very difficult to find any two firms producing exactly the same product. Thus deciding which firms to group as being one industry, or which outputs to group as being one market, can give rise to many differences of judgement and consequent differences of classification.

An approach might be to assess the substitutability by the consumers of goods or services, through cross-elasticity (see Chapter 2). Those goods or services which are highly substitutable in consumers' eyes (and have a positive cross-elasticity), may be deemed to be similar enough to be the 'same product' and thus constitute part of the same market, i.e. they compete with each other. Those outputs which are not substitutes (and have a negative cross-elasticity), are in different markets. But such an assessment of substitutability has problems of practical implementation.[17]

A single product (including close substitutes) may evidently be the output of firms in different industries. Likewise, each particular industry will contain firms which are multi-product and therefore multi-market operations. Each industry grouping will contain products which are not, therefore, identical with or close substitutes for, the main product.

The hotel and catering industry

What then is the hotel and catering industry? If it is a group of firms producing the same or similar products, what is that product? One authority has suggested that the product is 'accommodation, food and drink away from home'.[18] How does the UK Government's SIC relate to this? The SIC has altered in detail since it originated in 1948; the current version (1980) is as shown in Table 6.

Part of division 6 (distribution, hotels and catering; repairs) is Class 66 'hotels and catering' (see Table 7).

This definition differs from previous SIC classifications. For instance, the 1968 definition did not include take-aways (activity 6612) nor caravan sites (activity 6670). Thus any comparisons over periods of time of figures relating to hotels and catering in total, must be treated cautiously.

The 1980 classification does not include industrial or welfare catering, unless operated by catering contractors. Non-contractors' units dominate industrial and welfare catering (contractors' units are still numerically few[19]) and their omission could be considered to be a significant one.

Table 6 *Standard industrial classification 1980*

Division	
0	Agriculture, forestry and fishing
1	Energy and water supply industries
2	Extraction of minerals and ores other than fuels; manufacture of metals, mineral products and chemicals
3	Metal goods, engineering and vehicles industries
4	Other manufacturing industries
5	Construction
6	Distribution, hotels and catering; repairs
7	Transport and communication
8	Banking, finance, insurance, business services and leasing
9	Other services

Source: CSO, *Standard Industrial Classification – Revised Edition 1980* (HMSO 1979).

Table 7 *Class 66 – hotels and catering*

Group	*Activity*	
661		Restaurants, snack bars, cafés and other eating places
	6611	Eating places supplying food for consumption on the premises
	6612	Take-away food shops
662	6620	Public houses and bars
663	6630	Night-clubs and licensed clubs
664	6640	Canteens and messes
665	6650	Hotel trade
667	6670	Other tourist or short-stay accommodation (camping and caravan sites, holiday camps, holiday centres, conference centres, holiday houses, apartments, flats and flatlets, etc.)

Source: CSO, *Standard Industrial Classification – Revised Edition 1980* (HMSO 1979).

An industry, however, is a group of firms or organizations defined by major activity. Industrial and welfare catering, whether carried out by contractors or not, is usually only a minor activity of an organization such as a factory, office or school. If such catering is not provided by contractors, but by the organization itself (school or manufacturing firm) then its output and employment are included within that of the parent organization, e.g. the labour force of a canteen in a car factory would be allocated to employment in the car assembly industry rather than to the catering industry.

A classification of hotel and catering *occupations* or activity would clearly need to include all those in industrial and welfare catering but the hotel and catering *industry* is a concept which is more limited in its scope.

The 1980 SIC of the hotel and catering industry may be considered to be an advance upon the 1968 one in so much as the latter did not include those catering establishments which provided take-away services, nor did it include camping and caravan sites, or holiday houses, apartments, flats or flatlets. Thus, it comes closer to including all outputs which may be regarded as close substitutes and thus comprising the same product.

But are all those activities included under Class 66 'hotels and catering' really the same product? As already noted, there are some 'close substitutes' which are not included, e.g. much of industrial catering, and thus the SIC does not include all those outputs which could be considered the same or similar products.

Of the inclusions, each of the activities 6611 to 6670 provide quite different services, even though they are related – some primarily provide food, some drink and some accommodation and some provide varying combinations of any two or all three. But even within each activity the degree of 'sameness' about the outputs of the various firms depends ultimately upon consumers' judgement about the degree of substitutability between the outputs. 'Eating places', for instance, will include restaurants, snack bars and cafés, and there are obvious physical and technical differences between the establishments, their service, ethos and product, but if a consumer is indifferent between a whole range of such establishments, then they are (to him or her) completely substitutable and constitute the 'same product' – they are one market. However, if the consumers have strong preferences and some are prepared to eat in first-class restaurants and nowhere else, then competition between 'eating places' is reduced. The owners of the establishment may themselves succeed in creating within the consumer a degree of uniqueness about an establishment so that it no longer operates in the same market.

Thus, though the SIC may group together certain firms as being in the same industry, they need not be operating in the same market.

There is, however, an added dimension to 'markets' in the case of most services and hotels and catering in particular. The demand for a service in a particular location has to be met by establishments in that location; markets are thus essentially local markets, the limits of which will be defined by the willingness and ability of consumers to travel. Thus, there exists a multitude of separate markets which are defined not only by reference to the product, but also by reference to geographical area. Each market corresponds to a particular product *and* location. Any discussion of service markets and market structures must acknowledge this two-dimensional characteristic.

Table 8 *Hotel and catering firms, Great Britain, 1985*

	Number of businesses in each sector as % of all hotel and catering businesses		*Turnover of each sector as % of all hotel and catering turnover*
Restaurants, cafés, snack bars, etc. selling food for consumption on the premises only	11.3		11.4
Fish and chip shops, sandwich and snack bars and other establishments selling food partly or wholly for consumption off the premises	24.0		10.7
Public houses*	35.9		38.1
Clubs (excluding sports clubs and gaming clubs)	15.2		11.0
Catering contractors	1.3		5.2
Hotel and other residential establishments	10.8		21.0
Holiday camps, camping and holiday caravan sites	1.3		2.6
Number of businesses	117,788	Turnover (inc VAT)	£19271m

*Includes managed public houses owned by breweries in addition to businesses classified to the catering and allied trades such as tenanted and free public houses.

Source: Department of Trade and Industry, *British Business* (HMSO), 17 July 1987.

Hotel and catering sectors

The relative importance of the component parts of the industry is shown in Table 8.

These estimates are derived from inquiries by the Government's Department of Trade and Industry. The inquiries are based on the VAT register and since the smallest firms are not registered for VAT purposes it is probable that the figures underestimate, for instance, the number of unlicensed bed and breakfast boarding and guest houses.

Market structures

Each market may, in turn, be classified into one of several types of market structure, such as:

1 Perfect competition

2 Monopolistic competition

3 Oligopoly

4 Monopoly

A firm may be expected to behave in different ways according to which market structure it is believed to operate within. The term 'market structure' refers to the economically significant features of a market which *affect the behaviour* of firms supplying that market.

Which market structure a market is classified as, is determined by reference to a number of characteristics of that market:

1 Market concentration – degree of domination of the market by a few firms (or buyers).

2 Product differentiation – ability of firms to make their products appear different from others in the same industry.

3 Conditions of entry – ease of entry into an industry for a firm.

These and other characteristics are believed to influence the behaviour of firms and form the basis of market structure classification (see later discussion in Chapters 2, 3 and 4).

The greater the degree of market concentration and product differentiation and the more difficult entry is, then the more the market structure approaches a monpolistic one and the less it approaches a competitive one; the more control a firm can thus exercise in that market. Markets are likely to be more competitive where market concentration and product differentiation are low and entry easy.

Much depends upon how the markets are defined initially. Where a market is narrowly defined in terms of product and location, e.g. a 4-star hotel on the sea-front in Blackpool, there are likely to be few establishments which satisfy these requirements and they could thus be in a strong position. Where a market is widely defined, e.g. accommodation in North-West England, then there will be many establishments which operate in this market and they will be subject to a larger degree of competition than in the previous situation.

The Price Commission, when examining the share of the hotel market that Trusthouse Forte Hotels (THFH) had,[20] concluded that 'it is only when quite limited geographical areas or types of hotels are considered that THFH's market position appears at all significant', and 'on the basis of the AA star rating...we found that THFH had 50% of the available bedrooms in sixteen locations and 100% in three locations.' The Commission adopted a particularly wide definition of the market when it considered the Butlin's holiday camp operations.[21] The market was defined so as to include 'holiday camps... other types of low-cost summer holiday such as caravaning or camping...the less expensive holiday houses and hotels and... cheap holidays abroad'.

The economist is largely concerned with an analysis of markets, market structure and the consequent behaviour of firms.

Data on 'industries' does not always provide information suitable for such analysis, but it is rather more readily available to the analyst. Conclusions thus often have to be drawn from inappropriate data.

There are several definitions of the hotel and catering industry other than the SIC, such as those of the Wages Councils, HCITB and the HCEDC.[22] Each gives a different coverage of the industry from that given by the SIC and this can give rise to further complications. There is, however, no 'correct' definition of the industry; each is drawn up for a different purpose and none more closely approximates 'the market' than the SIC does.

Whatever definition is used, it is apparent that hotels and catering are part of an increasingly significant sector of the economy. Just how significant the hotel and catering industry itself is and an examination of the ways in which it operates, will be discussed in the following chapters.

Questions for essays and seminar papers

1 Discuss the different definitions of the hotel and catering industry. What difficulties might be encountered in deciding what to include in the industry?
2 Explain why the hotel and catering industry only emerges as a significant industry in the more recent stages of economic development.
3 Is the continued growth of 'the service economy' inevitable? Discuss the implications for hotels and catering.

Practical assignment

From the SIC find examples of products that compete but which are in different industrial groupings. Compare the UK SIC of hotels and catering with that in another country such as the USA. (The SIC for other countries may only be available in a few reference libraries.)

CHAPTER 2

Price mechanism

In seeking explanations of how economies operate, considerable use has been made of 'models'.[1] As reality is so complex, certain simplifications have to be made if that reality is to be described and analysed; basically a model is no more than a simplified version of reality. A good model will be one that yields sound results. Even if the simplified model itself appears somewhat removed from reality, it is still possible for it to yield results approximate enough to what actually happens to be a useful model. If results are not useful, then it may be that the wrong simplifying assumptions have been made.

The behaviour of firms is very complex and, consequently, economists have constructed models of their behaviour. In particular, models of market structure have evolved and were briefly mentioned in Chapter 1. In each of these market structures, the firm has usually been regarded as a profit-maximizing organization operating in a known and certain environment which includes knowledge of demand conditions and its cost structures, both present and future. The firm makes no effort to modify that environment, but responds passively to it. In addition, there is usually an assumption that the firm is owner-managed.

Much recent work has sought to review such a model of the firm and to establish other models of its operation, but none has so far obtained such universal acceptance as to completely replace this more 'traditional' view of the firm.

This chapter will examine that conventional view; as a consequence it may appear somewhat theoretical and abstract but is important none the less in order to make sense of other models and views of the firms and later chapters.

Market structure, conduct and performance

It was seen in Chapter 1 that market structure is believed to influence how firms behave; this behaviour (or conduct), in turn, influences the performance of firms. The relationship expressed in Figure 3 reflects this causal sequence. It is possible that this one-way, static relationship is too simple a model and, for instance, modifications need to be incorporated to allow for a two-way causal sequence, e.g. aspects of performance may influence conduct and structure.[2]

The characteristics of the market structures (including perfect competition) that were mentioned in Chapter 1 may be identified as those in Table 9.

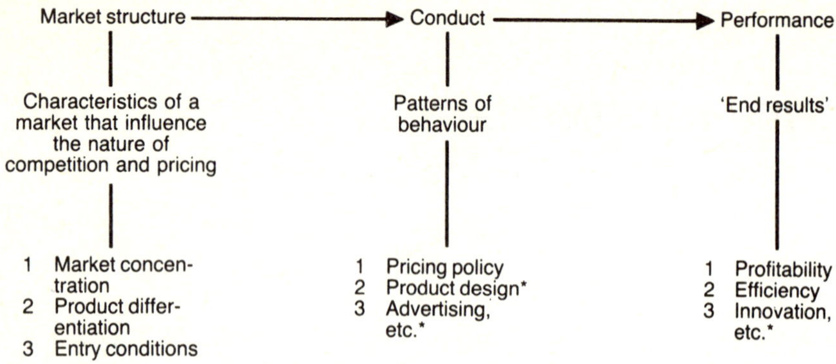

**Note*: The allocation of advertising, product design and innovation to these categories is arbitrary since it is possible, for instance, for them all to appear under market structure as an entry condition, and for 'innovation' to be a form of 'conduct' (see further discussion in Chapters 3 and 4).

Figure 3 *Relationship between market structure, conduct and performance*

Table 9 *Market structure characteristics*

1 *Market structure*	2 *Market concentration*	3 *Product differentiation*	4 *Conditions of entry*
Perfect competition	Low (many firms)	None (homogeneous product)	Easy (no barriers)
Monopoly	High (one firm)	–	Difficult (barriers)
Monopolistic competition	Low (many firms)	Exists	Relatively easy (low barriers)
Oligopoly	High (few firms)	Exists	Relatively difficult (barriers)

Each of the market structures in Table 9 will be discussed in more detail later, as will the methods of measuring market structure.

Perfect competition

Optimal resource allocation is desired because of the economic problem of scarcity; it is often defined by reference to the Pareto criterion. This indicates that optimal resource allocation is achieved if it is not possible to alter the allocation of resources between goods and services (the composition of output) so as to make someone better off without making someone else worse off, i.e. maximum economic satisfaction is achieved. If it *is* possible to alter the allocation (have a different composition of output) so as to make someone better off without welfare reductions elsewhere (i.e. a net gain), then a suboptimal situation exists.[3]

In addition to this objective of allocative efficiency, productive efficiency may also be considered desirable and this occurs when production is achieved at the lowest possible cost.

There has been a strong undercurrent to the development of economics which suggests that if the market structure of perfect competition prevailed throughout the economy then these desirable objectives could be achieved.[4]

At the heart of the perfectly competitive market structure is the owner-managed firm which seeks to maximize profits and which has perfect knowledge about its current and future cost structures. Additionally the product of each firm in any one market is undifferentiated and therefore indistinguishable from the products of all the others; the product is homogeneous (see column 3 of Table 9). Consumer choice is thus solely on a price basis.

The market structure assumes that there are sufficient firms in any one market so that no one of them can influence price of the product (see column 2 of Table 9) and each has to accept the price which is determined by forces outside of its own control (see page 50). Each firm is a small enough part of the market to ensure that its actions will have no effect on the other firms.

The firm not only knows its costs but also knows what current and future revenue it may expect at any particular level of output.

There are no barriers to the entry and exit of firms to and from the market (see column 4 of Table 9).

On the consumer side, each is considered to be seeking maximum economic satisfaction from his/her limited income and is seeking maximum economic reward for the services of his/her labour. Each consumer also has perfect knowledge about the range of products available, of prices prevailing in all parts of the market for a product and in the market for his/her labour services.

The outcome of all of these restrictive (and perhaps unlikely) assumptions is that resources will be allocated through the operation of the price mechanism according to the joint action of firms (supply) and consumers (demand), with firms responding passively to needs expressed by the consumer; the consumer is sovereign. The resources themselves are considered to be able to move effortlessly to produce whatever goods and services are currently demanded, i.e. resources are perfectly mobile, and they are capable of being used for producing any of these goods and services, i.e. they are substitutable between different uses.

Because of the characteristics of the market structure the firm's *conduct* is limited to passive reactions to an externally determined price. The *performance* is, however, according to the Pareto criterion, considered to be highly desirable.

Demand

As noted above, the price mechanism serves to allocate resources to their 'optimal use' under these perfectly competitive conditions. It is, therefore, now appropriate to look more closely at that price mechanism and its component parts, demand and supply.

The demand for any product, whether good or service, is influenced by a large number of factors (or determinants) and it is clearly of interest to the owners, managers and marketing specialists of firms to identify those factors. In economics the role of demand itself in the operation of the price mechanism has also been the focus of attention.

Demand, in the economic sense, is defined in a particularly rigorous way. It is not need or want for a product but the willingness and ability of a consumer to purchase a product at a particular price, i.e. 'effective demand'. No matter how great the need, the lack of money to back it will mean that it does not constitute demand or exert any pressure in the market.

As well as being an influence on the price of a product (see below), demand is also itself partially determined by price. At any particular moment it is likely that consumers will be willing to buy more of a product the lower is its price and vice versa. Underlying this fairly plausible suggestion is the 'law of diminishing marginal utility', where utility is the satisfaction derived from a good or service.[5] There are many examples in economics of so-called 'laws' including the 'laws of supply and demand' but in no sense should they be interpreted as rules of behaviour that always hold true. They are, more realistically, theories or hypotheses that may or may not prove to be useful in explaining the workings of the economic system. 'Marginal' concepts are also common in economics and will reappear several times throughout this book; 'marginal' refers to *change* in a variable (such as output, cost, revenue or utility) that results from a *one* unit change in another variable (such as inputs, sales or purchases). Thus the law of diminishing marginal utility may be stated as: 'the utility that any household derives from successive units of a particular commodity will diminish as total consumption of that commodity increases, the consumption of all other commodities being held constant'.[6]

If, for instance, a family had an evening meal out in a restaurant once a month, the utility (satisfaction) derived from that one meal would doubtless be high. As the frequency of such eating out increased, each extra occasion would probably give less and less utility to the family as it became less of a 'special treat'. While not denying the increased *total* utility that will result from eating out, the 'law' only suggests that each *extra* meal is likely to give less utility than the previous one. Assuming that utility can be measured in money terms then the relationships shown in Table 10, and represented graphically in Figure 4, might be expected. Note how total utility rises but marginal utility falls.

If the third meal per month gives £12.50 worth of utility but the price of meals is £13.50, then the meal is unlikely to be bought; the consumer will sacrifice more than he/she gains, which is an economically irrational thing to

Table 10 *Utility of eating out*

Number of evening meals in a restaurant per month	*Total utility (in £s)*	*Marginal utility (in £s)*
0	0	
		15.00
1	15.00	
		14.00
2	29.00	
		12.50
3	41.50	
		10.50
4	52.00	
		8.00
5	60.00	
		5.00
6	65.00	
		1.50
7	66.50	

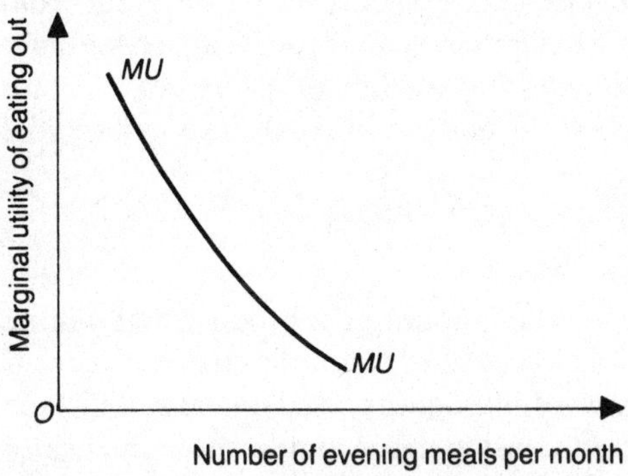

Figure 4 *Graphical representation of marginal utility*

do if it is assumed (see earlier) that consumers seek to maximize their satisfaction.

If the price is £12 then the consumer will purchase up to three meals per month and no more. If the price were to fall to £10 it would be economically rational to consume more (four meals) and if the price were to rise to £14.50, then consumption of meals would be reduced (to one meal). The marginal utility curve of Figure 4 can thus be transformed into the demand curve of Figure 5,

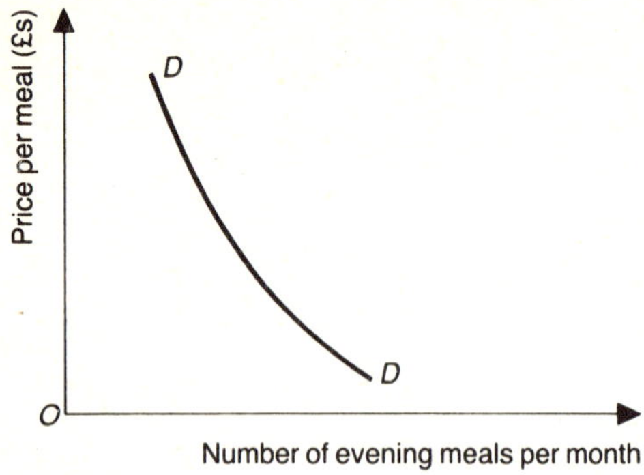

Figure 5 *Demand curve*

indicating an inverse (or negative) relationship between quantity demanded and price: as one rises, the other falls.

'Curves' such as this could, in practice, be straight lines and are conventionally labelled as indicated in order to avoid confusion with supply and other curves. The demand curve represents the situation at a *particular point of time;* it answers the question 'What would be the current number of meals consumed per month *if* price now was at a level of £*x*?'. This is rather different from determining what demand would be when prices actually do change over time. It is a restrictive condition but it is one that applies to a number of other economic concepts (such as the supply curve and cost curves) and is an essential part of 'model-building'.

Shifts in demand

There are other factors that influence the amount of a product that will be bought but these are assumed to be held constant when the demand curve is determined. These other determinants of (influences on) demand will include the prices of other goods, the level of consumers' incomes, the influence of advertising and of social pressures, and so on.

If any of these determinants other than price alters, such that more or less is being demanded at the same range of prices, then the existing demand curve is no longer representative of consumers' willingness to purchase; a new demand curve is required. If, for instance, incomes increased and consumers increased their demand for meals out as a result, there would be a shift in the demand curve shown in Figure 6 and the movement from the original demand curve D–D to the new one D_1–D_1. This is clearly different from asking what the increased demand would be if price was at a different level – the original demand curve would answer that question. The shift to D_1–D_1 arises because it is some influence other than price that has changed (in this case, incomes).

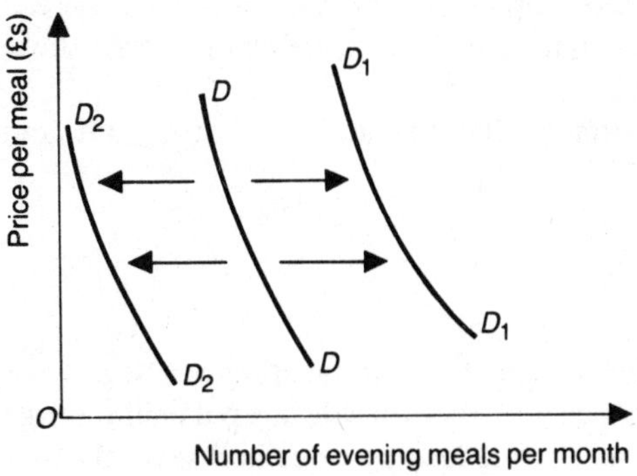

Figure 6 *Shifts in the demand curve*

A change in any of the other determinants such that demand at all prices fell, would cause the demand curve to shift in the opposite direction (to D_2–D_2 in Figure 6). For example, a fall in the price of video-recorders and the hire of video-films might cause families to stay in more and eat out less. There would be a change in demand for meals out which was not associated with a different price for meals out.

Market demand

The downward-sloping demand curve is usually to be interpreted as a 'market' demand curve, i.e. the demand arising from all purchases of a product, rather than as an individual consumers' demand curve. Market demand curves for most goods and services are probably downward-sloping[7] even though at any one time any individual consumer, family group or part of the market may exhibit behaviour which is inconsistent with an inverse price–quantity demanded relationship.

It might be, for instance, that high-price goods and services have a certain prestige value and the higher the price the more that is demanded. Consumers may gain a great deal of satisfaction from dining out in high-class, haute cuisine, expensive restaurants, not just because of the standard of service and food preparation but also because of prestige and social standing to be gained from dining in such expensive places. A lower price in these circumstances may not increase demand, as the analysis so far would suggest, but may actually result in fewer customers. In the case of hotels, where it is often difficult to judge the quality of the product before purchasing, price may be taken as an indicator of value. A low tariff in a previously highly-priced, high-quality hotel may lead consumers to believe quality has fallen and demand may fall off.

Behaviour in individual parts of the market such as these examples need not be reflected in the market as a whole. It is unlikely that if prices in *all* high-class restaurants or hotels were lower the demand would be less; total market demand may rise as new customers, who could not previously afford these products, are attracted to buy.

See page 43 for further discussion of the demand for eating out and accommodation.

Supply

Supply, the other of the two forces influencing price, is the amount of a good or service that a firm would wish to produce and offer for sale at a particular range of prices. Like demand, supply is itself influenced by price and several other factors. Supply is considered to be positively related to price, i.e. at any given point of time firms will only be willing to supply more at a higher price and vice versa. This relationship is illustrated as the supply curve in Figure 7; this curve, in a similar way to the demand curve, answers the question 'What would be the current number of meals supplied per month *if* price now was at a level of £*x*?'. The supply curve does *not* show how much will be actually sold at a particular price because that will depend on demand also; it shows only willingness to supply. The curve is labelled *S–S* to distinguish it clearly.

The supply curve is usually considered to be upward-sloping in this way because:

1 Existing restaurant owners are assumed to be operating on rising cost curves (see page 53 and Chapter 5) and a rise in price is necessary to cover the increased costs resulting from the extra output. (Owners experiencing constant or falling costs may be tempted to increase output as price rises in order to increase profits.)

2 Prospective entrants into the industry are assumed to be relatively high-cost

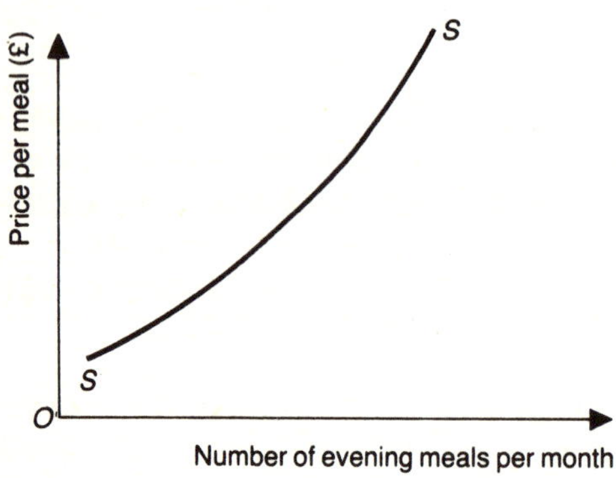

Figure 7 *Supply curve*

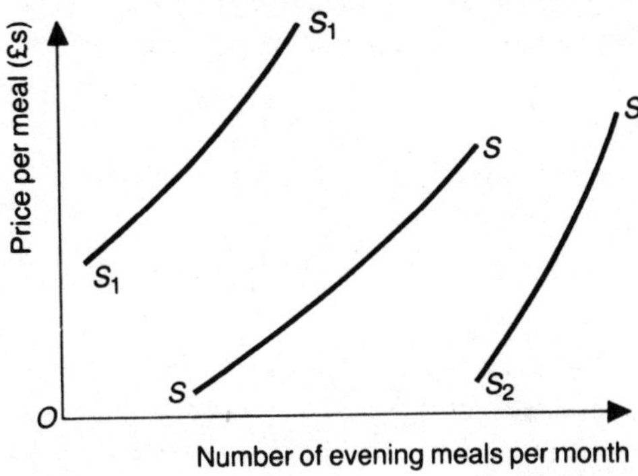

Figure 8 *Shifts in the supply curve*

producers and it is only as prices rise that it becomes worthwhile for them to enter the industry and thus increase supply.

The other factors that might affect supply – such as the price of other goods, price of factors used in production, changes in the state of technology, taxation on expenditure or on production – are considered to remain constant when the supply curve is determined. If any of these alters, however, so as to vary the amount firms are willing to supply at any particular range of prices, then there will be shifts in the supply curve in the same way as there are shifts in the demand curve.

Consider, for example, the imposition of a tax on hotel rooms. A tax of 50p per room per night might lead hoteliers to require prices 50p greater than the previous range of prices; the supply curve would shift (in Figure 8) to S_1–S_1, the vertical distance between S–S and S_1–S_1 being 50p.

A subsidy of 50p paid by governments to hoteliers would mean that hoteliers need only require prices 50p lower than previously in order to supply the same amounts. The supply curve would shift to S_2–S_2.

If hotelkeeping in a seaside resort became much less attractive because of the job opportunities, wages and salaries available in a newly-opened local car factory then the supply of hotel rooms could diminish as hoteliers and staff are attracted into car factory occupations. Over the current price range less would be supplied and the supply curve would shift leftwards (closer to zero, indicating a reduction in quantity) as represented by S_1–S_1 in Figure 8.

Market price

The interaction of the demand and supply as represented by D–D and S–S in Figure 9 determines market price of a product. (It is still assumed that perfectly competitive conditions prevail.)

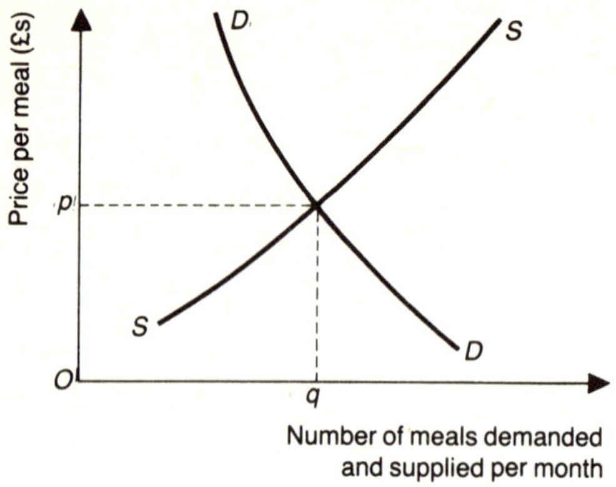

Figure 9 *Market price*

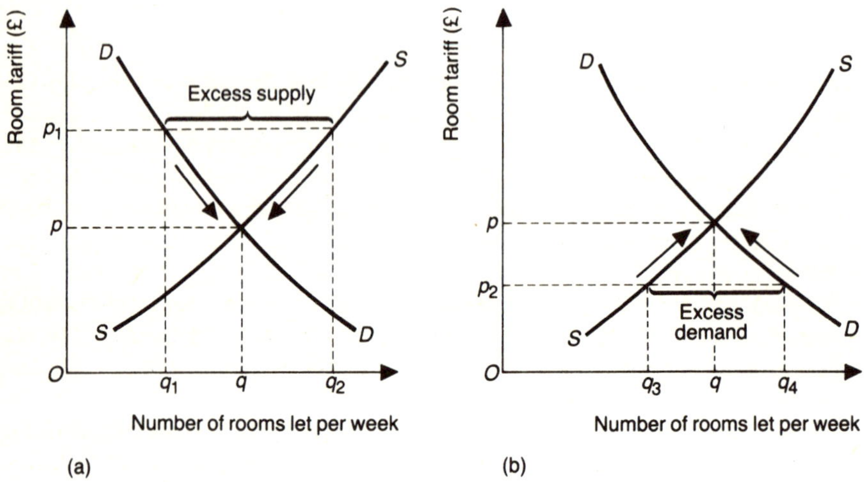

Figure 10 *Excess demand and supply*

Given the current market conditions of demand and supply (all other determinants remaining unchanged), the intersection of the two curves will indicate the equilibrium market price and quantity, i.e. that price (*op*) at which the amount consumers will buy (*oq*) is exactly the same as the quantity firms are willing to offer for sale (*oq*). At any other price demand would not equal supply and a disequilibrium situation would exist.

In Figure 10(a), at a price of op_1, the number of hotel rooms offered to be let (oq_2) exceeds that which consumers are willing to buy (oq_1). The possibility of unlet rooms will cause the price to fall in order to eliminate the excess supply.

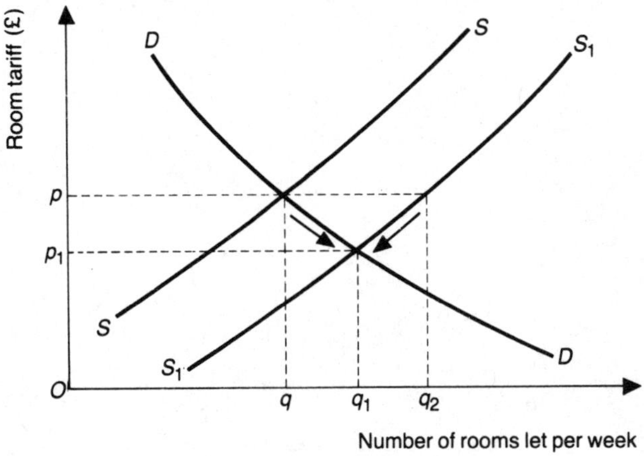

Figure 11 *Equilibrium price and a shift of supply curve*

Supply will fall along *S–S* and demand will increase along *D–D* until they are equal (*oq*) at a price of *op*.

In Figure 10(b) the number of hotel rooms offered to be let (oq_3) is less than that which consumers are willing to buy (oq_4). The possibility of unsatisfied demand causes price to rise, supply increases, demand reduces and equilibrium is achieved at a price of *op*.

Thus at any price other than *op*, excess demand or supply exists, but only temporarily for the operation of the price mechanism (assuming perfect competition) will be such as to eliminate the excess and return the situation to an equilibrium.

If, however, one or both of the curves shifts then a new equilibrium will be established. In Figure 11, for instance, an increased supply of hotels (to S_1–S_1) leads initially to an excess of supply (oq_2) over demand (*oq*) at the original equilibrium price of *op*. Pressure of excess supply would cause the equilibrium price to fall to op_1 (with demand and supply now being equal at oq_1).[8]

Consider what would be the outcome of an increased popularity of a particular hotel or resort (due, perhaps, to a successful advertising campaign). The demand curve would shift to D_1–D_1, as in Figure 12, and there would be an initial excess of demand over supply (at the original price of *op*), shown by the difference between *oq* and oq_1.

If the currently available hotel rooms are fully booked, then supply can only be increased by building new hotels or extending existing ones. This will take a long time – the supply is inelastic – and in the meantime, hoteliers could take advantage of the excess demand to charge a price of op_1 for the existing supply (*oq*) of rooms. Eventually, when the new supply is completed (to oq_2), a new equilibrium at price op_2 is established.

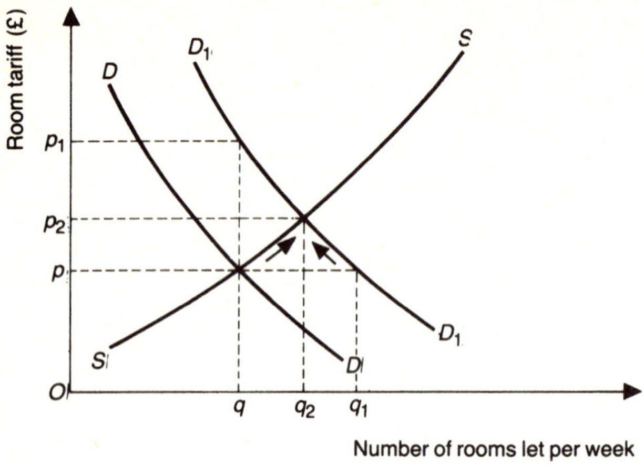

Figure 12 *Equilibrium price and a shift of demand curve*

If, for some reason, such as government intervention, price does not achieve its equilibrium level then excess demand or supply will continue. A government-enforced minimum price for agricultural products, which was above the equilibrium price would result in a continuing excess supply of these products, as seen in the so-called 'butter mountains' and 'wine lakes' associated with the agricultural policies of the European Economic Community.

A maximum price would have the reverse effect. If, for some reason, governments wished to keep the price of holidays lower than they are now, this could well result in an increase in demand which could not be satisfied by the existing facilities. Unless hoteliers could find some way of profitably supplying their hotel rooms at these lower prices the excess demand would persist.

Elasticity

It would be useful to know with some more precision what sort of reaction there might be on the demand or supply side to a change in price. In Figure 11, for instance, would the fall in price from op to op_1 result in a substantial increase in demand or a very small one? Similarly, in Figure 12, of what magnitude would be the response of supply to the increase in price? Assume experience (or market research) suggests the relationship between meal prices and quantity sold per night shown in Table 11.

If price fell from £11 to £7, revenue received would rise. The fall in price on each meal sold is more than compensated for by a rise in sales. If costs are unchanged profits will rise. A reduction in price from £5 to £1 would lead to a fall in revenue since the rise in sales has not been enough to compensate for the fall in price.

Table 11 *Revenue from meal sales*

Price per meal (£)	×	*Number of meals sold per night*	=	*Revenue (£)*
11		25		275
7		45		315
5		55		275
1		75		75

Table 12 *Price-elasticities of demand (UK)*

Food	0.52	Bread and cereals	0.22
Durable goods	0.89	Entertainment	1.40
Services	1.02	Expenditure abroad	1.63
		Catering	2.61

Source: D. Begg, S. Fischer and R. Dornbusch, *Economics* (McGraw-Hill 1984), Chapter 4.

These differences are referred to as differences in 'price-elasticity' of demand, i.e. the responsiveness of demand to a change in price. It is possible to give a numerical value to this concept by using the following formula:[9]

$$\text{price-elasticity of demand} = -1\left(\frac{\text{percentage change in quantity demanded}}{\text{percentage change in price}}\right)$$

The minus sign is placed before the bracketed formula as a matter of convenience in order that all the values will have a positive value. If the elasticity value is greater than 1, then the demand is termed 'elastic'. Thus in Table 11 between £11 and £7 demand is elastic. If the elasticity value is less than 1, demand is said to be inelastic (as between £5 and £1). There are other possibilities including values ranging from zero (completely inelastic) through one (unit elasticity) to infinity (completely elastic). The concept applies also to supply. Table 12 gives a number of estimated price elasticities.

Whether the demand for any particular product is elastic or inelastic is very much (but not solely) influenced by the availability of substitutes. For instance there are few substitutes for food (see Table 12) but for individual types of food there may be a large number. The more specific the product the greater the number of likely substitutes and the greater the elasticity. In Table 12 it is clear that the elasticities for individual services, such as entertainment and catering, are greater than for the broad category 'services'.

If the price of hotel accommodation rises then some consumers may shift their demand to guest houses or self-catering. Demand from businessmen and women might be expected to be less sensitive to price changes in hotels and the demand would be more price-inelastic than the demand from holidaymakers. Certainly the demand from foreign visitors is likely to be price-elastic, given that there are many holiday destinations world-wide that they could choose from.

There are, also, available substitutes for eating out in the form of meals at home; thus it can be expected that the demand for eating out would be price-elastic. This may not be so true in the case of industrial catering and school meals where there is a less obvious range of substitutes.

Income- and cross-elasticity

Other elasticity concepts include 'income-elasticity' and 'cross-elasticity'. This latter concept has already been mentioned in Chapter 1 and refers to the responsiveness of demand for a product to a change in the price of some other product.

$$\text{cross-elasticity} = \frac{\text{percentage change in quantity of product } x}{\text{percentage change in price of product } y}$$

A negative sign is not put in front of this formula for it is important to determine whether the elasticity value is positive or negative. A positive value (e.g. +0.3) would suggest that products are substitutes, whereas negative values indicate non-substitutes and possible complementary goods. The demand for meals in a staff restaurant may change considerably following a price reduction in a local sandwich bar or pub (i.e. substitutes). A reduction in the price of holidays in the UK may increase visitors' demands for another product such as meals in cafés and snack bars while on holiday (i.e. complementary products).

Income-elasticity measures the responsiveness of demand to a change in income and therefore can be calculated as:

$$\text{income-elasticity} = \frac{\text{percentage change in quantity demanded}}{\text{percentage change in income}}$$

Again a negative sign is not put before the formula: the value calculated will usually be positive since changes in income are usually (though not always) associated with changes in demand in the same direction. The demand for accommodation and for eating out is likely to be highly responsive to changes in income. When incomes are low, spending on hotels and eating out is low also, but as incomes increase consumers are enabled to go on holiday and eat out; income-elasticity values are therefore likely to be high. Demand for food generally is not so responsive to changes in income and income-elasticity values are likely to be lower (see Table 13: value of 0.45 for food). In some instances the demand for foodstuffs will actually fall as incomes rise and the income-elasticity value will be negative; these are known as 'inferior goods' (see Table 13: value of −0.50 for bread and cereals).

Table 13 *Income-elasticities of demand (UK)*

Tobacco	−0.50	Bread and cereals	−0.50
Food	0.45	Vegetables	0.87
Clothing	1.23	Travel abroad	1.14
Durable goods	1.47	Recreational goods	1.99
Services	1.75	Wines and spirits	2.60

Source: D. Begg, S. Fischer and R. Dornbusch, *Economics* (McGraw-Hill 1984), Chapter 4.

It is significant that the income-elasticity for both services and durable goods is high (see pages 16–17).

Demand for hotel and catering services

The overall (or aggregate) demand for hotel and catering services and the structure of that demand (type of accommodation or catering unit demanded within the aggregate) are characterized by fluctuations; the causes of these are many, complex and often interrelated. It is difficult to disentangle the effects of individual causes or determinants but the most significant economic determinants are likely to be prices (absolute and relative), and consumer incomes. Other determinants of a social, psychological and demographic nature are less the concern of economics, but may have an equally important influence on demand. There have been relatively few comprehensive and rigorous studies[10] of the accommodation and eating out markets which have successfully identified the influence of economic determinants of demand, possibly because of the lack of basic information about expenditure, especially in the eating out market.

Accommodation

Table 14 illustrates the fluctuation in overall demand for accommodation away from home in Britain, from both British and overseas residents.

These fluctuations can be partly explained by the background of economic activity in this country. The nation's GDP and consumer incomes do not grow at a constant rate (see Table 15) and they have an effect upon consumer expenditure.

There is not a direct and immediate connection between these items and the exact relationship between income and expenditure is difficult to determine (there are time lags in the effects and the complication of many determinants influencing expenditure at the same time). Purchasing power as expressed in real personal disposable income does, though, have a decisive effect on aggregate expenditure and the demand for individual goods and services. (See also Table 4.)

Table 14 *Rate of growth of demand for accommodation 1983–7*

	Domestic	*Overseas*
	Number of trips in GB by British residents for all tourism purposes	*Number of visits to the UK*
	(% change per annum)	
1983	6.5	7.1
1984	6.9*	9.5
1985	−10.0	5.9
1986	1.6	−3.8
1987 (provisional)	3.1	11.6

*New base for domestic statistics.

Sources: Department of Trade and Industry, Business Statistics Office, 'Overseas Travel and Tourism, Quarter 4 1987', *Business Monitor* MQ6, 1988; *Tourism Intelligence Quarterly*, Vol. 10, No. 1 (British Tourist Authority and English Tourist Board 1988).

An increase in unemployment (from 2.6 per cent of the labour force in 1974 to 12.2 per cent in 1982) will also have affected consumer expenditure through the overall loss of purchasing power and the effect on employees' long-term expenditure plans. Generally, recession and lack of economic growth in the economy may depress travel away from home but the demand overall has remained reasonably buoyant. Rather than abandon travel, consumers may have 'traded-down' in accommodation, made shorter journeys and trips, spent less, cut out shorter 'breaks', etc.[11]

Demand for business and conference trips will be similarly affected by fluctuations in GDP, real personal disposable income and unemployment.

Demand from overseas will be affected by fluctuations in the GDP and income in those overseas countries that generate visitors. Additionally, the cost of travel to and stay in the UK will be important. Changes in air fares will be particularly significant as will be changes in the exchange rate. This rate is basically the price of pound sterling expressed in terms of some other foreign currency such as the US dollar; this price is determined like any other price by the demand and supply of the product (in this case, the pound sterling). As the exchange rate fluctuates (see Table 16), so the price of the stay in and/or

Table 15 *Rate of growth of GDP, consumer expenditure and personal disposable income*

	% increase over previous year		
	GDP	*Personal disposable income*	*Consumer expenditure*
1981	−1.0	−1.5	−0.1
1982	1.1	−0.1	0.8
1983	3.6	2.2	4.0
1984	1.8	2.5	2.1
1985	3.8	2.5	3.7
1986	2.7	4.0	5.8

Note: Growth rates are of the variables expressed in constant (usually 1980) prices so as to remove the effects of inflation.

Source: Central Statistical Office, *UK National Accounts, 1987* (HMSO 1987).

Table 16 *Value of some foreign currencies against the pound 1985–7*

	1985	*1986*	*1987*
Spanish peseta	219.55	205.31	201.90
US dollar	1.30	1.47	1.64

Source: *Tourism Intelligence Quarterly*, Vol. 10, No. 1; Vol. 9, No. 4; Vol. 9, No. 3 (British Tourist Authority and English Tourist Board 1988, 1987).

travel to the UK becomes relatively cheap or expensive. For example, if the value of the pound falls in terms of the US dollar (e.g. from $2.03 in 1981 to $1.75 in 1982) then British goods and services become cheaper for the American citizen to purchase (i.e. he/she has to offer fewer dollars for each pound's worth of goods and services). The net effect of exchange rate fluctuations will be the outcome also of the US dollar's exchange rate against other currencies; the American citizen might obtain a much more favourable exchange rate against Caribbean countries' currencies, in which case demand may shift to these destinations.[12]

It has been estimated[13], for instance, that international travel expenditure by US citizens falls by just over 1 per cent for each 1 per cent rise in relative prices

Table 17 *Holidays in Britain and abroad by British residents 1971–86*

	Holidays (4 or more nights duration) taken by residents of GB (millions)	
	In GB	*Abroad*
1971	34	7
1981	37	13
1985	33	16
1986	32	17

Source: Central Statistical Office, *Social Trends*, No. 18 (HMSO 1988).

(price-elasticity of −1.1); also, expenditure in any one area such as Europe falls by 2 per cent for every 1 per cent rise in prices relative to those in areas such as the West Indies and Central America (elasticity of 2.03). Income-elasticity was estimated at 0.7.

The demand from British residents for accommodation in the UK will be influenced by the relative costs of domestic and overseas visits, as well as the background determinant of income. Income-elasticity for overseas travel by British residents[14] has been estimated at 1.2 with price-elasticity at 0.5. (The income elasticity for demand at any one location may be low since as incomes rise, consumers may search for 'new' destinations, e.g. 0.62 in part of British Columbia, Canada.[15])

It is clear that the growth of visits abroad by British residents has been considerably greater than the growth of domestic tourism (see Table 17), largely due to the combination of a long-term rise in incomes and the introduction of inclusive tours (package holidays) which has served to keep the real cost of travel and stay reasonably low.

The greater the number of potential destinations that consumers can go to, the more responsive is the demand at any one destination to a change in its price, e.g. price-elasticity of 2.1 in British Columbia.

The large rise in fuel costs in 1974 (and thus cost of travel) undoubtedly contributed to the fall in the rate of growth of visits abroad in that year (see Table 18).

It is clear from Table 18 that by 1974, the world export price of crude petroleum had risen to nearly seven times its level in 1970, whereas the export price of all other primary commodities had only just doubled. The effect on air transport costs was particularly devastating; effects on car transport within the country were also evident.

Table 18 *World export price index of crude petroleum and all primary commodities excluding crude petroleum 1962–81*

	Price index of crude petroleum	*Price index of all primary commodities (excluding crude petroleum)*
	(1975 = 100)	
1962	16	n/a
1970	15	47
1974	100	107
1979	170	138
1980	295	157
1981	325	146

Source: *1981 Statistical Yearbook*, 32nd issue (Department of International Economic and Social Affairs, United Nations 1983).

As exchange rates have altered, so have the relative attractions of going abroad and of different destinations abroad; an elasticity of 2.8 has been estimated for the UK, signifying that a reduction of 1 per cent in prices (internal or exchange rates) in any one country would lead to an eventual increase of 2.8 per cent more British travellers to that country.[16]

A study of tourism by Austrian residents[17] estimated an income-elasticity of between 1.0 and 1.2 for domestic and 2.5 for international tourism. The elasticity of domestic tourism with respect to prices and of international tourism with respect to exchange rate fluctuations were estimated at between 0.3 and 0.5 and 0.9 respectively. One American study[18] suggested that the price-elasticity of demand for accommodation for business travellers was greater than that of holidaymakers (1.50 and 0.3 respectively).

Eating out

Data comparable to that for accommodation does not exist for the eating out market but the data in Table 19 illustrates fluctuations in aggregate demand.[19]

Once more, the underlying economic determinants of GDP and real disposable income will have had an effect upon the industry.

It has been estimated[20] that the income-elasticity for meals in restaurants (USA) is about 1.0 with the price-elasticity ranging from 1.0 in the short term to 2.0 and more in the long term (see also Table 12). Cross-elasticity with the price of meals at home ranged from +0.4 in the short term to −0.5 in the

Table 19 *Rate of growth of eating out by UK residents 1982–7*

	Rate of growth: % change in expenditure per annum
1982	−1.9
1983	4.0
1984	4.6
1985	4.7
1986	2.8
1987	5.3

Note: Growth of expenditure in constant (1980) prices.

Source: *Leisure Futures, Summer 1988* (Henley Centre for Forecasting 1988).

Table 20 *Index of retail prices: average 1986*

All items	*Food* (15 January 1974 = 100)	*Meals bought and consumed outside the home*
385.9	347.3	439.5

Source: Central Statistical Office, *Annual Abstract of Statistics, 1988* (HMSO 1988).

long term, i.e. likelihood of eating at home decreased with time after a rise in the relative cost of eating out.

Changes in energy costs (petrol prices) appeared to have little long-term effect upon restaurant demand.

Eating out, at least in the American market, has appeared to suffer in recession less than might be expected because consumers have 'traded-down' and continued to regard eating out as an occasion that cannot be dispensed with. Much eating out may be 'necessity' anyway.[21]

In the UK the overall demand for eating out will have been affected by the more rapid rise in cost of eating out than of food and prices in general (see Table 20). Prices of all retail items were 3.8 times higher in 1986 than the level in 1974 and food prices 3.5 times higher, whereas prices of eating out were 4.4 times higher.

The imposition of VAT, a tax on expenditure, on take-away foods in 1984 will have caused some change in relative prices and may affect demand.

The few studies that there have been of the accommodation and eating out markets do not always give conclusive and consistent results about the effects of income and prices upon demand, nor do the results always bear out what might be intuitively believed. There is general agreement though that the

Table 21 *Average bed occupancy 1987 (England)*

	%		%
January	26	July	57
February	34	August	58
March	36	September	56
April	42	October	51
May	45	November	39
June	51	December	32

Source: *English Hotel Occupancy Survey, 1987* (English Tourist Board 1988).

Table 22 *Average bedspace occupancy 1985–87 (England)*

	%
1985	44
1986	43
1987	45

Source: *English Hotel Occupancy Survey 1987* (English Tourist Board 1988).

influence of prices and incomes is substantial despite the existence of a large number of other possible determinants.[22]

Demand fluctuations

The demand for hotel and catering services usually exhibits marked fluctuations. During the day there are peaks of demand for meals at a few well-defined times and perhaps very little or no demand at other times. For accommodation there may be peaks of demand during the week for business-hotels and little demand at weekends.

Over the year there is a distinct pattern to the demand for holiday accommodation in particular. Hotels in most locations have occupancy rates that peak in summer months and slump in the winter (see Tables 21 and 22). Even London hotels experience seasonal fluctuations, with a 1987 peak bed occupancy of 74 per cent (July) and a low of 44 per cent in January.

Because of the inability of the hotel firm in particular to adjust supply, these fluctuations in demand cause problems.[23] A manufacturing firm might be able to cut back its production (and thus costs) if demand falls, or can place produced goods in stock holdings. Conversely, when demand rises it may be able to meet that demand by shift working, working overtime or reducing its stock of finished products.

This flexibility is denied to the hotel firm and therefore a fall in demand does not necessarily lead to a fall in costs nor can stocks be built up. The room unlet on a Saturday night cannot be 'stored' until Sunday to be sold along with the Sunday night letting of the same room!

A certain amount of flexibility of supply can be built in through the use of part-time staff and shift working, but it still leaves a high proportion of costs other than labour to be met when demand falls.

The inflexibility of supply exists also in the locational sense. Since this is a personal service industry, establishments need to be located where the consumer demand arises. As the demand moves to another location, it is impossible for the existing hotel and catering establishment to supply the product in that new location; a manufacturing firm, however, could continue producing and transport its product to the consumer in a different location.

The firm under perfect competition

This section is rather more abstract than others but is part of the model that is necessary for a complete understanding of perfect competition. (It could be omitted at a first reading, in which case the section titled 'A view of perfect competition and the price mechanism' on page 53 should be read next.)

1 It has been seen earlier that price under perfect competition is determined by the interaction of market demand and supply; price will therefore be an already-determined variable for the individual firm. No one firm is able to influence price and there is no joint action or collusion between firms to bring about such an influence. Thus the price facing the firm may be represented as the horizontal line at *op* in Figure 13. Also on this figure are represented the cost curves of the individual firm; these will be discussed in more detail in Chapter 5, but the curve *AC* shows what the cost per unit of output or sales (per meal or room) will be at any level of output or sales, i.e. average cost. The curve *MC* shows marginal cost; earlier in this chapter the 'marginal' concept was introduced and in the present context it refers to the addition to total cost resulting from an increase in output or sales of one more room or meal. (The characteristic shape of these curves will be analysed in Chapter 5.)

It is important to note that 'price' is synonymous with 'average revenue' (*AR* in Figure 13), i.e. the amount of revenue received per unit of output/sales.

Marginal revenue is the extra revenue received from the sale of one more room or meal and is represented by *MR*. Under conditions of perfect competition (but not in other market structures) *MR* is equal to price; every unit can be sold at the current market price and thus the extra revenue is equal to that price (or *AR*).

2 If it is assumed that the firm is seeking to maximize profits, then at what level of output will the firm produce? (It has no decision to make about price,

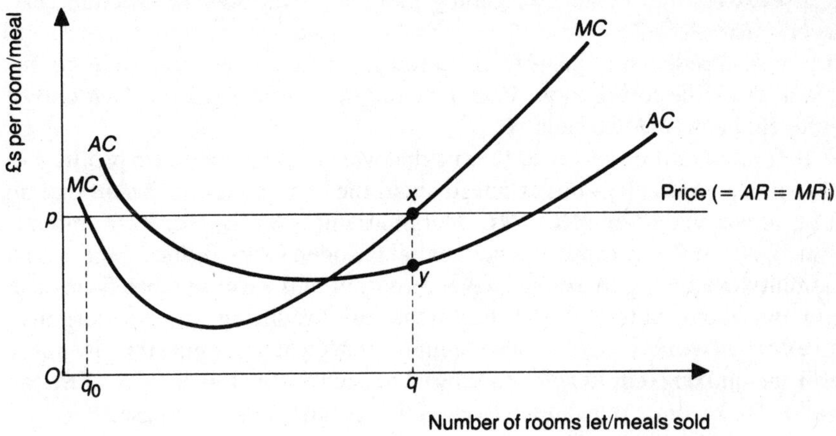

Figure 13 *Cost and revenue curves of firm in perfect competition*

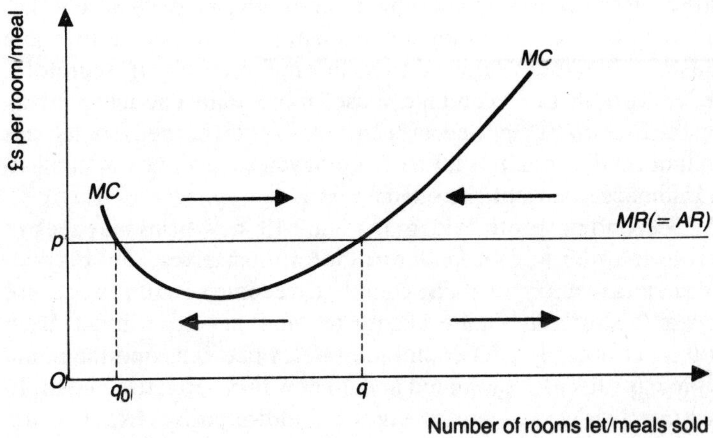

Figure 14 *Profit-maximization output of the firm*

of course.) Consider, initially, the marginal curves only, *MR* and *MC* as in Figure 14.

At any output level between oq_0 and oq it would be in the interests of the firm to increase its output, for as it did so, for every extra unit of sales it would be adding more to its revenue than it would be adding to its costs (i.e. *MR* exceeds *MC*) and thus profits would be rising. Beyond oq profits would be reduced because extra units would be adding more to costs than to revenue (*MC* exceeds *MR*).

If the firm reduced its sales from *oq* towards oq_0 it would reduce its profits since it would be losing more from revenue than from costs for each unit of output cut back (*MR* exceeds *MC*).

The level of output *oq* would thus be that which would maximize profits, i.e. where $MR = MC$. (It is important to avoid the erroneous conclusion that no profits are earned when $MR = MC$. Marginal concepts relate to 'extra amounts of' and when $MR = MC$ profit is neither being added to nor reduced; there is no possibility of moving to another level of output and earning more from each extra unit of output than it costs to produce or of reducing costs by more than the extra revenue.) *MR* is also equal to *MC* at oq_0 but this is not a profit-maximizing output level since by increasing output towards *oq*, more can be added to revenue than added to costs, i.e. profits can be increased.

3 By referring back to Figure 13, it will be noted that at this level of output *oq*, average revenue (*AR*) exceeds average cost (*AC*) (shown by *xy*). The revenue accruing to the firm for every room/meal is greater than the cost per room/meal and thus an 'economic' profit is being earned. This concept will be developed further in Chapter 5, but it is necessary at this stage to accept that 'costs' as defined by the economist include enough profit to keep a firm in a particular industry (sometimes referred to as 'normal profits'). If, therefore, revenue exceeds costs in this economic sense, more than enough is being earned to keep the firm producing and an economic profit is earned (sometimes referred to as 'abnormal profits'). A level of output where revenue was equal to costs in this economic sense would be satisfactory.

Because of this economic profit evident in Figure 13, new firms may seek to enter the industry in order to gain similar profit for themselves. This entry of new firms (no barriers to entry, enabling complete freedom of entry) will cause supply to increase (a shift as in Figure 11) and the market price will fall. Each firm will now face a lower price (*AR*) and thus *MR*. Price will continue to fall until the economic profits are eliminated and no new firms are attracted in. In Figure 15 the price/average revenue changes are indicated by *AR*, AR_1 and AR_2.

As price falls from *op*, (*AR*) economic profit is reduced (and, of course, profit-maximizing output altered as a new *MR* and *MC* intersection occurs). At a price of op_1 (AR_1) and output of oq_1 average revenue is equal to average cost and no economic profit is earned. (It will be recalled that sufficient profits are being earned here, however, to keep the firm in the industry; thus profits are maximized given the prevailing price and cost conditions.)

If price was at op_2 (AR_2) then the firm would need to adjust its output to oq_2 (to keep $MR = MC$) but *AR* would be less than *AC* and insufficient profit would be earned to induce the firm to remain in the industry. As firms move out, the market supply will reduce and price will rise (back towards op_1).

Thus equilibrium of both firm and industry is established at price op_1 and

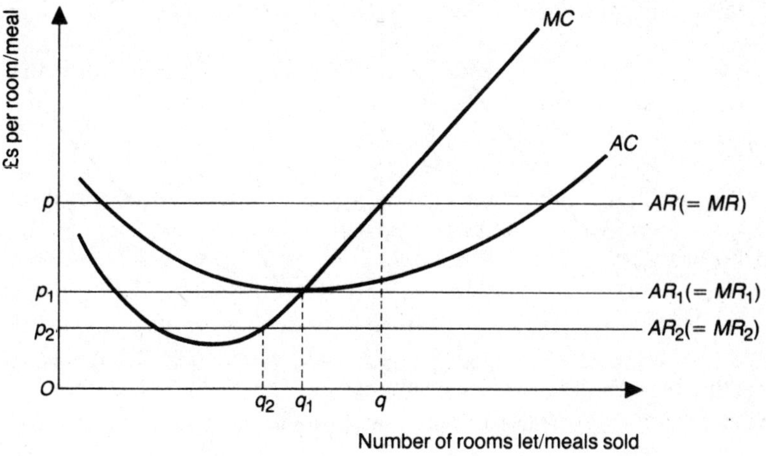

Figure 15 *Equilibrium of the firm and industry under perfect competition*

output oq_1 where $MR = MC = AR = AC$. There is no incentive for the firm to alter its output and no incentive for new firms to enter or existing firms to leave. At any other level of price and output the firm may well be in equilibrium (with $MR = MC$) but the industry will be in disequilibrium because of the movement of firms in and out.

4 It is now possible to see how the upward-sloping supply curve noted earlier is derived. In Figure 16(a) the marginal cost and marginal revenue curves are isolated once more. As price, and therefore *MR*, falls new profit-maximizing output levels for the firm are established.

At price levels between *op* (*MR*) and op_3 (MR_3) the firm would produce the outputs oq, oq_1, oq_2 and oq_3 rather than oq_0, oq_5 and oq_4 because, as has been shown above, profits can be increased by choosing the higher levels of output. Thus a graphical representation of the supply curve of the individual firm – price against quantity produced – would be as in Figure 16(b). When such supply curves of all firms in an industry are added together the slope of the market supply curve is explained.

A view of perfect competition and the price mechanism[24]

It is now possible to gain an overview of how the price mechanism is believed to operate under perfect competition to achieve allocative and productive efficiency.

Mechanism

Consumer preferences for particular goods and services are expressed through

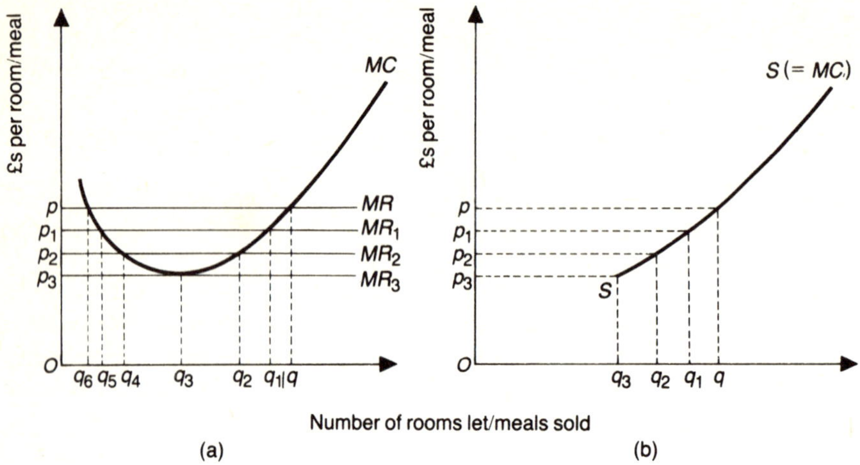

Figure 16 *Derivation of supply curve*

the pressure of demand and as those preferences alter so the demand curves for individual products will shift – some will experience rising demand and some falling. Prices will, consequently, alter and act as a 'signal' to firms to respond in appropriate ways. Products experiencing an increased demand will rise in price, existing firms will increase their output and new firms will be attracted into the industry. Profits act as a necessary part of the mechanism to ensure supply matches the demand but any excessive (economic) profits are competed away.

Resources of land, labour and capital are switched from producing products experiencing reduced demand to products with growing demands by firms offering increased payments (e.g. wages) to the suppliers of the resources. In the same way as there is a price mechanism for goods and services, there is a price mechanism for the resources (see Chapters 6 and 7).

Changes in consumer preferences therefore lead to alterations in relative prices in the economy (prices of goods and services and of resources used in production) and these changes in price lead to a re-allocation of the economy's scarce resources. Price acts as a 'signal' to producers and also provides the incentive to induce them to respond to consumer preferences.

The essence of price is that it is a 'rationing' device and without it some other means of rationing out or allocating resources would need to be found.

Performance

Allocative efficiency is ensured by price being equal to marginal cost, for all products.[25] If the price of product *X* is £8 and marginal cost is £10, the utility (or satisfaction) derived by the consumer (measured by the price the consumer is willing to pay) is less than the cost of the resources used to produce the last unit of that product. Output of the product should be reduced and the £10 worth of resources transferred to produce a product *Y* that *will* give utility of £10, i.e. that has a price of and is valued by consumers at £10. There will thus be a loss to consumers of £8 of utility from reduced output of *X* but a gain of £10 utility from increased output of *Y*, i.e. a net gain of £2 of utility. It was therefore theoretically possible to make some consumers better off (increase utility) without making others worse off (given the willingness of those who gain to compensate those who lose).

If the price of product *Z* is £15 and the marginal cost is £11, output should be increased by attracting resources from other uses. For as long as marginal cost does not rise above £15 as resources are transferred from elsewhere, then units of products giving utility of say, £12 or £13 will be lost but units of product *Z* giving utility of £15 will be gained. A net gain will be possible.

Once price is equal to marginal cost it would no longer be possible to re-allocate resources between different products without reducing net utility. By transferring resources, gains will equal losses and one group of businesses could gain only by making others worse off.

Perfect competition, as seen above, gives a situation where price does equal marginal cost (since price = *MR* and profit-maximization requires *MR* to equal *MC*), and thus allocative efficiency is ensured.

Productive efficiency is achieved as output occurs at the lowest point of the average cost curve (output oq_1 in Figure 15). Competitive pressures ensure that output cannot persist at any other level of costs.

The perfectly competitive market structure seems, therefore, to give a desirable performance. Additionally, the consumer is sovereign and production is determined solely by the needs of the consumer. Firms are but passive agents of the consumer and receive their 'instructions' through the price mechanism.

The system is an impersonal one and it decentralizes and delegates power and decisions since no one consumer or firm is able to influence the allocation system. There are not the costs of administering the system that there would presumably be in a 'planned' or 'command' economy. Adam Smith, an eighteenth century economist, used the term 'the invisible hand' to describe the operation of the price system as it co-ordinated the decision-making of many individual consumers and producers, each one of whom is seeking to maximize his/her own satisfaction. Smith and other 'classical economists' saw little reason for there to be any interference by government in the workings of this price mechanism, for left to its own devices it would allocate resources efficiently; they advocated *laissez-faire* policies with the minimum of government interference.

Government attempts, through subsidies and expenditure taxes, to alter the relative prices of products would distort consumers away from what they would have 'freely' chosen to purchase. (It could also mean unfair competition between products.) The price mechanism gives equilibrium prices which are a reflection of both consumer utility and production costs. A reduction of price through subsidies would mean that price would be less than costs and there would be 'overconsumption' of the product.

Intervention in the price mechanism

It is evident that the price mechanism does not, in reality, operate in conditions of perfect competition; there are many imperfections in any economy (see Chapters 3 and 4). Governments often try to remove these imperfections and introduce more competition into the economy (see Chapter 8). It is by no means certain, however, that anything short of universal perfect competition will bring about the desired results;[26] piecemeal attempts to increase competitive pressures may actually make the situation worse.

Even if all the conditions of perfect competition were present in an economy, there may well be certain circumstances where some intervention is justified:[27]

Externalities

Firms base their decisions upon the costs they bear themselves, i.e. private costs, whereas they might inflict costs on persons and organizations other than themselves, i.e. social costs. The most obvious example is pollution in its varied forms. The firm is unlikely to take these costs into account and some intervention may be necessary to avoid or reduce the cost. These social costs are known as externalities as are any social benefits that might occur: benefits which accrue to those other than the immediate consumer. In the case of industrial catering, the consumption of appropriate meals during the working day may not solely benefit the worker but also the employer, whose profits might rise because of increased productivity, and also the consumer of the product being made if the product's quality is improved. Holidays might confer a social benefit in the form of a 'more stable society' or 'enhanced contribution to work performance'.

Few, if any, of these social benefits are likely to be recognized by the consumer and thus a level of consumption/output which is best from society's point of view may not be achieved. Some encouragement of further consumption by the individual so that the 'socially desirable' level is achieved might therefore be appropriate: a subsidy.

Public goods

These are a limited number of goods and services which are not 'marketable' and are a special case of externalities; the benefits from their provision are spread over the whole community regardless of who actually purchases or finances them. If, for example, the armed forces are established to defend a country, then all who dwell therein will be defended whether they wish it or not. Exclusion is impossible and if some 'private' individuals or groups agree to finance the provision, 'free-riders' (those who benefit but have not paid) will be evident. Any individual who does not pay towards the product can still obtain the full benefits of that product. Besides the armed forces, other examples include the provision of a police force, a judicial system, radio and TV signals, and lighthouse services. There is, therefore, a serious risk of non-provision or underprovision given that financiers will be unwilling to accept free-riders. To overcome this, government financing, through taxation, will be the only practical solution.

The promotion of a tourist destination, such as a seaside resort or a whole country, may be considered a public good, too. It will be difficult to ensure everyone helps finance the advertising and difficult to exclude any one hotelier, caterer, transport operator or other tourist business from the benefits if they choose not to contribute.

Merit wants

These are goods and services that in some way are considered to be so important to the well-being of the individual, that consumers should not, because of low income or ignorance, be prevented from consuming them. Education and health services, in particular, may be considered to be in this category. Industrial catering may give benefits to employees (ignoring external effects). Holidays may be 'good' for the individual (ignoring external effects) because they contribute 'substantially to both physical and mental well-being'. If so, then it might be appropriate for some 'paternalistic' body (firm, trade union, government) to encourage consumption through subsidies.

Alternatively, prices could remain at their market level and consumers' incomes altered (through the tax and social security system) or consumers advised of the benefits of consumption.

Income distribution[28]

Although the goals of allocative and productive efficiency might be achieved, it is possible to have reservations about the resulting allocation of goods and services if the distribution of income is, in some way, considered to be unsatisfactory. There may, at the extreme, be a few consumers receiving most of the economy's income and the majority of consumers receiving a very small share of that income; this might be considered to be 'unjust', despite the achievement of allocative efficiency. There are very many different distributions of income possible and allocative efficiency can be achieved at any one of them. Governments might then intervene, through the tax and social security system, to bring about an income distribution which is considered to be 'equitable'.

When government intervention is felt to be justified, it may take several forms.[29] Governments can arrange for the goods and services to be supplied to consumers without direct charge (such as primary and secondary education), or on a flat-rate charge which bears little or no relation to usage (charges for medical prescriptions in the UK). It may be, however, that such policies could encourage a greater usage of these products than consumers really 'need', i.e. wastage occurs. The absence of a 'true market' price denies consumers the opportunity to assess the worth of these products in relation to other priced products and they continue consuming without considering the cost involved to society as a whole.

The intervention in price need not mean that government actually produces the good or service though this will often happen, in practice. Education and health services in the UK are largely provided by the Government, but it is conceivable for them to be provided by private firms though at prices decided by government.

A further instrument of government intervention is 'compulsory consumption', as in the case of education up to the age of sixteen in the UK.

(See also Chapter 8.)

Questions for essays and seminar papers

1 Discuss and evaluate the operation of the price mechanism under conditions of perfect competition.

2 Tourist attractions such as cathedrals, museums and art galleries often allow free admission. Consider whether it would be more desirable for them to charge a price for admission.

3 How far is the continued growth of demand for UK hotel and catering services dependent upon a fall in the foreign exchange rate?

4 Explain how knowledge of the elasticity of demand for hotel and catering services might be of use to hoteliers and caterers.

Practical assignment

Prepare statistics of the volume, value and structure of demand for accommodation and eating out in the UK over the last twenty years. (Information about eating out may be relatively difficult to obtain.) The structure of demand should include information about types of consumer, timing of demand, types of hotel or restaurant etc., transport used, and so on.

CHAPTER 3

Market structure

This chapter will examine the model of the firm and the price mechanism developed in Chapter 2 and develop less theoretical, more 'realistic' aspects of it, and, in particular, the market structure component of the structure, conduct and performance relationship.

Size structure of firms

The perfect competition model envisages that firms are owner-managed, they seek to maximize profits and are not large enough to have an influence over price. The existence of a large number of small firms in any industry may suggest the existence of something close to perfect competition.

With regard to manufacturing industries in the UK, small firms certainly dominate (data for service industries is much less readily available). They were defined by the Bolton Committee[1] as being those which had a small market share, were managed by the owners and which were legally independent. Small firms are, in practice, distinguished in a number of ways in each industry, e.g. in manufacturing the Bolton Committee used 200 employees as the cut-off in defining the small firm, in road transport firms with five vehicles or less were 'small', in construction twenty-five employees was the cut-off point, and in catering all firms were included except multiples and brewery-managed public houses.

The vast majority of manufacturing firms (97.9 per cent) employ fewer than 200 people (1985).[2] But in terms of total employment and net output, their contribution is comparatively limited (30.3 per cent and 25.3 per cent respectively) and is not proportional to their numerical importance.

There may well be relatively few large firms in manufacturing, but they dominate the employment and output scene. Firms that employ more than 200 employees are only 2.1 per cent of the total number of firms, but they account for 69.7 per cent of manufacturing employment. They also dominate manufacturing output and there is a strong tendency for that domination to increase; in 1909 the 100 largest manufacturing companies accounted for about 16 per cent of manufacturing output and by 1985, the proportion was 37 per cent.[3]

The number and size of the largest firms seem to be increasing. The Bolton Committee commented upon the decline, up to that time (1971), in the number

Table 23 *Relative importance of small firms in different industries 1963*

	Small firms as % of all firms		
	Numbers employed	*Net output*	*Number of firms*
Miscellaneous services	82	68	99
Retail trades	49	32	96
Road transport	36	26	85
Hotel and catering trades	75	73	96

Source: *Report of the Committee of Inquiry on Small Firms*, Cmnd 4811 (HMSO 1971).

and relative importance of small firms in manufacturing, but the small firm sector remains significant and it may well be that the sector's decline has been reversed recently.[4]

Although data for the service sector is limited, the Bolton Committee did provide some relevant information which is now somewhat dated (see Table 23).

It is apparent from Table 23 that in the hotel and catering industry, small firms not only dominate in terms of numbers, but also in terms of their contribution to employment and output. This is in marked contrast to manufacturing and there is apparently a lack of domination by a few large firms.

Table 24 relates to 1976 and, while not showing the hotel and catering industry as a separate sector, does illustrate the relative importance of small firms in the service industries generally.

The number of large or small firms in industry as a whole, however, does not give any indication of the market power of those firms. It may be that the large firms in manufacturing, although dominating the overall industrial scene, have little power in the individual markets they serve, e.g. all of the large firms could be competing in the same market. Similarly, it could be that the large firms in services, although apparently unimportant overall, do exercise a great deal of market power.

Market concentration

Market concentration is a measure of the extent to which a market (or more usually, in practice, an industry) is dominated by a specific number of the largest firms. The domination is measured by reference to employment, sales or capital employed, and the specific number of largest firms may be taken as, for instance, the top five.

A concentration ratio is thus the proportion of sales (or other variable) accounted for by the five (or other number) largest firms. Many manufacturing industries (if not markets) appear to be dominated by a few large firms, i.e.

Table 24 *Employment in small firms by sector 1976 (UK)*

	Employment in small firms as % of total employment in each sector
Manufacturing	22
Agriculture, forestry and fishing	30
Distributive trades	39
Miscellaneous services (includes hotels and catering)	43
Construction	49
Professional and scientific services	48
Insurance, banking, finance and business services	20

Source: G. Bannock, *The Economics of Small Firms* (Basil Blackwell 1981), Chapter 3.

concentration ratios are 'high' and the top five firms account for a large share of total sales. The UK Census of Production for 1985 lists 106 industries for which five-firm net-output concentration ratios are given. Six per cent of the industries had a concentration ratio of over 90 per cent and for 17 per cent it was over 70 per cent. One per cent had a concentration ratio of less than 10 per cent and for 49 per cent it was less than 40 per cent.[5]

These concentration levels have been increasing over time and are higher than in several other industrialized economies; the evidence does, however, point to a levelling-off of concentration since the late 1960s.[6]

Concentration ratio values that have been calculated for the hotel and catering industry have usually been well below those common in manufacturing. Rogers and Phipps[7] estimated a four-firm concentration ratio of 11 per cent in the hotel sector, and 6 per cent in the catering sector. Both were calculated by reference to ownership of 'physical capacity' rather than by reference to sales, employment, etc., and in the case of hotels that capacity was measured by reference to 'beds'. Ryan[8] estimated a four-firm hotel ratio of 1.1 per cent by reference to number of hotels, 10.3 per cent by reference to number of bedspaces, 8.2 per cent by number of rooms and 23 per cent by reference to sales value. Ryan suggested that the four largest catering firms controlled less than 3 per cent of all units. Another source[9] reports that only just over 2 per cent of catering outlets are owned by 'restaurant' chains, though the picture is probably different in the case of take-away fast food where franchised operations are common. (In the USA, the top 100 chain restaurant companies have increased their share of total commercial eating out sales from 24 per cent in 1970 to 48 per cent in 1982.)[10]

Table 25 *Relative importance of 'multiple' organizations in the 'catering trades' 1977*

	'Multiples' as % of:		
	Businesses	Establishments	Turnover
Licensed hotels, motels and guest houses	0.37	7.2	31.3
Unlicensed hotels, motels and guest houses	0.25	4.0	13.2
Licensed restaurants	0.54	11.4	27.2
Unlicensed restaurants, snack bars, etc. (on-premises consumption)	0.42	9.9	22.9
Catering contractors	20.40	92.9	92.3

Note: The inquiry defined 'multiples' as operating six or more establishments.

Source: Business Statistics Office, *Catering and Allied Trades, Business Monitor SDO 29* (HMSO 1981).

Akehurst estimated a four-firm hotel ratio of 1.3 per cent (by number of hotels), a restaurant ratio of 4.6 per cent (by number of units) and a ratio for catering contractors (five firms) of 75 per cent.

Sales concentration ratios (five firms) for 1977 have been estimated by Horsburgh at 19 per cent for hotels, 7 per cent for restaurants and fish and chip shops and 49 per cent for contract catering. It is believed that these values are lower than 1969 values but this is not certain.[11]

It is not an easy task to derive concentration values for this industry. There are few up-to-date and/or reliable figures for total sales value, of total number of bedspaces, of total stock of accommodation or of catering outlets, or total employment, etc. Such data is necessary if the influence of any number of firms is to be assessed.

Further related data may be derived from a statistical inquiry into the industry undertaken in 1977[12] (see Tables 25 and 26).

Numerically, therefore, except for contractors, large multiple firms are not important in the hotel and catering industry, accounting for less than 1 per cent of firms, but reference to numbers does understate their true importance in respect of contribution to total turnover and ownership of all establishments. The relative unimportance of multiples compared with manufacturing is, however, confirmed by these tables. The 'Pickering' research report[13] of the Bolton Committee concluded that 'when compared with concentration ratios in other industries, particularly manufacturing, the data we have on hotel and catering concentration may seem to indicate that this is not particularly significant'.

In Chapter 1, it was noted that markets for hotel and catering products are

Table 26 *Hotel and catering businesses: by number of establishments 1977*

	Percentage of businesses having:
1 establishment or branch	97.1
2 establishments or branches	1.8
3–5 establishments or branches	0.7
6 or more establishments or branches	0.4

Source: Business Statistics Office, *Catering and Allied Trades, Business Monitor SDO 29* (HMSO 1981).

essentially 'local' markets; as a consequence, national concentration ratios may have little value. Even if there appears to be little overall market domination by the largest firms, it may well be that there exists considerably more domination within particular areas of the country by even small hotel or catering firms. Some of the bigger firms are not competing in the same markets as small firms and thus it might be appropriate to estimate concentration in those 'large-firm markets'.[14]

One snack bar in a busy town shopping-centre could exert significant market power. Conversely, national or local market power can be modified by foreign competition; the hotel industry in the UK does experience the competitive effects of hotels in tourist destinations abroad. Although such an influence will not be as significant in the case of catering, it does illustrate that measurement of concentration and market power can depend critically upon the definition of market that is adopted.

Data relating to a popular North Wales seaside resort (Llandudno) and a large conurbation suggests that while large hotel firms may control a larger share of the bedrooms in the latter location, they certainly do not dominate the overall accommodation scene even here (see Table 27).

A study of Scarborough[15] indicated a pattern similar to that in Llandudno for serviced (traditional) accommodation; for self-catering accommodation, however, 44 per cent of Scarborough capacity was owned by persons/companies owning more than one establishment.

There is no doubt that the multiples do have a firm grip on certain parts of the market. Of the AA 2-star and above hotels in Manchester city centre, about 70 per cent are multiple-owned, but in Llandudno, only 30 per cent are so owned.

Discussion in Chapter 1 also indicated the difficulties surrounding the concepts of 'industry' and 'market'; data for industries or parts of industries is not, of course, necessarily appropriate for information about markets. The largest hotel and catering groups provide a range of different products (different grades of accommodation at different locations) sold in different markets. Thus they may sell some of their product (e.g. city-centre 5-star

Table 27 *Relative importance of large hotel firms in Llandudno (North Wales) and in Greater Manchester County (1981–82)*

	Llandudno	*GMC*
Total number of accommodation units*	243	117
Total number of bedrooms*	3199	5742
(Average number of bedrooms per unit)	13	49
Multiples' units as % of total†	6%	13%
Multiples' bedrooms as % of total†	25%	33%

* Does not include self-catering accommodation.
† Estimates only due to incomplete availability of 'ownership' data.

Sources: *Llandudno Accommodation List, 1982* (Aberconwy Borough Council Leisure and Amenities Dept. 1981). *Your Hotel Key to GMC, 1981* (Greater Manchester Council 1981).

hotels) in conditions which are less competitive (and thus they may exercise more control) than the markets in which they sell other of their products (e.g. unclassified seaside accommodation). 'Thus Trusthouse Forte Hotels (THFH) has only a very small market share which is positioned in the top quarter of the market but, in the market in which it operates and in some localities at least, THFH possesses some degree of influence'.[16]

Concentration ratios in isolation should be treated cautiously in that the relative size of the firms outside the top few is not taken into account, as such. Other firms may be similar in size to the largest or there may be a great number of much smaller firms. It is believed, of course, that there are a large number of very small firms in the hotel and catering industry but the exact size range of firms (as opposed to units/establishments) and structure is not known. Ryan[17] has observed, however, that the four largest hotel firms are very much larger than their nearest rivals (over three times as large). There do exist other relative concentration measures which attempt to allow for the number of firms in an industry and their relative size, but they have been rarely calculated for the hotel and catering industry.[18]

In conclusion, one element of market structure, namely seller concentration, is not yet readily determined in the case of the hotel and catering industry. It is not yet possible, therefore, to deal entirely satisfactorily with an analysis of the competitive structure of the industry and the way in which it contributes to the 'optimal allocation of resources'.

Other elements of the market structure will be discussed later in this chapter.

The small establishment

It is, however, possible to consider rather more satisfactorily the size range of establishments within the hotel and catering industry and to provide some

Table 28 *Size distribution of establishments in hotel and catering and in manufacturing*

Size of establishment (number employed)	*Hotels and guest houses (1981)*	*Restaurants, cafés and snack bars (1981)*	*Manufacturing (1985)*
1–10	57.8	75.2	69.0 (1–9)
11–49	34.7	23.4	21.2 (10–49)
50–99	5.0	1.4	4.0
100 and over	2.5		5.8

Sources: Business Statistics Office, *Report on the Census of Production 1985, Summary Volume, Business Monitor PA1002* (HMSO 1988) and *Hotel and Catering Establishments in Great Britain: A Regional Analysis, Part 1* (HCITB 1985).

explanation for the large number of small establishments (and thus of small firms).

'Establishments' are the productive or sales unit such as the individual hotel, restaurant or factory, whereas the 'firm' is the unit of ownership and as such, it may be made up of one or more establishments.

The Pickering research report confirmed that 'the key to the identification of the small firm (in hotels and catering) should be that it was owner-managed'. Many of the firms in this industry are believed to be owner-managed, i.e. they are one or a very small number of establishments owned by an individual or small group of persons who take active day-to-day control in the detailed running of the establishment(s). Establishments are thus usually 'small'. Table 28 gives a broad indication of the size of hotel and catering establishments and also compares them with manufacturing establishments/plants. It is noticeable that the typical establishment in both this industry and in manufacturing is 'small', although the largest establishments are more common in manufacturing.

By other size criteria, such as number of bedrooms, more data exists for accommodation establishments than for catering establishments.[19] Data from tourist boards[20] confirms that the majority of accommodation establishments are 'small' in terms of numbers of bedrooms. Table 29 reinforces this.

Even the largest companies are thus characterized by ownership of a large number of establishments, small and large, rather than ownership of just a few large establishments. This reflects, in part, the many different types of market (both geographical and product) that characterize the industry.

The larger firms are more likely, however, to own a higher proportion of large establishments than are small firms and those large establishments do account for a large part of the large firms' total business, e.g. the 30.6 per cent of Trusthouse Forte's establishments that have 101 or more bedrooms in fact accounted for nearly 60 per cent of the company's total bedrooms (UK).

Table 29 *Size structure of various accommodation establishments*

	Llandudno					
Number of bedrooms	*Fully licensed hotels*	*Full board hotels*	*B, B & evening meal*	*B & B only*	*Greater Manchester County*	*Trusthouse Forte (UK)*
	(% of establishments in each size range)					
Up to 10	–	37.9	81.9	80	18.8	0.5
11 to 20	–	24.1	15.1	20	27.3	8.2
21 to 30	–	10.3	3.0	–	18.8	12.6
31 to 40	7.1	13.8	–	–	6.8	7.8
41 to 50	28.5	13.8	–	–	4.3	7.3
51 to 60	21.4	–	–	–	4.3	9.2
61 to 70	–	–	–	–	5.1	7.3
71 to 80	21.4	–	–	–	1.7	9.2
81 to 90	7.1	–	–	–	0.8	3.9
91 to 100	–	–	–	–	1.7	3.4
101 and over	14.9	–	–	–	10.2	30.6

Sources: *Llandudno Accommodation List, 1982, op. cit. Your Hotel Key to GMC, 1981, op. cit.* R. Tiltscher, *An investment review of the UK hotel industry* (Sector Investments 1983), appendix.

The 'smallness' of hotel and catering establishments may be explained in several ways:

1 In the case of many services and the hotel and catering industry in particular, the market demand is highly stratified and is not always readily standardized. The basic products (the establishments) are differentiated by their different locations, their different mix of sales (food, drink and accommodation) and their different standards. The diversity of demand is best satisfied by a wide range of different small establishments, rather than by one large establishment.

It is possible to standardize the demand for hotel and catering products and to have several standardized establishments within any one firm. The other characteristics, however, of the hotel and catering product combine to mean that there will probably still be several smaller establishments rather than one larger establishment.

There may well be cost advantages in building and running one large hotel or restaurant rather than several smaller ones, but the cost advantage is not great enough to outweigh the necessity to serve several local markets and the advantages to be obtained by meeting the stratified demand of the consumer and operating on a small scale.

2 In fact there are probably fewer (technical) economies of scale to be achieved in the hotel and catering industry than in many manufacturing

industries. These economies will be discussed in a later chapter, but simply they are advantages of operation on a large scale; such operation is usually dependent upon the ability to produce and sell a long run of standardized output. By their very nature, many service industries are limited in their ability to produce significant technical economies of scale (see Chapter 5 for further discussion of this) and thus there may be little to lose by producing on a small scale.

There is probably not much of a cost disadvantage in building and operating three or four small hotels or restaurants rather than one big one.

3 Hotel and catering markets are local markets. Service outputs must be produced in the same place and at the same time that they are demanded; production and consumption occur simultaneously. The service cannot be stored or transported. As the consumer must usually travel to the service establishment in order to obtain the product, service establishments are located within 'easy' travelling distance of consumers. Demand itself is widely dispersed because of the dispersal of the population, transport facilities, tourist attractions, etc. Each local market is thus limited in size and large hotel and catering establishments would, in many cases, be too large for a particular market. Large establishments exist only where the market is large enough to justify them.

4 The nature of hotel and catering services is such that the small establishment may be better suited to satisfying the wants of consumers. The manager (owner or not) can give attention to detail and can facilitate the co-ordination of interconnected services. Hotel and catering services depend on close and flexible day-to-day management; the personality of the proprietor or manager can have an important effect on customer and employee satisfaction. The large hotel and catering firms recognize this, of course, and seek to combine a degree of independence at their establishments with an element of central control and co-ordination.

5 Small establishments may well be as cheap or cheaper to run than many a large establishment.

The small firm

Why so many small firms?

1 It is, in practice, relatively cheap for owner-managers to establish themselves initially. Because of the dominance of small establishments, relatively little capital is required in order to set up, compared with many manufacturing industries, for instance. It is therefore possible for owner-managed firms to come into existence easily. Undoubtedly, costs of building new hotels and restaurants in city-centre locations are very high, but there exists an extensive

market in existing properties and many opportunities for set-up in other 'cheaper' locations. Much entry into the 'hotel' industry has, in the past, taken the form of converting private houses; sufficient funds have often been available for set-up from private savings or a gratuity. The Scarborough study, previously mentioned, estimated that 20 per cent of 'traditional' accommodation and over 30 per cent of self-catering had been converted from private housing.

2 A firm comprised of but one or a few small establishment(s) can exist and survive in the hotel and catering industry. There may well be distinct advantages over the large firm in being such a small and/or owner-managed firm. For instance, they may provide a personal service and atmosphere that may be lacking even in the small establishments of large firms; this is often a critical marketing feature. The owner-manager will probably be highly motivated and keen to make a success of the business. Also, he/she may be able to directly supervise the establishment's activities. If family are involved in running the business, then there may be added advantages of greater flexibility in staffing, fewer personnel problems, reduced wage bill, longer hours worked, and so on.

Furthermore, the large firms may not possess significant advantages over the smaller ones. Whatever economies of scale do exist in the hotel and catering industry (see Chapter 5), they do not seem to have been great enough to overcome the advantages of the owner-manager and the nature of the hotel and catering market. Some of the smaller firms may exist, however, only by operating at a 'loss' which would only be evident if the owner drew and paid economic salaries.[21]

Such owner-managed establishments can, in practice, be run by a single person perhaps with family or very little outside staff; such small establishments/firms would not require a complex supervisory structure. It is the belief, too, of many entrants to the industry that the skills and expertise required for hotel and catering management are not very great and such as they are, they can be easily acquired and effectively applied by one or two persons without recourse to much outside expertise. A small establishment can exist independently without having to rely on back-up services from 'head office' or the strength of being one of many establishments within a large firm.

3 It is also an attractive industry to enter. There are attractions of being an owner-manager and the hotel and catering industry offers one of the few opportunities of becoming 'one's own boss'. This attraction is reinforced by the inherent attractions of working in the hotel and catering industry itself which can provide much human interest and job satisfaction. There are no real restrictions on the ability of individuals to enter the industry in the sense of essential professional qualifications, for instance.

4 The small firm can survive too because of the wide variety of markets to be served, some of which the large firms may not be interested in.

5 The existence of so many small firms is made easier, too, by the lack of significant barriers to entry.

Barriers to entry[22]

These constitute another element of market structure (along with market concentration and product differentiation). Low barriers to entry of new firms into a market/industry mean that it is relatively easy to establish in that market/industry. Thus any control that is exercised by a dominant firm over the market may be competed away by new entrants. Any attempts by a dominant firm to earn 'high' profits by, for instance, charging high prices, could be short-lived if those high profits provide an incentive for new firms to establish themselves in that market.

Conversely, if barriers to entry are high, then a dominant firm may safeguard its dominance because there is a reduced threat of competing entrants.

Thus the behaviour of firms may be influenced not solely by the number of existing firms but by the entry of new firms or by the prospect of entry. The barriers themselves may be of several types:

1 If a firm succeeds in 'differentiating' its particular product so that it is made to appear unique, then a degree of brand loyalty will result. The differentiation of basically similar products (see later in this chapter) usually occurs by establishing different brand images and can entail extensive expenditure in the form of advertising outlays, for instance. Any new entrant would probably have to equal (if not exceed) such expenditure in order to compete successfully with established firms. The more successful the product differentiation and the greater is the brand loyalty, the higher is the barrier to entry.

Product differentiation exists among smaller owner-managed hotel and catering firms but is probably not at such a level as to mean that a newcomer would have to spend a lot of money in order to equal it and successfully enter the industry.

Among the bigger firms dominating some parts of the industry the situation is such that a large amount of money might have to be spent by newcomers to create an 'image' and advertise it. For hotels, in particular, a brand image can be important as a reassurance to potential customers: customers cannot inspect the product before purchase and have to buy 'on trust'.[23] Hotel and catering products are 'experience goods' and a reassuring, well-known brand image can encourage custom.

Product differentiation may not be so noticeable in hotels and catering as in many other consumer goods industries such as cosmetics, washing powders and cars, but there are many instances of successful product differentiation, for example, in the fast food sector (McDonalds and Wimpy) and short-break

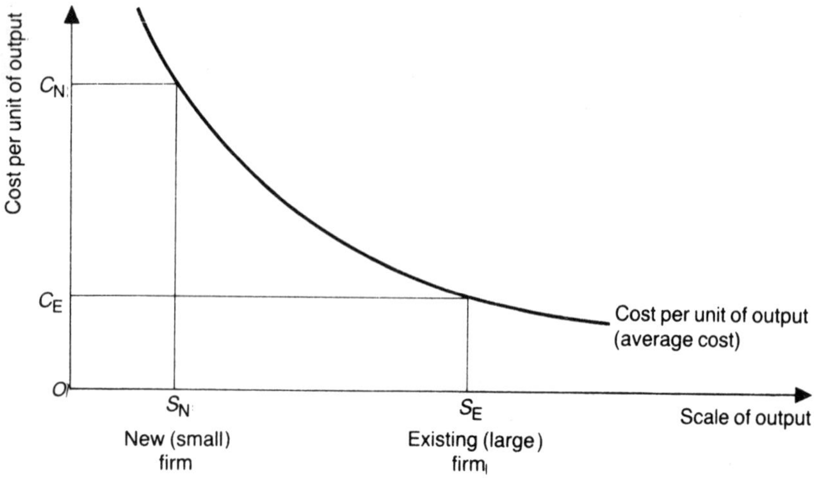

Figure 17 *Relative costs of new and existing firms*

holiday markets (Stardust). The 'good-will' of a business may well also be a barrier to entry and owe its strength to a form of product differentiation.

2 Another barrier may be economies of scale. If these are of some significance in an industry, it means that the largest firms have substantial cost advantages over the smallest. Any new firms entering an industry would usually start at a comparatively low-level of production (S_N) and would thus incur higher costs (C_N) than the existing, larger, firms (S_E and C_E) (see Figure 17).

It has, however, already been suggested that the scope for achieving economies of scale is limited in the hotel and catering industry and this, too, is unlikely in most markets to create much of a barrier to the entry of new firms (i.e. in Figure 17, C_N is not likely to be much above C_E).

In so far as there are economies of scale in being able to differentiate and advertise products successfully, then a real barrier will exist in favour of the larger, established firm. Trusthouse Forte Hotels (1979) was considered to have advantages in group purchasing and booking facilities which could make entry more difficult for new firms.[24]

3 Further barriers include those which might be termed 'absolute cost disadvantages'. These arise when costs for the entrant are higher at all levels of production (and not just at the lower levels) than for the existing firms (see Figure 18).

At all levels of output, such as *oq*, costs of the new firm are higher (C_N) than those of the existing firm (C_E); such a disadvantage might arise because the existing firms possess knowledge that is not available to the entrant or because

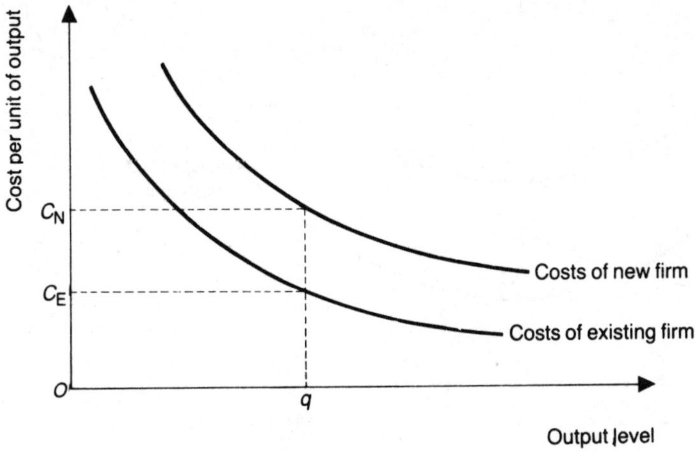

Figure 18 *Relative costs of firms in the presence of absolute cost disadvantages*

they have control over or favourable access to suppliers of inputs. In the hotel and catering industry there is little to suggest that knowledge and skills are very specific to particular firms – there are few 'trade secrets' or patents. Even though existing firms may have established their credit-worthiness with suppliers and are able to negotiate discounts for supplies, such advantages may not be significant in terms of a barrier. Even existing firms' knowledge of the market is likely to be a short-lived advantage; few of the absolute cost disadvantages are likely to be permanent, in fact. Large multinational corporations may be able to achieve and maintain such advantages, however.

The ownership by one firm of many hotel and catering establishments could act as a barrier in that, for instance, brewery-owned establishments could be dealt with more favourably than the 'free trade' in terms of price and reliability of supplies of beer and related products. In practice, this has not always been the case.[25]

4 Trade associations in the hotel and catering industry (such as the British Hotels, Restaurants and Caterers' Association), i.e. associations of firms, do not operate very restrictive entry conditions which could serve to keep any advantages of membership to the select few.

As existing firms could be at a cost advantage compared with new entrants, they could choose to jointly set an 'entry-forestalling' price or 'limit' price. In such a case, the existing firms would each set a price for the product (*op* in Figure 19) which was high enough to ensure that they earned a profit, but not high enough for a newcomer to earn a profit. Thus they would deliberately lower their own profits and keep prices low so as to avoid attracting others.

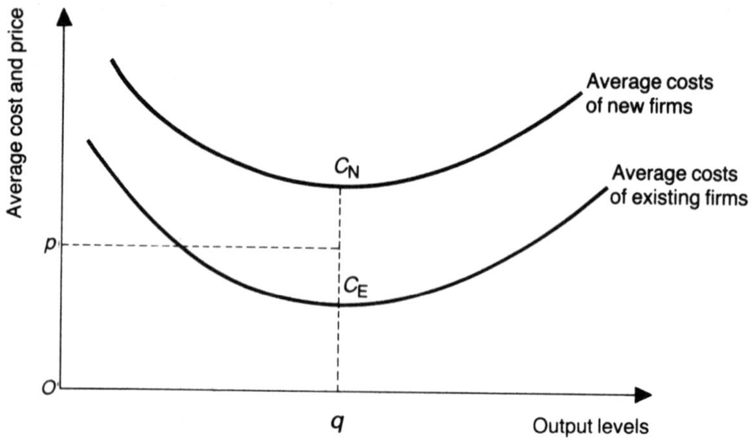

Figure 19 *'Limit' or 'entry-forestalling' price*

Such action is only likely, however, in markets where there are few firms which are able to easily communicate and co-operate, and as such is not likely in most hotel and catering markets.

Undoubtedly hoteliers and caterers may have kept each other informed of their tariffs and may have implicitly agreed to keep them in line but the effect of government legislation (see Chapter 8), has been to make such activities illegal.

Membership of neither the trade associations nor the professional association (Hotel, Catering and Institutional Management Association), i.e. association of individual managers and owners, is necessary before entry into the industry.

5 It has already been suggested that 'finance' and initial 'set-up' costs are not a very important barrier to the entry of firms in the industry as a whole.

Other barriers will include licensing legislation, if the sale of alcoholic liquor is required, and town and country planning legislation. Both Butlins and Trusthouse Forte Hotels Ltd were believed to be protected to some extent by the difficulty of obtaining planning permission for new holiday camps and the planning constraints in central London.[26]

Barriers to entry are not easily measured in practice but some indication can be obtained from estimates of economies of scale (see Chapter 5) and of advertising and product differentiation (see later in this chapter).

Because of the undoubted costs of entry into most markets, entry is often by firms already established in other markets/industries rather than by newly-established firms. They often have some existing links with the market into which they are moving and will have the financial resources to withstand the costs of entry. Certainly there are many instances of already-established firms with some links with the hotel and catering industry entering this industry, e.g. airlines, breweries, leisure companies, food firms, etc.[27] (See also Chapter 4.)

Overall barriers to entry in the hotel and catering industry are low, certainly if compared with many technologically-based manufacturing industries. Thus the ability of any one firm to exercise effective control over a market is restricted and the behaviour is likely to be more competitive in outcome. However, there are, of course, many different hotel and catering markets and while it may well be true that entry into the industry as a whole may not be difficult, some hotel and catering markets may prove more difficult to penetrate than others.

Some of the fast food take-away and 'eat-in' chains located in many urban areas may be partially protected by their attempts to establish brand-loyalty, and by some ability to achieve economies of scale (e.g. in bulk purchasing). In addition the specific (and in some cases, well-guarded) nature of the product and its ingredients (including sauces) and technical know-how often contribute towards the ability to restrict entry. Certainly the sort of markets that the larger hotel and catering firms supply are often characterized by higher barriers to entry than are the markets supplied by the owner-managers. In the former case there may well be substantial advertising costs to match, high capital costs to incur and significant economies of scale may be achieved.

Entry overall, is easy because of the ability to meet the needs of consumers in any one of many different sections of the market; if entry into some parts of the market proves difficult, then entry elsewhere may be easier.

Prospects for the small firm

The Report of the Committee of Inquiry on Small Firms (Bolton Committee) concluded that the absolute number and relative importance of the small firm in the British economy were declining. Concern was expressed about this contraction because the small firm sector was seen as a valuable source of innovation and a contributor to the provision of a variety of products. Such firms were seen also as being flexible and responsive to changes in consumer needs, and as providing a 'breeding ground' for new firms and industries; they were considered, too, as providing a means of entry into business for new talent. Finally, the sector can provide a competitive stimulus to large firms.

More recently the small firm sector of industry has been regarded as valuable in its contribution to employment and the regeneration of inner urban areas and depressed regions.[28]

If small firms are so valuable (and this is something that all governments since have emphasized) then the contraction ought to be halted or reversed. As a consequence of the Bolton Committee, the Small Firms Service was established. Since that time a number of further government policies have

Table 30 *Change in hotel and guest house population of Great Britain 1977–81*

% change in number of establishments, categorised by number of employees					
1–10	*11–24*	*25–49*	*50–99*	*100+*	*All*
−19	+6	+11	+6	−9	−10

Note: Data excludes establishments run by self-employed proprietors.

Source: *Hotel and Catering Establishments in Great Britain: A Regional Analysis, Part I* (HCITB 1985).

sought to give particular forms of assistance to small firms, especially in manufacturing[29] (see Chapter 8).

It is possible that the contraction has now slowed down, if not stopped. In the hotel and catering industry there is no comprehensive data about the small firm sector and especially about changes in its size and composition. However, there are undoubted problems that the small firm sector in this industry faces and the future of the hotel and catering small firm is not secure.[30] Data in Table 30 does suggest that small hotels have diminished in number and the Scarborough study (Table 31) points to an overall decline in units in one location.

Apart from the difficulties faced by small firms in all industries in raising finance (see Chapter 7), such firms face competition from the larger chains. Such large chain groups have access to finance, techniques, specialist management knowledge and skills, which are not available to smaller firms; they are more able to meet the demands for higher standards of catering and accommodation. They are more able to meet high interest charges and they are more likely to diversify and be less reliant upon one establishment or location. They are less likely to be dependent upon the talents of only one or a few people.

Small firms continue to survive, however, and their position may be strengthened by their success in marketing their particular assets. Individuality and the personal touch can generate much repeat business; the owner-manager can direct the firm with strong motivation and can generate personal loyalty in his/her employees.

Additionally, small firms may co-operate in a marketing consortium,[30] many of which are now well established in the hotel sector, in particular. Consortia such as 'Best Western' are groupings of geographically-separate independently-owned hotels which seek to compete with the large chains by engaging in marketing activities which individually they would not be able to afford (e.g. national and international advertising campaigns, promotional brochures, central reservation systems, referrals within the group, tours using hotels within the group, and so on). Other hotels, guest houses and boarding houses may rely upon the 'spin-off' from the efforts expended by local authorities and tourist boards to promote their particular resorts and tourist destinations.

Many of the large hotel firms co-operate in joint marketing efforts, especially of cheaper winter attractions, e.g. Highlife (1980) – Crest, Centre, Embassy and Thistle holidays; Breakaway weekend holiday breaks – Swallow, Anchor and Greenall Whitley hotels.

Caterers may operate under a franchise system which effectively allows many to remain as independent firms.[32] The exact detail of each franchise system (such as Wimpy or Kentucky Fried Chicken) varies, but generally the caterer contributes financially towards the setting-up of an establishment. The 'parent' organization (the franchisor) may also contribute and give assistance in setting up and running the business and will be responsible for the overall marketing of the product for all of the franchisees and for supplying precise specifications for the product, service and environment. Thus the independence of owner-manager is restricted, but he/she gains the financial, technical and specialist assistance of a large organization. This sector of catering has grown rapidly in recent years and is also a limited feature of hotels (e.g. Holiday Inn).

Although large firms are not typical of the UK hotel and catering industry, some of the industry's larger firms are among the 'giants' of British industry as a whole, e.g. Grand Metropolitan is ranked as the thirteenth largest firm in the UK (by turnover, 1987) and Trusthouse Forte the seventy-fifth largest firm. Large firms such as Allied Lyons (rank 23), Bass (37) and Ladbroke (63) are active in hotel and catering activities.[33]

Grand Metropolitan owns one of the largest restaurant chains in the world, Berni, ranked fortieth by number of units in 1987, and up to 1988 one of the largest hotel chains (eighteenth by number of bedrooms, 1987). Bass and Ladbroke, however, were in thirteenth and seventeenth positions respectively with their acquisitions of Holiday Inns International and Hilton International. Trusthouse Forte was the ninth largest hotel chain and owned the thirty-fourth largest restaurant chain (Little Chef). Two of the largest restaurant chais, Wimpy and Pizzaland (thirty-first and forty-first ranking) were controlled by the UK company United Biscuits whose other interests include snack and biscuit manufacture.

Product differentiation[34]

This is a further aspect of market structure, along with market concentration and barriers to entry, in that it may influence the conduct of firms, especially in pricing. As noted earlier, product differentiation (and advertising) can act also as a barrier to entry.

Product differentiation is the ability of producers to distinguish basically similar products from each other so that *in the eyes of the consumer,* they are no longer perfect substitutes (compare perfect competition). The reduction in substitutability may arise from the use of brand names, different packaging and appearance, creation of brand image, etc. If successful, such a policy creates brand loyalty and an element of a firm's control over the market and over price. Consumers may be willing to pay more for goods or services because 'price-consciousness' is reduced.

If a firm has successfully undertaken a market-segmentation exercise it may find it profitable to offer several brands of the same product aimed at the different consumers in each segment. The multiplication of brands by any one producer (especially evident in the case of washing powder) will also reduce the likelihood of any shifting consumer expenditure being captured by other producers.

In practice, the extent of product differentiation in industry is not clear because of the difficulties involved in measuring it. One approach is to assess the number of physical varieties of a product, but this is a subjective assessment and does not take into account the perceptions of the buyers of the products who may or may not see them as different products.

Cross-elasticities as a measure of product differentiation (Chapters 1 and 2) would give an indication of product substitutability. Such measures, however, are not widely available.

'Advertising intensity' (ratio of advertising expenditure to sales) is therefore often used as an indication of differentiation and is interpreted as a barrier to entry rather than as a separate aspect of market structure. (Advertising intensity is, however, subject to many influences and may reflect differences in firms' profits rather than differences in product differentiation.)

Although it can be claimed that product differentiation does have advantages for the consumer in that consumer choice is widened, it may be that many of the differences between products are more 'contrived' than real. Thus it might be considered to be a waste of society's scarce resources. It may, also, by creating a number of small markets rather than one larger standardized one, restrict the ability of firms to achieve economies of scale (see Chapter 5). Successful product differentiation can restrict the ability of new firms to enter an industry, as seen earlier in this chapter.

Advertising[35]

Advertising is closely associated with product differentiation and there are mixed views about its economic function and effects.

Advertising has an informative role to play in communicating information about the range, quality and price of products to consumers and thus serves to make markets more competitive and consumer-responsive.

It is arguable, however, just how far advertising is informative and how far it is 'persuasive'. If advertising succeeds in persuading consumers to purchase goods and services they would not otherwise have purchased, then consumer choice is distorted and consumer sovereignty reduced.

On the other hand, successful advertising should lead to increased sales and thus the achievement of economies of scale (the advantages of large-scale

Table 31 *Change in number of accommodation units (Scarborough) 1921–75*

	1921–31	*1975*
'Traditional' accommodation units	874	530
All accommodation units (including self-catering)	874	760

Source: C. Stallibrass, *Seaside Resorts and the Holiday Accommodation Industry: a Case Study of Scarborough*, Progress in Planning, 13 (3) (1980).

Table 32 *Advertising expenditure 1983 (£m)*

Top ten advertisers (GB)			*Top ten hotel and catering advertisers*		
1	Procter and Gamble	52.9	1	Kentucky Fried Chicken	5.3
2	Mars	33.9	2	McDonalds	4.1
3	Kelloggs	28.5	3	Butlins Holiday Camps	2.9
4	Imperial Tobacco	26.9	4	Wimpy	1.9
5	Rowntree Mackintosh	26.5	5	Pontins	1.7
6	British Telecom	24.4	6	Trusthouse Forte	1.2
7	Pedigree Petfoods	23.6	7	Pizza Hut	0.6
8	Cadbury	23.5	8	Watney Combe Reid	0.5
9	Electricity Council	21.7	9	Burger King	0.36
10	Gallaher	21.2	10	Berni Inns	0.32

Source: The Financial Times, 'Advertising Survey' (2 October 1984); *MEAL Digest*, 4th Quarter (1983).

production; see Chapter 5). It could also reduce restraints on innovation and the introduction of new goods and services in so far as it assists the rapid penetration of markets and the earning of profits. Although advertising is associated with non-perfectly competitive market structures, it can produce effective competition in terms of the quality of goods and services produced;[36] as such, it is an aspect of 'conduct'.

Advertising can act as an effective barrier to entry and thus result in higher profitability (see Chapter 4).

From Table 32 it can be seen that hotel and catering firms are not among the 'leaders' in advertising expenditure. Total expenditure by catering outlets (as recorded by Media Expenditure Analysis Ltd (MEAL)) amounted to £14.5m in 1983, below any one of the top ten advertisers. Total hotel advertising expenditure recorded by the same source amounted to £4.0m. (MEAL only records advertising expenditure by firms where it has exceeded £40,000 in the previous twelve months.)

The 'low' hotel and catering figures are, in part, due to the fact that there are not many large firms in the industry anyway. However, some of the advertising

Table 33 *Advertising by hotel and catering companies 1977–81 (£m)*

	Hotels	*Catering*
1977	1.15	1.82
1978	1.95	2.40
1979	2.25	3.02
1980	3.05	5.73
1981	3.65	8.38

Source: British Hotel and Catering Companies (Jordan & Sons 1982).

leaders (non-hotel and catering) have a smaller turnover than the bigger hotel and catering firms, e.g. Trusthouse Forte is the eighty-sixth largest firm (by turnover) in the UK in 1982, whereas Procter and Gamble was ranked number 242, Mars 121 and Kelloggs 309. The interfirm and interindustry differences will lie more in the nature of the products and the market structures of the industry. The more oligopolistic the industry the greater is likely to be the advertising intensity.

Advertising expenditure and intensity has, during the 1960s and 1970s, tended to be greatest in firms producing toiletries, soap and detergents, pharmaceuticals, food and drink, and domestic electrical appliances.

Advertising by catering firms has exceeded that by hotels for some years and has grown rapidly in recent years (see Table 33), largely because of the activities of fast food companies. Kentucky Fried Chicken, Wimpy and McDonalds accounted for 60 per cent of all hotel and catering advertising recorded by MEAL in 1983 (55 per cent in 1982).

A high proportion of hotel advertising expenditure appears to be directed at the business and conference and 'weekend break' markets where the establishment of a corporate image may well be important in stimulating demand. Many hotels in resort areas may consider that the promotion of the resort as a whole is more important. Advertising by some resorts is high with the top ten advertisers (recorded by MEAL) spending a total of £2.7m in 1983 (Blackpool: £0.9m). Other hotels may rely on marketing consortia for their advertising (see earlier in this chapter), e.g. Best Western expenditure of £0.2m in 1983.

Objectives[37]

Earlier in this and previous chapters it was noted that the 'traditional' model of the firm was one which saw it as a profit-maximizing owner-managed enterprise. It is evident that most hotel and catering firms are owner-managed, but how far is the 'profit-maximization' objective a satisfactory feature of the model?

'Survival' will be the ultimate goal of all firms and any other objectives will be dependent upon it; in turn, survival will be dependent upon achieving some of these goals.

'Growth' rather than profit-maximization has been identified in recent years as an important objective of many firms. The earliest models of the firm considered profit-maximization to be the objective of firms because firms were considered to be typically owner-managed and the owner, like all participants in the economic process, would be seeking to maximize his/her own personal financial gain. Further, the pressures of the competitive price mechanism in such a model would ensure that only the most profitable firms would survive.

A firm's conduct – its price and output decisions in particular – was considered to be the outcome of the policy of profit-maximization.

As the owner-managed firm is not necessarily the typical firm in British industry, a re-examination has occurred to construct different models, postulating other objectives and explaining firms' conduct or behaviour by them.

1 The Bolton Committee concluded that 'the underlying motivation (of owners of small firms) can best be summarized as "the need to attain and preserve independence". This need for "independence" sums up a wide range of highly personal gratifications provided by working for oneself and not for anybody else. It embraces many important satisfactions which running a business provided – the personal supervision and control of staff, direct contact with customers, the opportunity to develop one's own ideas, a strong feeling of personal challenge and an almost egotistical sense of personal achievement and pride – psychological satisfactions which appeared to be much more powerful motivators than money or the possibility of large financial gains'.

The 'Pickering' research report suggested that some owner-managers in the hotel and catering industry 'may have high leisure preference rather than an objective stated in terms of something nearer to the idea of the maximization of cash, income or profits....The particular nature of this industry means that operators with such a personal goal can often survive quite happily in view of the non-monetary benefits available'.

2 Thus even most owner-managed firms and many hotel and catering firms in particular are believed to have objectives other than profit-maximization. Most attention, however, has been directed by economic theorists towards an examination of the objectives of larger firms. These are usually public limited liability companies and as such, they are generally owned and managed by different people. The owners will be a large number of shareholders who may take little or no active interest in the company at all and the managers may own no shares but be very much in control of the company's fortunes. Because of this apparent separation of ownership and control, it becomes possible for management to pursue objectives other than those which interest the owners. It may be that while shareholders would be expected to be interested in profits, managers are more interested in their own levels of income, their status and power and are more concerned with security, a 'quiet life' and the avoidance of uncertainty (in these respects they may be akin to owner-managers). These

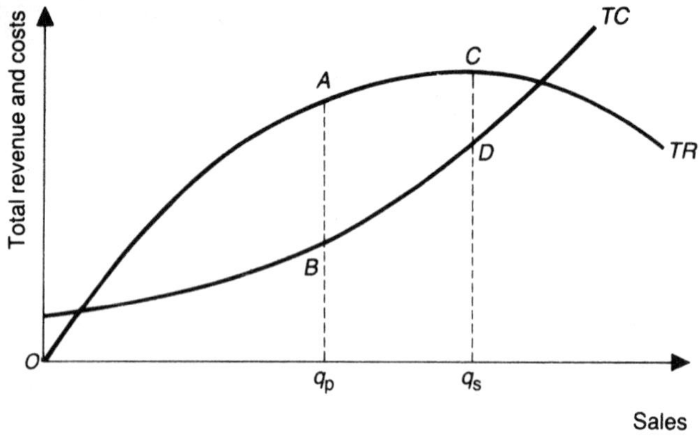

Figure 20 *Sales-revenue-maximization model*

factors of interest to managers have been considered to be more closely related to the size or rate of growth of a company than to its profitability.

Also, the environment within which such firms operate is believed to give some discretion to managers in the objectives they pursue. If firms do not operate within a 'perfect competition' market structure but within an imperfect world, then profit-maximization is no longer a necessary condition for survival; size, market dominance, financial resources, product differentiation and advertising may be more important in this respect.

Trusthouse Forte Hotels claimed to allow some discretion to their hotel managers in their actions subject to a 'constraint of maximizing sustainable profitability'.

3 One model of the firm that has been developed as a result is that of 'sales-revenue-maximization' (see Figure 20).

Profits are maximized where the difference between total costs (*TC*) and total revenue (*TR*) is greatest, i.e. at sales level oq_p where profit is indicated by *AB*. Sales revenue is maximized at oq_s, i.e. *TR* is at its highest here and profit is rather lower at (*CD*) than at oq_p. If there is a minimum profit level, greater than *CD*, considered necessary to satisfy shareholders, maintain the firm's survival and future growth, then the output level of a sales-maximizer may well be lower than at oq_s and may even coincide with oq_p.

Rather more complex models, including models of growth-maximization, have also been constructed.

But the division between owners and managers and their objectives may not be as clear-cut and absolute as such models would imply. In many cases small groups of shareholders can and do exercise effective control over their company, especially where there are 'institutional' shareholders (pension funds, insurance companies, banks, etc.). Some managers are also shareholders, and there is some evidence to suggest that the effect of profitability on management salaries has been previously underestimated. Finally, the discretion of management to pursue other objectives is limited by a requirement to achieve at least some minimum profit level. When a firm is not fully exploiting its assets to earn profits, share prices could fall and the threat of a takeover could emerge. This threat may be enough to ensure that profits are close to the 'maximum' level.

Thus the profit-maximization model has not been wholly displaced. However, the determination by a firm of the price-output level which maximizes profits is a difficult task in practice. As has been seen, determination of this level requires data (i.e. marginal data) that is not usually easily available to most businesses. Additionally, it assumes knowledge of current and future costs at all potential levels of output and knowledge of sales levels at all possible prices under all possible internal and external circumstances. Such knowledge is clearly impossible given the degree of risk and uncertainty attached to possible courses of action. The uncertainty arises, in part, because the reactions of rival firms to any one firm's proposed price-output levels are not known. That reaction, however, is likely to mean that the outcome of any particular chosen price level will not be as expected.

4 An alternative model of the firm which does not rely upon the 'maximization' of any variable is that of 'behaviourism'. Models of the firm, whether profit-, sales- or growth-maximization, have usually been considered to have universal application regardless of the individual characteristics of any single firm. The behavioural models consider the firm as an organization that is made up of many individuals and interest-groups, none of whom has perfect knowledge of (actual or future) costs and revenues or of the nature of the market environment. As a consequence, a significant part of the activity of the individuals and groups will be 'search', i.e. for such information. The many individuals and groups are also likely to have different objectives and the 'firm's objective' will alter as the balance between these individuals and groups alters. It will be a complex amalgam of several, possibly conflicting, individual and group objectives and will usually be of a suboptimal/non-maximizing nature, reflecting the compromise between these several individual and group objectives.

Any two firms will thus have different objectives according to how their internal organization differs; non-behavioural models assume that objectives are unaffected by the individual characteristics of the firm.

The firm in the behavioural models does not seek to maximize a specified variable, but rather it 'satisfices', i.e. it seeks to satisfy a number of different suboptimal or non-maximum goals. As such goals are achieved and the individual or groups satisfied, further goals are pursued. If goals cannot be or are not, in practice, attained, then alternative routes to such goals may be considered and pursued or the goals abandoned and new ones established. New goals will also be established as new problems and opportunities present themselves. This behaviour is what would be expected where uncertainty and lack of knowledge prevail.

5 Despite the existence of this and a number of other alternative models of the firm, 'profit-maximization' remains the basis of the most widely-accepted model. As indicated previously, the value of a model depends upon its predictive power and the superiority of other models in this respect has yet to be demonstrated.

It is clear that profit has a part to play in all models if only as a constraint upon the other objectives, and a satisfactory model must incorporate it.

Perhaps the greatest deficiency of all models, however, is the failure to allow for uncertainty and interdependence. Price-output decisions are taken with a lack of perfect knowledge in an environment often characterized by a great deal of interdependence between firms. Thus it is probably not sufficient to explain how any one firm behaves by reference to that firm alone. A successful model must, in some way, deal with all firms together. The decision of any one will affect others and the outcome of those decisions will be influenced by the reactions of those others.

Questions for essays and seminar papers

1 Consider whether 'maximizing profits' is likely to be an important objective of hotel and catering firms.

2 Consider the view that barriers to entry are low in the hotel and catering industry and therefore firms can exercise little control over markets.

3 Discuss the level of market concentration in the hotel and catering industry. How significant is a concentration ratio that is calculated for the industry as a whole?

4 Examine the reasons for the predominance of the small firm in the hotel and catering industry. What future do you believe such firms will have?

5 Consider the economic case for and against advertising and product differentiation. Assess their effects on market structure and performance (with Chapter 4).

Practical assignment

Estimate the number and size of hotel and catering firms in your locality. (Local tourist brochures, trade directories, *Yellow Pages*, etc., will help.) Into how many and what sort of markets can they be divided? Can you estimate local concentration ratios for each market?

CHAPTER 4

Conduct and performance

In Chapter 2 it was noted how the market structure of perfect competition was considered to achieve allocative and productive efficiency. Market structures, as noted in Chapter 3, are less than perfect and this chapter will attempt to examine the effect of those imperfect market structures upon the conduct and performance of firms and judge the consequences.

Monopoly and monopolistic competition[1]

The models of monopoly and monopolistic competition (see Table 9 in Chapter 2) emphasize the ability of firms to influence price (unlike perfect competition) because, in the case of monopoly, the firm is the only supplier of a product. In monopolistic competition, the product of each firm is differentiated and thus each firm can exercise some control over price.

Each firm, therefore, does not face the horizontal average revenue (or price) curve of perfect competition but a downward-sloping average revenue (price) curve, reflecting the influence of the firm's sales on price and vice versa. This downward-sloping curve showing the relationship between price and sales is, of course, the demand curve (see *AR* in Figure 21).

Because each firm is now faced with this particular curve, the marginal revenue (*MR*) will no longer equal price (*AR*). Demand curves are 'point of time' curves (see Chapter 2) and indicate the potential price and sales combinations that are currently possible. In Figure 21 price must be £10 per unit to sell 100 units per week and if 101 units were to be sold *in any one week*, then the price might need to be £9.95 per unit. That lower price will apply to all those 100 units that could have been sold for £10 each as well as to the extra unit. There will be an increase in revenue equivalent to the price of the extra unit but there will also be a loss of revenue equivalent to the reduction in price of the other units. This is shown in Table 34.

The consequences of the downward-sloping *AR* (price) and *MR* curves is that a profit-maximizing firm seeking to equate *MC* and *MR* will sell at a price (*AR*) that is no longer equal to *MC* and production is not at minimum average cost. (Compare perfect competition.) See Figure 22 also.

In both cases profits are maximized ($MR = MC$) but price (op_m and op_{mc}) is greater than $MC(R)$, and average costs (S) are greater than the minimum (T). In the monopoly situation (Figure 22(a)) price is also greater than the

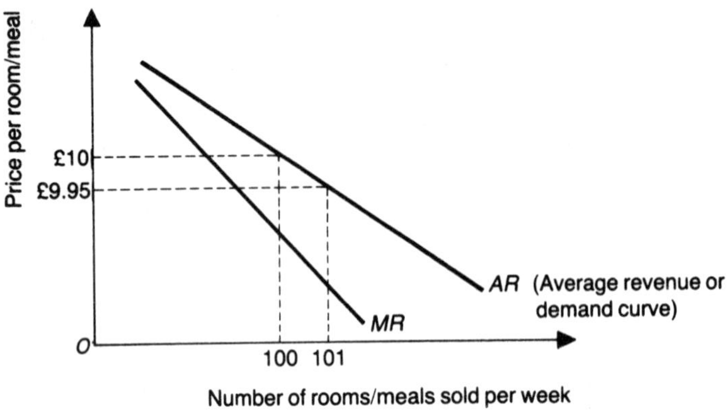

Figure 21 *Average and marginal revenue in monopoly or monopolistic competition*

Table 34 *Marginal revenue and price*

	100 units at £10 each	= £1000 revenue
	101 units at £9.95 each	= £1004.95 revenue
∴	Marginal revenue	= £4.95
or:		
	Addition to revenue from extra sale	= 1 unit at £9.95
	'Loss' of revenue from price reduction on other units	= 100 units at £0.05 = £5
∴	Net addition (marginal revenue)	= £9.95 − £5 = £4.95

average cost of production (op_m exceeds S) and thus an economic profit (or abnormal profit) is earned. If a monopoly firm can protect its position, that profit can persist.

In monopolistic competition, however, such profit will attract in new firms because the product differentiation is not enough to keep competition out completely. The entry of new firms causes the demand for the product of any one firm to shift to the left and this will continue until the profit no longer exists (i.e. where $AC = AR$). This is shown in Figure 22(b) as sales level oq_{mc}. Even here, production is not at the lowest point of the average cost curve (T).

Oligopoly

It is likely that most industries and markets in western industrialized countries fall within the market structure of 'oligopoly'. This structure is the least well formulated as an economic model and there is no one generally agreed model

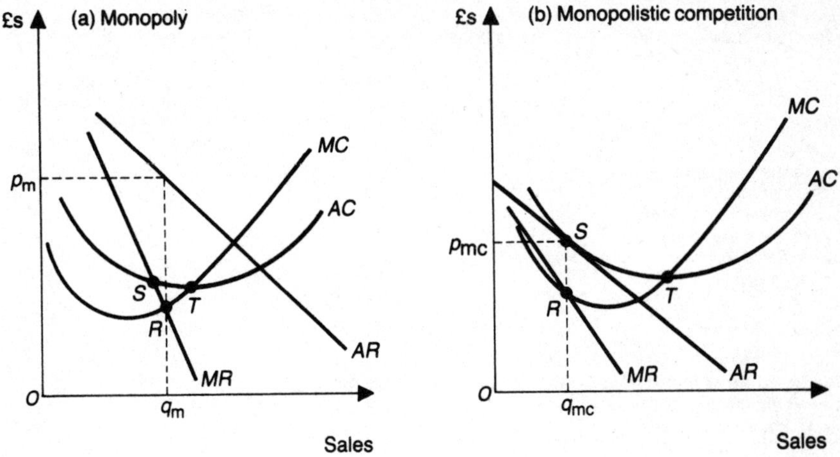

Figure 22 *Equilibrium of firm operating under monopoly or monopolistic competition*

of oligopolistic conduct. Thus an analysis of oligopoly is less a consideration of a model than a set of observations and possibilities. Its predictive value is therefore currently limited.

Oligopoly is considered to exist where there are a 'few' firms in a market.[2] 'Few' is taken to mean a situation where the number of firms is such that whatever any one of them does has an impact upon the others. (Under perfect competition there are so many firms that no one of them is significant enough to influence the others.) Therefore the fortunes of any one firm are related to the policies and activities of the others; the essential characteristic of oligopoly is *interdependence.*

Although firms in a market may be expected to react to policy changes by any of the others, these reactions are unknown beforehand to the firm initiating the changes. Therefore the firm does not have perfect knowledge of the revenue that it will receive at any particular price level. Each firm will need to make assumptions about the likely reactions of rivals before it can attempt to assess potential revenue (see Figure 23).

This uncertainty leads to firms following policies that are uncertainty-reducing. Firms are likely to move away from using price as a competitive weapon and towards forms of competition that will reduce the uncertainty of the environment within which they operate. Product differentiation (and advertising) is an example of this since, if successful, it enhances the differences between products and reduces their interdependence.

Non-price competition will occur also through new product development and product improvement. Such competition may be no less intense than price competition. The attraction lies in the ability to reduce interdependence and

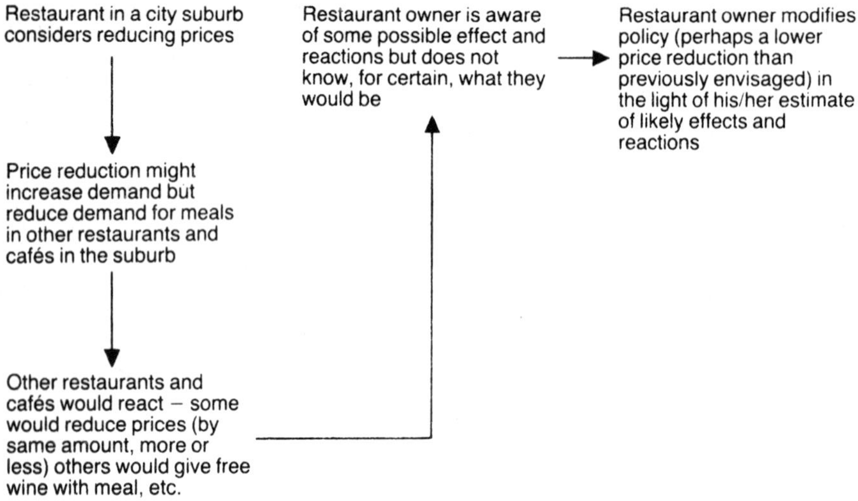

Figure 23 *Oligopolistic interdependence*

thus expand 'strategy space'. Advertising, for instance, can shift a firm's demand curve outwards and reduce cross-elasticity of demand. There is often likely to be a delay before a rival's responses occur to a non-price move and such responses are not normally as complete or direct as a price reduction. Non-price moves are also less easy to copy than are price changes.

Conduct

Pricing[3]

1 Where firms are aware of their mutual dependence, prices may remain relatively stable. The English Tourist Board's report on hotel pricing policy indicated that room tariffs in its sample were changed only twice a year and menu items reviewed two to four times a year. This is rather different from what could be a constantly changing price under perfect competition.

Whichever way a hotel or restaurant changes its price the outcome may be unfavourable since rivals will not allow the firm to benefit from its actions: a price rise may not be matched by rivals whereas a price reduction could be matched completely. (This is frequently illustrated by reference to the 'kinked' demand curve.)[4]

Oligopolistic firms are soon likely to appreciate that price-competition is time-consuming, wasteful and costly. In a price war all firms are likely to be losers and prices may no longer correspond with costs but may fall below them. The end result may not be the survival of the most efficient supplier but of the firm with the strongest financial resources. Firms may also be reluctant to alter prices so as to avoid the administrative costs of making frequent price changes, the problems of dealing with stock re-valuation and the effect on consumers of frequent price changes.

Prices, when they do move, may move in the same direction and by similar amounts for all firms in an industry or local market. Hoteliers in a seaside resort or city centre could join together to do this (collusion) or they could simply follow the conduct of a 'price leader'. Sometimes collusion between firms is formalized as a 'cartel' such as the International Air Transport Association (IATA) which has a membership of many of the world's leading airlines.[5] IATA determines the fares for many air routes thus reducing price-competition. Similar tariffs for hotel rooms, for instance, may be achieved by less formal means but the likelihood of success of such schemes is greatest where the hotels offer similar rooms and services, and are similar in size and costs. Such firms could, as noted in Chapter 3, attempt to set 'entry-forestalling' or 'limit' prices to create an entry barrier.

A price leader may emerge among hotel firms where one of them currently dominates the market or because it has a better ability to recognize changed market conditions (of demand or supply).

It is quite likely, of course, that local hotels may move tariffs up by the same amount simply because costs have risen by the same amount for all. Hoteliers may also hold similar views about what cost increases there will be in the future and therefore set tariffs that they hope will cover those costs.

2 Costs seem to be an important influence on price, in practice. (Compare the influence of demand and supply in perfect competition.) The practice of 'full-cost' or 'cost-plus' pricing has been widely observed in hotel catering and many manufacturing industries.[6] The restaurateur may estimate the food cost per meal for instance, and then add on a percentage to cover overheads and profit. It is unlikely, however, that this full cost pricing is adopted mechanically since the percentage mark-up does seem to vary according to market conditions. An English Tourist Board report[7] on hotel pricing concluded that hotel prices were closely related to costs but prices would be adjusted to take account of market demand and supply, and tariffs in other hotels. If demand was less than supply (because of an increase in hotel building or because of a decline in demand), then tariffs often fell below 'rack rates'. When demand was buoyant room rates were increased. Interestingly, the report confirmed how price was seen by some hoteliers as an indicator of quality (see Chapter 2).

Rogers' earlier study[8] of hotel prices confirmed the tendency for hotel tariffs to be cost-related and pointed to the fact that few owner-managers had any real pricing policy other than following what others do.

The differences in the tariffs of individual Trusthouse Forte hotels were, however, considered by the Price Commission[9] to be due more to differences in 'local market opportunities' than to differences in costs.

The 'pure' view of 'full-cost' pricing is that prices would be unlikely to alter unless costs altered. Given that there is a certain amount of 'stickiness' about

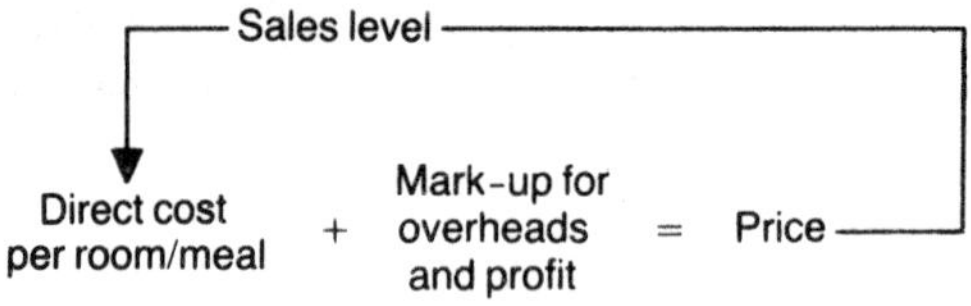

Figure 24 *Full-cost pricing*

prices in that they do not respond rapidly to changes in supply and demand, it is none the less clear that prices are affected by market conditions.

There is, though, a certain element of indeterminacy about 'full-cost' pricing, for the direct cost per meal/room may not be known with certainty until the sales level is known (unless it can be assumed that this average cost is constant at all levels of sales – see Chapter 5). The level of sales will itself be determined by price which is what the approach is seeking to establish (see Figure 24).

There is a large number of studies in industry generally which confirms how widespread this cost-related pricing practice would appear to be. The conclusion is then often drawn that 'marginal analysis' is inappropriate[10]; firms apparently do not make their decisions in the way that economic models would suggest. Additionally, firms do not have access to data in a 'marginal' form and even if they did, it is suggested that they would not make the fine adjustments to output (by one unit at a time) that the models suggest. It is clear from Chapter 3 that firms may have 'discretion' in their objectives and therefore cannot be assumed to be fixing prices as if they were profit-maximizers.

The arguments about the relevance of marginal analysis continue. The supporters of the concepts claim that firms do not have to follow the marginal approach in practice in order for the theories to still be relevant and have predictive value.[11]

3 The determination of price by a firm is a complex process and will be influenced by many considerations.[12] It has already been noted how firms may have a number of objectives and pricing policies will reflect these objectives. A firm seeking to maximize profits could have higher prices than one which was concerned with obtaining a large volume of sales.

Given the firm's objectives, costs and marketing strategy then pricing policies will also vary according to market conditions, consumer characteristics, demand elasticity, extent and nature of competition and so on. Penetration prices (low prices) may be appropriate, for instance, when a new restaurant opens, where there is a great deal of competition or where the firm can achieve economies of scale. Market skimming (high prices) might be considered for long-established and well-patronized, haute cuisine restaurants with a low-elasticity of demand and city-centre hotels where there is little to fear from the entry of new competition. Appropriate prices will change over the life-cycle of hotels and restaurants; as they move from 'birth' to 'maturity' it may be that prices shift from 'penetration' to 'skimming'.

Firms may decide to price some of their products below cost to act as 'loss leaders' and thus introduce consumers to the whole range of products. A hotel might offer a function room free of charge for certain banquets or conferences in the hope that revenue from, say, meals and drinks will compensate.

There may be deliberate cross-subsidization of products within a firm's range in order to keep some prices low to fight off competition. Hotel and catering chains would certainly have the opportunity to support loss-making units from their total profits if they wished to eliminate local competition.

4 Hotel and catering firms have successfully followed a policy of price discrimination.[13] This is a policy of charging different prices to different customers where relative prices do not reflect relative costs.

A demand curve assumes that the whole of output in any one time period will be sold at the same price regardless of any one individual's willingness to pay a higher price. If the output could be sold at prices that relate to each individual's willingness to pay, then higher profits may be obtained. In Figure 25(a), sales of oq_1 occur at price op_1; to have sold more of the product during that particular time period would have required a price of op_2 or op_3. If the price was, in fact,

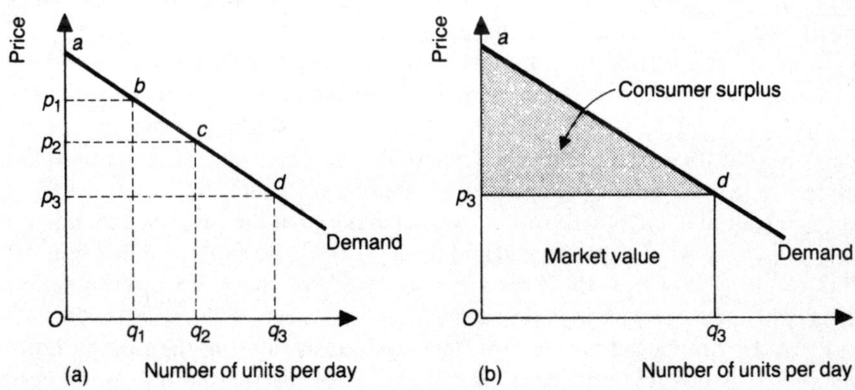

Figure 25 *Consumer surplus*

at op_3 then all of those consumers who were prepared to pay op_1 (a demand of only oq_1) are receiving a 'bonus'. Similarly, those who were willing to pay op_2 will also receive a (lower) 'bonus'. This bonus is referred to as 'consumer surplus', i.e. the excess of total utility over total market value (shown also in Figure 25(b)).

In Figure 25(a) and (b):

Total utility is represented by adq_3o

Total market value is represented by p_3dq_3o

Therefore, total consumer surplus is adp_3

At any given price level there will be those who are receiving more utility (because they were willing to pay a higher price) than they are sacrificing, in terms of cost incurred (price). Each of these purchasers will be receiving a consumer surplus.

If firms are able to charge these different prices to the different consumers then this surplus is transferred from the consumer to become 'producer surplus': profits can be increased. Such a policy is only possible, however, under certain conditions.

There must exist groups of consumers who are willing to pay different prices for the same hotel room or restaurant meal, these different groups must be identifiable and distinguishable from each other, and they must be prevented from re-selling to each at the lower price.

In the hotel market there are differences, for instance, between business and holiday visitors in their willingness to stay in hotels in most (but not all) city centres. Low tariffs may be necessary to encourage the holidaymaker to stay there. Many holidaymakers may, however, be willing to pay a higher price to stay in resort hotels during the summer than they are during the off-season. Discounts for group and contract bookings may be greater than cost-savings justify and thus constitute price discrimination.

In most instances in the hotel market there is little difficulty in identifying and distinguishing a particular category of consumer because of the source (a company) or nature (large number of guests) of a booking, or the time of the week or year for which a booking is made. If consumers were able to buy at the low price (a company, a group, off-season holidaymaker) and re-sell to others (persons, individuals, peak-season holidaymakers) at the low price then price discrimination would not succeed and revenue would be diluted. While some of this resale is possible, the time-basis for much of the price discrimination effectively prevents resale in those instances.

Price discrimination is, perhaps, less obvious in catering than in the hotel sector but is possible and does exist there. Price discrimination can be very important in manipulating and stimulating demand in an industry where supply is fixed for long periods of time. It is important in a high fixed-cost activity (see Chapter 5), such as hotels, that maximum use be made of the facilities and price discrimination can help do that.

Innovation[14]

Innovation covers all those technical, industrial and commercial steps which lead to the marketing of new products (such as motels or fast food take-aways) or use of new processes (such as free-flow food service areas, convection and microwave oven cooking). It includes both the initial invention and the subsequent development of the product ready for sale (i.e. research and development (R & D)).

Innovation can be an aspect of conduct or of performance. It can be a competitive weapon (like product differentiation) in oligopolistic markets, but it may also be regarded as a criterion alongside profits, for judging the performance of firms.

Measuring the extent of innovation is considered to be easier than measuring product differentiation but it is sometimes difficult to distinguish between the two. Innovation has the potential to add to consumer welfare by expanding the range of available products, by improving quality and lowering the cost of production. Some 'innovation', however, may lead to little more than relatively minor product differentiation such as changes in packaging or image with the object of convincing consumers that existing products are now obsolete.

Innovation may be measured by reference to its inputs, i.e. the expenditure on R & D or the numbers of R & D employees. The problem with these is that not all formal programmes of R & D actually produce results and not all innovation is organized in this way.

Alternatively, measures of output in the form of numbers of patents issued may be used. Not all innovations are, however, patented and not all patents actually find their way into commercial use.

Bearing these reservations in mind, the UK devotes less than 3 per cent of its GDP to R & D, whereas the USA devotes between 3.5 and 4 per cent. Private industry carries out most of the work in both the USA and the UK, but much of the finance is from government sources (47 per cent in the UK in 1978). In the UK R & D activity is concentrated in a few firms and industries (electrical engineering, aerospace, chemicals, mechanical engineering, motor vehicles and increasingly electronic components and computers).[15] Information about innovation in the hotel and catering industry is lacking but much of the innovatory effort seems to have come from the larger firms and also from supplier firms outside the industry (supplying equipment). Fast food firms have been particularly instrumental in introducing innovations in the 'eating out' product (limited menus, self-service, finished-goods inventories and specialized production equipment). It has been suggested that many of these innovations originated in smaller rather than large firms.[16] R & D expenditure by all service industries amounted to less than 4 per cent of total R & D expenditure in 1980.[17]

It may be that oligopoly is particularly likely to produce innovation because of the preference of firms for non-price competition, because firms have the money necessary to finance it, and they can ensure that the benefits of R & D accrue to them by preventing newcomers entering the market. However, it is claimed by others that more price-competitive market structures may be necessary to generate the competitive pressures that ensure innovation. There is also an unresolved argument about whether large or small firms are more likely to be responsible for innovation.

Product-differentiation and advertising

See Chapter 3.

Growth[18]

Few firms are of a constant size and size at any one time will be a result of growth. In many recent 'models' of the firm, the process of growth has been promoted to a position of central importance. This reflects the influence of growth and size upon the status, salary, prestige and promotion prospects of management. (In Chapter 3 it was noted how managerial objectives could prevail within an organization.) Growth is regarded as a universal and necessary characteristic of firms; if some firms grow large then there is an incentive for others to do the same to maintain their relative positions and survive.

The economy is characterized by firms experiencing differing rates of growth and decline, but there is no clear tendency for any particular size of firm to experience the highest rates of growth (or profitability). High rates of growth are evident in all firm size-ranges. There is some relationship, however, between rates of growth and profitability, with both tending to rise together. It is not clear whether growth influences profitability or vice versa, but there is certainly a close interdependence between the two.

It is probable that profits are necessary for growth to occur, but beyond a certain point where customer resistance/saturation to a product occurs, further growth may erode profits. This may be due to a reduction in prices which will adversely affect profits or it may be that there are limits to management's ability to find new areas of expansion sufficient to maintain profitability. Thus restraints upon a firm's growth rate will result from such demand or managerial limitations. In addition, there may well be a 'financial' restraint in that if profitability falls too much with growth, other firms may well seek to take over the 'weakened' firm; that threat may be sufficient to limit the rate of growth.

There are other growth restraints but these three have been most often incorporated into theories explaining firms' growth.

Firms' growth may take one of two forms:

1. Internal growth, whereby a firm grows independently of any other firm and retains its original identity. Such growth may be by expanding sales of existing products, expanding the range of products, or by moving into related or completely new products. It can be a relatively slow means of achieving growth
2. External growth, whereby a firm joins with another to achieve 'instant' growth. Such external growth may be a merger (firms agreeing to join,

Table 35 *Percentage of proposed mergers (UK) by type of integration 1965–84*

	1965–69	*1970–77*	*1978–84*
Horizontal	82	71	62
Vertical	6	6	6
Diversified	12	23	32

Source: D. Begg, S. Fischer and R. Dornbusch, *Economics*, 2nd Edition (McGraw-Hill 1984).

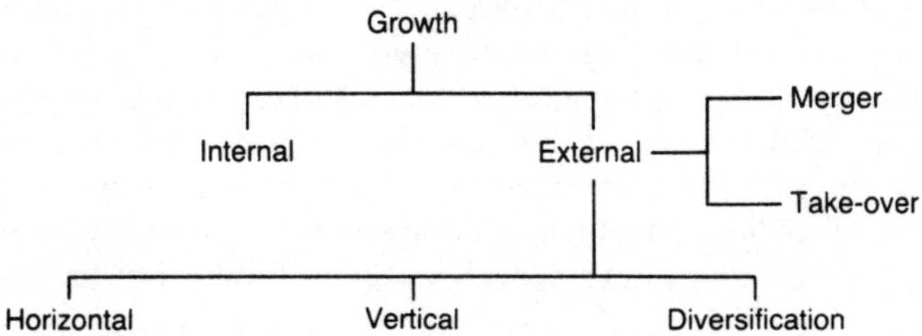

Figure 26 *Forms of growth*

usually to form a 'new' organization) or a take-over (a firm acquires a controlling interest in another firm and the latter is usually absorbed into the former).

External growth may, in turn, be in a horizontal or vertical direction or of a diversified nature (see Table 35). Internal growth may also take these forms, but is less often described in these terms (see Figure 26):

1 Horizontal growth occurs when a firm joins with another in the same stage of production; they are producing the same or similar products, e.g. two hotel firms joining together.
2 Vertical growth occurs when a firm joins with another at a different stage of production of the same or similar products. A firm may move closer to the retail outlet/customer (vertical forwards), e.g. a brewery owning public houses or tour operators owning hotels, or further away from the customer (vertical backwards), e.g. a caterer owning a manufacturer of catering equipment.
3 Diversified growth occurs when firms producing different products with no underlying connection, join together. A variation is 'lateral' growth when the products of the firm are dissimilar, but there is some connection such as the utilization of similar labour skills or raw materials. A diversified firm may also be known as a 'conglomerate' firm.

From Table 35 it is evident that in recent years there have been few notified vertical mergers. Horizontal mergers are still the most important, though diversified or conglomerate growth has become much more important.

Consequences of growth

1 External growth is often justified by reference to the opportunity to achieve 'economies of scale'. There may certainly be increased ability, through 'size', to raise finance more easily, to utilize managerial skills more effectively, and to engage in more effective marketing and R & D activities. In horizontal growth there may well be opportunities to achieve economies of scale by concentrating production into a smaller number of larger establishments. In this way output may be achieved at a lower cost per unit of output. The scope for this is rather limited in the case of hotels and catering (see Chapters 3 and 5) and indeed it is doubtful whether it happens often in practice in the case of external growth in manufacturing. Many companies which join together remain a collection of loosely-linked divisions which are no more effective together than apart.

In the case of vertical growth, there may also be scope for achievement of economies of scale through integrating several stages of production on the same site.

Most studies suggest that merged companies perform badly when compared with the average industrial performance or the previous performance of the unmerged firms. Additionally, the performance of large firms is not always as satisfactory as that of smaller ones. However, the threat of a take-over by another firm may be sufficient to encourage a firm to improve its efficiency.

2 Horizontal external growth (two hotel companies joining together) may have the added advantage of eliminating direct competitors. This, in turn, could lead to a more effective control over the market and higher profits.

Horizontal growth could be beneficial by rationalizing or eliminating duplicated facilities, e.g. existing facilities might have been unable to operate at the most economic level – perhaps two hotels in the same area, neither of which is able to achieve high occupancy rates. More intensive use of existing facilities such as central reservations systems can occur and they might become economic to set up.

Vertical external growth similarly may deprive competitors of sources of supply (a caterer taking over a supplier of meat in a local area) or, if 'forward', may deprive them of retail outlets (a hotelier owning a large number of travel agencies). On the other hand, it can ensure for the initiating firm a closer control over its suppliers (quality, price, etc.) and, if 'forward', a closer involvement with the direct marketing of the product to the consumer.

External growth can lead to more effective competition by the establishment of firms that are more equal in size.

3 External growth can gain for a firm those resources, often managerial or financial, which it currently lacks and much external growth appears to be motivated by this. Resources such as hotels may be obtained at a lower cost

Table 36 *Activities of a number of hotel and catering firms and firms with activities in the hotel and catering market 1985–8*

Company	*Some of the company's main activities*
Grand Metropolitan	Catering inc. Berni; milk and dairy products; brewing and public houses (Watney and Truman); bookmaking.
Bass	Hotels including Crest and Holiday Inns International; catering; brewing; public houses; Coral Leisure; etc.
Trusthouse Forte	Hotels; catering (including Little Chef and Happy Eater, and stake in KFC (UK)); contract catering (Gardner Merchant); Puritan Maid; Lillywhite; etc.
ITT	Hotels (Sheraton); telecommunications and electronics; engineering; insurance; finance; etc.
United Biscuits	Food and biscuit production; catering including Crawford, Pizzaland and Wimpy (franchise); etc.
Ladbroke	Hotels including Hilton International; bookmaking; leisure; property; retailing (including DIY), clubs; catering; publishing; etc.
International Leisure Group	Intasun tour operators; Air Europe; Merit hotels (GB)
BAA	Heathrow, Gatwick and other airports; majority holding in Ramada hotels
Pleasurama	Hotels, casinos; gaming machines; discos; coach holiday operators (Smiths, Shearings and National Holidays); theme restaurants; etc.
Whitbread	Brewing and public houses; Beefeater steak houses; Pizza Hut restaurants

Sources: Trade and national press and Kleinwort Grieveson Securities, *Hotel Companies in the UK, Spring 1987*.

than the cost of building. Some growth may be motivated by a desire to obtain undervalued assets and some to sell off at a profit the assets acquired.

4 Diversification is the spreading of activities to dissimilar products (see Table 36). There is some difficulty about measuring diversification within firms but the single-product firm is rare (only six out of the 100 largest manufacturing firms are in this category).

Diversification may be measured in several ways including:

(a) The percentage of a firm's activity that is outside its main activity industry.

(b) The number of industries that a firm is active in.

These and other measures point to the fact that it is common for manufacturing firms/establishments to be diversified though most firms remain with over 70 per cent of their activity in one industry (1985 Census of Production). The largest firms tend to be the most diversified: 3 per cent of the activity of small firms and 22 per cent of large firms' activity is in 'other' industries. The degree of diversification also tends to increase the more 'science-based' a firm is: it tends, perhaps to have more opportunities to 'find' new products.

Much diversification is, in fact, within 'related' fields where the products have links through similar or common technological or marketing expertise and knowledge. Many hotel and catering firms are diversified into the 'leisure' field rather than into activities totally removed from their initial activity, i.e. 'narrow spectrum' diversification.

Diversification does provide a means of growth for firms should existing products be facing 'saturated' markets, and it also spreads the risks of dependence upon one or a few products. It may mean that firms are more able to withstand economic recession and/or intense price-cutting competition between themselves and others.

However, diversification does not offer much scope for rationalization and standardization; the firm itself may prove difficult to effectively manage because of the very diversity of activities. Grand Metropolitan has made a decision to reduce its diversification by selling (1985–88) its hotels (Intercontinental), contract catering (Compass), leisure interests (Mecca) and tobacco, and concentrating on a core of food, drink and gaming.

5 External growth of whatever form is a response by firms to an uncertain environment. Rival firms' policies create change and uncertainty and external growth is a means of stabilizing that environment through enabling the firm to control a larger share of the market. Diversification illustrates well the extent of such uncertainty – reducing activity and the constant striving to maintain a competitive edge.

Each combination of two or more firms will, however, create further uncertainty for remaining firms who may, in turn, engage in 'defensive' combinations.

This explanation of external growth is confirmed by the fact that the rationale for mergers is often in practice more to do with managerial objectives than with industrial efficiency. Growth decisions do not usually appear to be made on a 'rational' financial basis.

Those firms which survive merger and take-over activity are not necessarily the most efficient but may be the strongest (and even the least efficient).

6 External growth has been a conspicuous feature of British manufacturing in recent years, though the rate has slowed down compared with the early 1970s (see Table 37), and a great deal of the increase in market concentration may

Table 37 *Mergers and takeovers (UK) 1972–85*

	Annual averages
(1972–73)	(1208)
1972–78	590
1979–81	414
1982–83	395
1984–85	495

Source: D. Begg, S. Fischer and R. Dornbusch, *Economics*, 2nd Edition (McGraw Hill 1987).

have resulted from it, as has the increased size of firms.[19] It is not clear, however, that advantages to the firms in the form of increased profitability, or to consumers in the form of lower prices, have resulted.

Imperfections[20]

This review of oligopolistic conduct clearly points to the very real distance between the perfect competition model and 'reality'.

1 The 'free' operation of the price mechanism is inhibited by the manipulation of prices and output by firms. Price is not free to fluctuate and respond to changes in demand and supply.

Firms do not necessarily rise or disappear according to the desires of consumers, but they seek to exercise some degree of control over their own destinies.[21]

2 Firms have objectives other than profit maximization. Additionally profits do not necessarily act as an index of consumer wants but may simply reflect powerful and protected market positions.

3 Consumers do not have perfect knowledge of the markets for goods and services or for their own labour. Decisions about what to buy may be made on the basis of habit and consumers do make 'wrong' decisions. This may arise from ignorance on the part of consumers or from manipulation by firms. Because hotel and catering services often cannot be 'sampled' beforehand, consumers may well end up not making the 'best buy'.

Like firms, consumers may 'satisfice' rather than maximize utility. Consumers will be satisfied by a 'minimum' level of utility and will be unlikely to devote time and effort to improve the situation. Comparing the range of services offered and tariffs across the large number of hotels or guest houses in a resort may be particularly time-consuming and may be considered not worth the effort.

4 Resources of labour, land and capital are not as fully mobile as the perfect competition model assumes. They do not move swiftly and effortlessly into the most desired areas of production and this inertia prevents the rapid adjustment of output to consumer wants. Hotels and restaurants, in particular, are assets which are difficult to alter to meet changed demands, especially if the new demands arise in different geographical areas. Therefore hotels and guest houses may continue in existence in a particular seaside resort long after the demand has begun to shift away to, say, foreign resorts.

Resources are not perfectly substitutable and they are usually specific to a particular field of activity. It is more difficult, for instance, to adapt hotel and restaurant buildings to other uses than it is to adapt a factory for other manufacturing purposes. Similarly, skilled chefs cannot easily become skilled electronic engineers should the demand for products shift accordingly.

As well as these and other imperfections, it was noted in Chapter 2 how the existence of externalities and merit wants, etc., restricted the ability of any economy, even with universal perfect competition, to achieve desirable economic objectives.

Perfect competition *v* the imperfect world

It is clear that the 'real world' is far removed from the perfect competition model; thus, it would appear, that allocative and productive efficiency may not be achieved. It is common for comparisons to be made between the models of monopoly and perfect competition as two extreme market structures in order to highlight the shortcomings of anything less than perfect competition. These comparisons have some validity and are made implicitly in everyday discussion of competition. It is not a wholly useful comparison, however, in so far as neither pure monopoly nor perfect competition exists and societies are not faced with a choice of either one or the other.

In reality government policy-makers are more likely to be faced with situations where they might succeed in encouraging a little more or less competition in a particular market. Actual market structures are found along a broad spectrum between perfect competition and monopoly and are usually impossible to classify precisely.

Medlik[22] suggests that certain hotel and catering markets do resemble perfect competition (a large number of boarding houses in a seaside resort) and monopoly (where there is only one restaurant or hotel in a wide geographical area). He concludes, however, that the 'great majority of markets for hotel and catering services lie between the two extremes of perfect competition and monopoly'.

As noted previously in Chapter 2, if perfect competition cannot be achieved throughout all sectors of the economy, then achieving perfect competition in just some sectors will not necessarily move the economy closer to allocative efficiency. It is a case of all or nothing.

Policy-makers may therefore content themselves by seeking to achieve

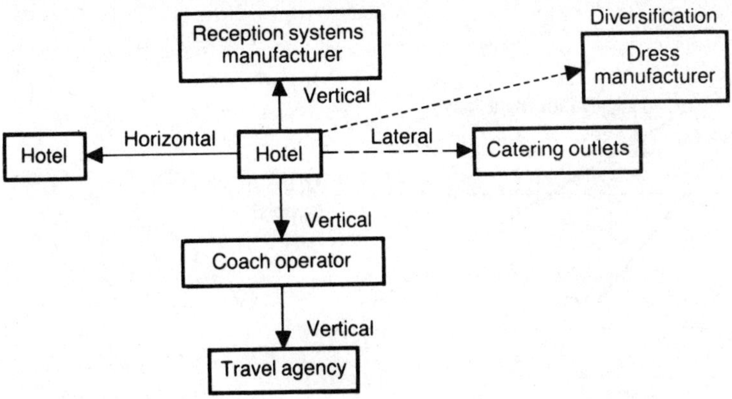

Figure 27 *Growth by a hotel firm – a hypothetical example*

'workable competition'.[23] Perfect competition is recognized as unattainable and also, by some, as being undesirable. (There are those who do not like perfect competition on political or ethical grounds.) 'Workable competition', therefore, involves the setting of guidelines for judging individual markets. These guidelines are vague and indeterminate but they highlight areas of performance (profitability, advertising, product quality, etc.) to be examined rather than establish standards to be achieved. 'Workable competition' is less concerned with market structures and more with the end-results that are achievable in practice in oligopolistic markets, in particular.

Resource misallocation[24]

Estimates have been made of the cost to an economy of the imperfections within it.

1 It can be demonstrated in Figure 28 that price under imperfect conditions will be higher and output lower than under perfect competition. In a perfectly competitive industry price is determined where demand is equal to supply. In Figure 28 the supply curve, which is the sum of the marginal cost curves of the firms, is represented for convenience as the horizontal line *MC*. It can be shown that if *MC* is constant then so too will be *AC*. Price is at the intersection of the supply curve (*MC*) and demand, i.e. price of op_c and output of oq_c.

Under monopoly, with *no change in costs,* the market demand becomes the firm's demand curve and in order to maximize profits, the firm will produce at an output level that equates *MC* and *MR*. This occurs at an output of oq_m and price charged is op_m: output is less than oq_c and price is above op_c. (It has already been noted in this chapter that price is greater than *MC* and exceeds minimum average cost and thus allocative and productive efficiency are not achieved.)

In the perfectly competitive situation, consumer surplus (excess of total utility over market value) was represented by EGp_c in Figure 28. Under monopoly the

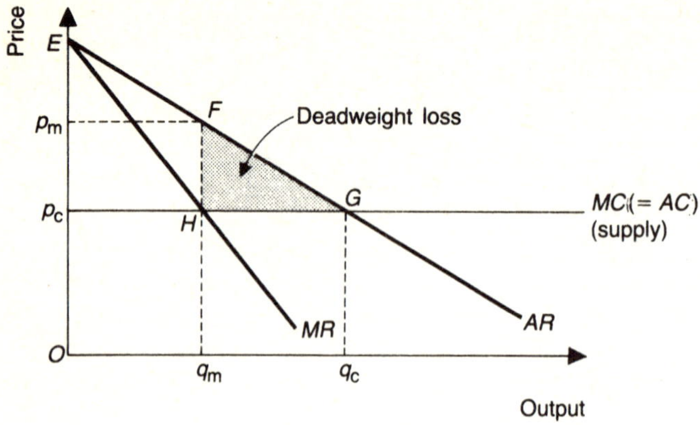

Figure 28 *Comparison of price-output levels under perfect competition and monopoly*

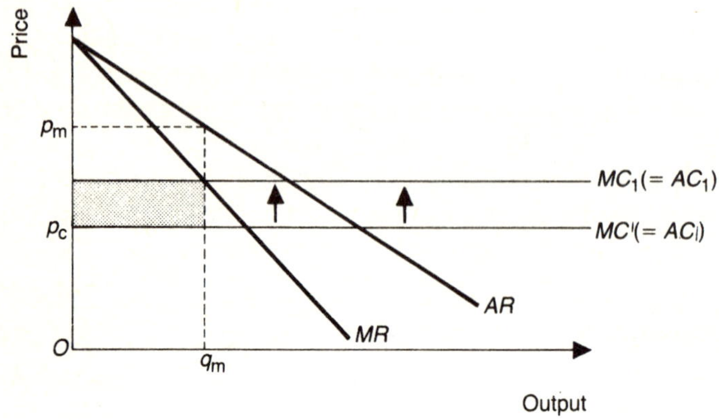

Figure 29 *'X-inefficiency'*

consumer surplus has fallen to EFp_m with a gain in producer surplus of p_mFHp_c (excess of receipts over cost). There is, therefore a net loss of welfare known as the 'deadweight loss' of monopolization, represented by *FGH* in Figure 28.

Imperfections in the UK economy may account for such welfare losses equivalent to up to 10 per cent of manufacturing output or GNP (similar to GDP; see Chapter 8).

2 As well as these undesirable features of the imperfect economy, there can be additional sources of resource misallocation. '*X*-inefficiency' arises whenever resources are not being used in the most productive way and thus costs are higher than they need be – at MC_1 rather than *MC* in Figure 29. These higher costs may arise for many reasons but have been particularly associated with the failure of firms to search out and eliminate waste and

inefficiency. This may be due to a poorly organized production process and a lack of competitive pressures. The extent of the *X*-inefficiency is represented by the shaded area in Figure 29. The diagram is similar to that in Figure 28 except that there is an additional cost curve ($MC_1 = AC_1$) representing the higher level of costs in an imperfect market.

X-inefficiency may be a greater source of welfare loss than is allocative inefficiency and its effect may be up to three times greater than that of 'deadweight loss'. It is, however, possible that costs under monopoly and other forms of imperfect competition may be lower than under perfect competition (because of economies of scale) and it may be that innovation is more likely.

3 The existence of economic profits, associated with the ability of firms to preserve their market positions, will encourage other firms to attempt to enter that particular market and earn a share of the profits for themselves. Under perfect competition the existence of 'high' profits would signify unsatisfied consumer demand which would be met by the entry of new firms. When these profits are, however, a reflection of market power, there is a real cost to society. This cost arises in the form of the resources used by firms to protect that position (product differentiation, advertising, etc.) and used by new firms seeking to compete for the profits. The resources could be considered to be wastefully used and better used elsewhere – in producing more goods and services.

This form of cost has been estimated at about 7 per cent of the output of a sample of UK firms (13 per cent in the USA).

Performance[25]

The preceding discussion suggests that the real world of imperfections may not be considered as 'satisfactory' as perfect competition. That discussion was largely theoretical and it is appropriate to consider what the 'end results' of the imperfect world actually are.

There is some difficulty, in practice, in attempting to establish relationships within the structure, conduct and performance model. As previously noted, data is more readily available for industries than for markets. The economic meaning of 'costs' and 'profits' (see Chapter 5) is not reflected in the available data. There may be a lack of data (especially for the hotel and catering industry) and there are difficulties of comparing data over time (as the SIC definitions change, for instance).

Profit is a common measure of performance but firms may calculate profits in different ways. Profit figures, if they are to be meaningful, need to be related to some other variable such as sales, or capital employed, but there are variations in how these might be calculated also.

Even where there is data sufficient to establish relationships between structure, conduct and performance, problems of interpretation of the data may arise. High profits, for instance, may be seen as the outcome of market domination but these profits could equally be temporary, reflecting adjustment in a competitive situation and eventually be competed away.

The structure, conduct and performance model as indicated earlier is primarily seen as one in which the causal direction is one-way, with structure influencing conduct and performance. There can, however, be a reverse sequence with, for instance, low profitability (performance) leading firms to alter prices (conduct), or attempting to modify structure by raising barriers to the entry of new firms. Low profitability could also stimulate merger activity (conduct) and thus influence structure.

It is not, therefore, altogether surprising that studies of the structure, conduct and performance model, in practice, have not always provided firm conclusions. Unfortunately, the evidence does not exist for performance in the hotel and catering industry to be judged within the context of the structure, conduct and performance model. The results of studies in the UK and the USA relating mainly to manufacturing are summarized below.

Concentration and profitability

Studies have found no strong and definite relationship between concentration and profitability, though profits of firms in highly concentrated industries might be less variable than in other industries.

There is rather more evidence in the USA of a positive relationship between concentration and profitability, especially when high concentration is combined with high barriers to entry.

It is clear that there are many possible influences on profitability other than market structure. Firm size in itself may be influential: profitability tends to decline with firm size, in fact. Firms in low concentration industries could collude and achieve high profits that way.

Market structure and innovation

Large firms and concentrated markets do not have an obviously better record on innovation than do others. Major technological breakthroughs come from a variety of sources, both large and small firms, in high and low concentration industries. Much of innovation is possibly the work of individuals and small firms, but it might be that subsequent development is undertaken by large firms. Small firms find it difficult to engage in expensive R & D programmes but studies do not show that there are clear advantages of large-scale R & D activity.

It is likely that the opportunity for innovation is a greater influence than is market structure – the opportunity is greater the more technologically-based is the firm or industry. 'Moderate' concentration and barriers to entry and a high and growing output also appear to provide some incentive to innovate.

Concentration, advertising and profitability

Some studies suggest that advertising is an effective barrier to entry and leads to higher profits. Other studies point to a different causal sequence: firms in the more concentrated (especially oligopolistic) markets being more likely to be able to afford advertising because of their profits.

Growth and profitability

Studies have found a strong positive association between growth and profitability with profits more likely to affect growth than vice versa.

Questions for essays and seminar papers

1 Examine, within the context of the hotel and catering industry, the reasons for the growth of firms.

2 Explain why firms in hotels and catering may prefer to engage in non-price competition rather than compete through price.

3 Discuss the view that imperfections in an economy lead to undesirable economic results.

4 Consider what the strengths and weaknesses of a 'command' or 'planned' economy might be (with Chapter 8).

5 Discuss and explain the features of pricing by hotels and catering firms operating in oligopolistic markets.

Practical assignment

From press advertisements and other material, give examples of how local hotel and catering firms compete. How does this relate to your results in the practical assignment to Chapter 3?

CHAPTER 5

Costs

This topic is of considerable interest and concern to accountants and the significance of cost data as collected by that profession is substantial in the managing of a firm. Data and textbooks on 'costs' from an accounting perspective abound, so much so that it may not be immediately clear what contribution economics might be able to make to the subject.

The contributions are two: the first concerns what happens to costs as output alters, and the second concerns the definition of 'costs'.

Cost structure

It will be helpful if, first, some typical hotel and catering cost structures are considered (see Tables 38 and 39).

The relative importance of particular costs will vary according to the sales-bias of the establishment and according to its size, occupancy and type of product sold.[1] However, it is clear that in most cases, a substantial proportion of costs may be regarded as fixed or semi-fixed, which must be incurred regardless of the volume of sales.

Fixed costs are those which do not vary in total as output changes, e.g. rent, insurance, depreciation, as well as much of administrative, marketing, maintenance and energy costs. Variable costs are those which do alter in total as output changes, e.g. cost of food and beverages. Some costs, such as labour costs, may be semi-fixed in that they cannot be adjusted readily to changes in output but can be adjusted eventually. (The Price Commission Report on Butlins noted that the holiday camps 'cannot be operated with less than 60 per cent of the full staff complement, regardless of how few guests there are'.)[2]

In the tables, cost-fixity (if labour costs are included) varies between 41 and 59 per cent in restaurants and is approximately 74 per cent in the hotels. This compares with less than 40 per cent in the car assembly industry,[3] approximately one-third of expenses of tea-blending firms[4] and just over half of the expenses of a brewery.[5]

This proportion of costs which is not readily variable is particularly high in the case of hotels and despite being less so for restaurants, is still relatively high. There are a number of implications of this cost-fixity:

1 As the scope for cost-reduction is limited, it is important that hotels in particular should be market-orientated,[6] i.e. seeking to influence demand.

Table 38 *Restaurant expenses (USA) 1976*

	Fast food restaurants	*Traditional table service restaurants*
	Expenses as % of sales revenue	
Cost of sales	42.0	34.3
Operating expenses		
Payroll and related	19.0	38.5
Advertising and promotion	3.0	1.5
Other	9.0	11.0
Occupancy costs		
Rent	8.0	4.5
Depreciation	2.2	3.5
Insurance	0.6	0.3

Source: D. Wyckoff and E. Sasser, *The Chain Restaurant Industry* (Lexington Books 1978).

Table 39 *International hotel expenses*

	Expenses as % of sales revenue
Food and beverage costs	11.5
Operating expenses	
Payroll and related	33.3
Departmental expenses	13.1
Marketing	3.0
Administration and general	6.3
Property operation and maintenance	3.4
Energy costs	4.7
Occupancy costs	
Property taxes and insurance	2.4
Rent	6.3
Interest	3.5
Depreciation and amortization	3.8

Source: Horwath and Horwath International, *Worldwide Lodging Industry 1983* (Horwath & Horwath, 1983).

Fluctuations in sales become important as a major determinant of profitability. As sales rise, total costs do not rise as rapidly whereas when sales fall, total costs do not diminish in the same proportion; thus high occupancy rates become crucial influences on profitability. (It has been demonstrated that managers in the industry have attempted to cope with problems associated with inflation by trying to reduce costs rather than increase sales.[7])

2 Demand for hotel and catering services is irregular and exhibits seasonal, weekly and daily peaks and troughs. To meet the peaks, capacity (and therefore fixed and semi-fixed costs) is often greater than it would be if the total demand was more evenly spread on a time basis. Thus the need to stimulate off-peak demand becomes more acute than in other industries, in order to avoid the wastage and underutilization of assets. Decisions about the size of units will involve a trade-off between meeting peak demand and the need to minimize waste through capacity underutilization.

3 Cost-fixity does, however, mean that the short-term discretion for price variation is greater. Prices must, over a long period of time, cover all costs but firms may occasionally offer prices at below cost in order to stimulate demand. The floor to such price reductions is given by the variable costs, i.e. those extra costs incurred by supplying the customers. Fixed costs may be temporarily disregarded because they have to be met whether there are sales or not; thus if the reduced price at least covers the extra costs of sales, then some contribution is being earned towards these fixed costs. If the reduced price does not even cover these extra costs, then it makes no sense to charge that price since not only are fixed costs not covered, but there will also be additional variable costs which are not covered.

If variable costs are the floor to these short-term price reductions, then the high proportion of fixed costs would imply that this floor is 'low'.

Output and costs

Returning to the specific contribution of economics to the topic of costs, consider the relationship between output and costs.

It is convenient and logical to divide this discussion into two:

1 The relationship over those periods of time during which one, or several, of the inputs of factors are fixed in supply. Such a situation is referred to as the *'short-run'*.

   An increase in output during the short-run will thus require an increased input of some factors working with fixed inputs of others.

2 The relationship over those periods of time during which none of the inputs is fixed in supply. This is a *'long-run'* situation.

   An increase in output in the long-run can result from an increase in all inputs.

These two concepts are not fixed in terms of days or years but will vary in duration according to the productive process under consideration. If, at any stage, an input is fixed in supply then a short-run situation prevails and if no input is fixed, a long-run situation prevails. It may be that in some industries short-run situations can last many years; it would certainly take several years for an existing hotelier or caterer to sell his/her existing establishment and bring to completion a new hotel and catering complex built from nothing. Until all of this can be done, the businessperson is working with some factors of production which are fixed in supply (such as the building itself, or equipment within it) and thus is operating within the 'short-run'. Output is constrained by the productive capacity of the existing resources.

As will be seen later in this chapter, the relationship between output and costs is believed to differ according to whether the situation is short-run or long-run. Additionally, the relationship will differ according to whether fixed or variable costs are considered.

It was noted in Chapter 2 that the conventional economic model of the firm assumes that the firm has perfect knowledge of its cost structures, both present and future. It is thus deemed to know the consequences of whatever level of output it chooses to produce and when it comes to long-run decisions, it is fully aware of the options available to it.

Short-run variable costs

1 Accounting models[8] of cost/output relationships often depict variable costs as being proportional to changes in output; as output increased by 10 per cent so do the variable costs (see Figure 30(b)). Underlying this is the assumption that as resources are put into production, the resulting output changes in direct proportion to the inputs (see Figure 30(a)). If this is so and the cost of each unit of input remains unchanged, then evidently the variable cost of production will rise proportionately also.

In Figure 30, the input of labour is increased by 25 per cent, resulting in a

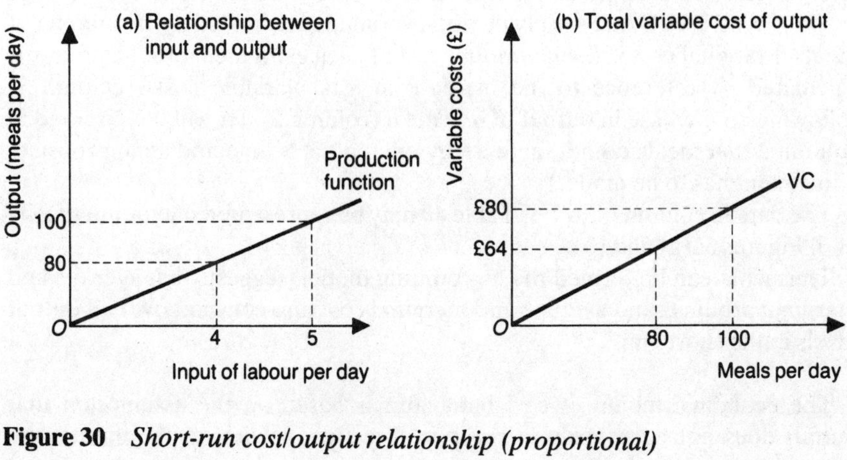

Figure 30 *Short-run cost/output relationship (proportional)*

Table 40 *Short-run outputs and costs (proportional cost/output relationship)*

1 *Labour input*	2 *Meals per day*	3 *Total variable cost*	4 *Average product*	5 *Marginal product*	6 *Average variable cost*	7 *Marginal cost*
1	20	£ 16	20 meals		80p	
				20 meals		80p
2	40	£ 32	20 meals		80p	
				20 meals		80p
3	60	£ 48	20 meals		80p	
				20 meals		80p
4	80	£ 64	20 meals		80p	
				20 meals		80p
5	100	£ 80	20 meals		80p	
				20 meals		80p
6	120	£ 96	20 meals		80p	
				20 meals		80p
7	140	£112	20 meals		80p	
				20 meals		80p
8	160	£128	20 meals		80p	

Each worker is paid £16 per day.

25 per cent increase in output. If each unit of labour is paid a wage of £16 per day, then it is possible to determine that the total cost of producing the meals (excluding, rather unrealistically, all other variable costs) rises from £64 to £80, also a rise of 25 per cent (see also Table 40, columns 2 and 3).

The average product (output) per unit of labour may be determined by dividing the total product by the number of labour units (see Table 40, column 4).

The marginal product, i.e. the *additional* output per *extra* person employed is also twenty meals (see Table 40, column 5). This is calculated by reference to the increase in total output (column 2) following on an increase in labour of *one* person (column 1).

These average and marginal products can be translated into the corresponding cost concepts of average and marginal costs (see columns 6 and 7). Average variable costs (AVC) are simply the total variable cost divided by the number of meals. Marginal cost is the *additional* cost of each *extra* meal produced; this is calculated by reference to the increase in total variable costs (column 3) following an increase in output of *one* meal (column 2). (It will be observed in column 2 that meals do not increase by one unit at a time and an appropriate adjustment has to be made.)

The data in columns 4 to 7 of Table 40 may be represented diagrammatically as in Figures 31(a) and (b).

Thus what can be termed the 'accounting model' suggests that average and marginal products and average and marginal costs are constant over all output levels in the short-run.

2 The economic model of cost behaviour is based on the assumption that output does not necessarily increase in direct proportion to the inputs; the

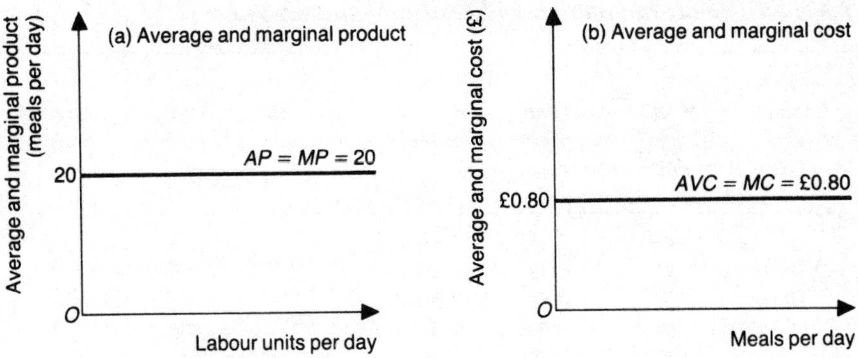

Figure 31 *Average and marginal outputs and costs*

consequence of this is that average and marginal outputs and costs will not be constant.

The assumption is formalized as the 'law of diminishing returns' or of 'variable proportions'. This has its origins in an agriculturally-based model, where increasing amounts of variable factors, such as labour, were applied to a fixed factor of land. It is less certain and obvious how far it may hold in other forms of economic activity, as will be discussed below.

The law states that as 'increasing quantities of a variable factor are applied to a given factor, the marginal product and the average product of the variable factor will eventually decrease'.[9]

As units of labour increase, the proportions in which all the factors of production are used alter. It is likely that there is some 'optimal' combination of the variable factor (labour) and the fixed factor (such as kitchen equipment) and if changes are made in the amount of labour around that optimal combination, then a less than ideal output will result. If the variable input of labour is increased, with all else remaining equal, then the law suggests that disproportionate changes in output will result (see Table 41).

From column 4, it is evident that the average product first of all rises, reaches a maximum at an input of seven workers, and then starts to fall. The marginal product (column 5) follows a similar path but reaches a maximum at a different input (as the labour input is increased from five to six workers). The maximum points in both the average and marginal cases are the points of diminishing returns (see Figure 32(a)).

The costs are shown in columns 6 and 7. It will be noticed that the paths of average and marginal costs are a direct 'mirror image' of the average and marginal products: the minimum average variable cost occurs at an input of seven workers and the marginal cost reaches a minimum as labour input is increased from five to six workers (see Figure 32(a) and (b) and compare with Figure 31(a) and (b)).

Table 41 *Short-run outputs and costs (diminishing returns)*

1 *Labour input*	2 *Meals per day*	3 *Total variable cost*	4 *Average product*	5 *Marginal product*	6 *Average variable cost*	7 *Marginal cost*
1	12	£ 16	12 meals		£1.33	
2	30	£ 32	15 meals	18 meals	£1.07	89p
3	51	£ 48	17 meals	21 meals	94p	76p
4	80	£ 64	20 meals	29 meals	80p	55p
5	125	£ 80	25 meals	45 meals	64p	35p
6	192	£ 96	32 meals	67 meals	50p	23.8p
7	245	£112	35 meals	53 meals	45.7p	30.2p
8	264	£128	33 meals	19 meals	48.5p	84.2p

Each worker is paid £16 per day.

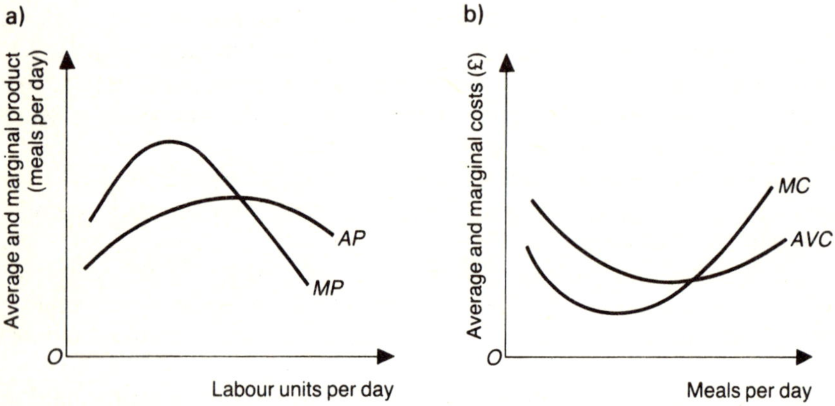

Figure 32 *Diminishing returns*

The economists' cost curves, like the demand curve, are to be interpreted carefully. The cost curve answers the question 'What will be the current cost of production *if* output now were at a level of *x* meals?' All points on the cost curve thus refer to the same period of time; this is rather different from determining what costs would be when output actually does change over time.

3 Why might such U-shaped cost curves be expected to occur? Given the size, quality and quantity of the fixed factors (such as kitchen equipment), output may initially be expected to rise more than proportionately if the variable factor (labour) was increased. Output per person would rise and variable cost

per unit of output (*AVC*) fall. This is because at low levels of output there are 'too few' staff employed to ensure the efficient utilization of the fixed factors. If extra labour were added the fixed factor would become more efficiently used and the combination of variable and fixed factors would be more appropriate.

Eventually a stage would be reached when output would increase more and more slowly in response to additional labour inputs. Output per person would fall and *AVC* rise.

The fixed factor would be overutilized and there would be too many staff in relation to the fixed factor. The combination of variable and fixed factors would be less and less appropriate.

Such relationships would seem to have some intuitive appeal in so far as there must be some 'correct' combination of labour and equipment and any deviation from that combination would result in less than ideal output. But how far is it likely to be a significant relationship such that cost curves really do have a marked U-shape?

Before answering that question, it is necessary to appreciate a few of the restrictive assumptions under which the law operates:

(a) That the efficiency of all the factors and the techniques of production are unchanged, so that persons of equal ability are combined with an unaltered stock of kitchen equipment. If an additional person proved to be a 'better' worker than previous ones or if the kitchen equipment was replaced or modified to become more effective, then diminishing returns need not occur.

(b) That the factors operate in varying proportions. If factors are variable in the same proportion or if all factors are variable, though not necessarily in the same proportion, then the possibility of combining variable factors with a fixed factor no longer holds. It may be that the 'fixed' factors are, in fact, divisible.

(c) That the prices of the inputs remain constant. It could be, however, that extra labour could only be employed by offering higher wages.

Evidence does suggest[10] that, in practice, the short-run *AVC* curve may have the following shape (see Figure 33) with the *AVC* virtually constant (and equal to *MC*) up to capacity, when it rises sharply.

The shape of the 'curve' over the levels of production usually experienced or considered is such that the accounting model therefore can serve as an adequate working model. Often the 'fixed' factor is, in practice, divisible and the proportions in which capital and labour operate can be kept reasonably constant.[11]

4 Consider aspects of hotels and catering. In the accommodation sector, what would be likely to happen to costs in practice if occupancy rose? The largest single component of the costs of the 'rooms' department of a hotel is payroll expenses (19 per cent of room sales revenue).[12]

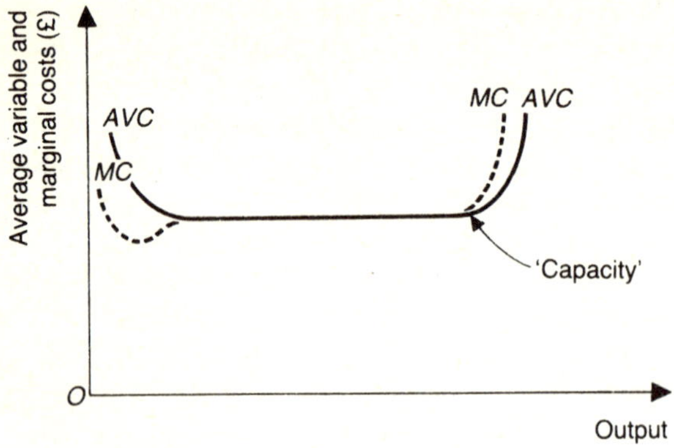

Figure 33 *Empirical variable cost curve*

If a hotel were to employ more roommaids than a given occupancy rate justified, then diminishing returns would be expected to occur, e.g. if roommaids are employed on the basis of one per ten rooms, then when seventy rooms are let seven maids are required. The employment of extra maids would be unnecessary and would reduce the average output (rooms) per maid. Doubling the number of roommaids without a corresponding doubling of rooms let would lead to diminishing returns.

In reality, it may be that a pool of labour will be available to attend to whatever number of rooms are let; if the number of rooms let is less than ten per maid, then average output will be lower (and average variable cost higher) than if rooms let were ten per maid. Conversely, if rooms let were greater than ten per maid, average variable costs would be reduced. *AVC* would be as in Figure 34(a).

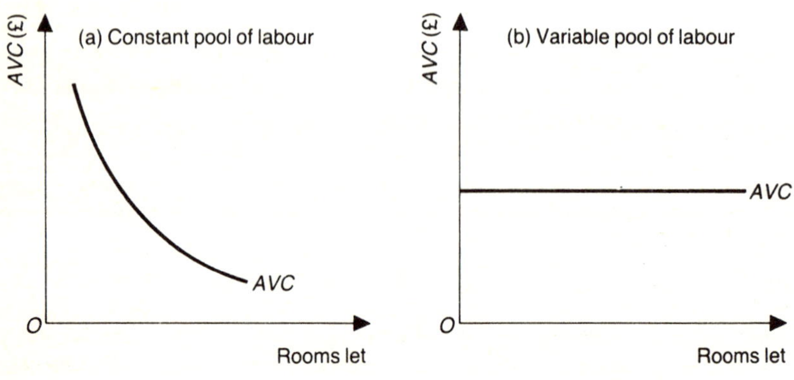

Figure 34 *Possible AVC curves for accommodation units*

If roommaids are employed on a casual or part-time basis so that the input is directly variable with rooms let, then average variable costs will be constant (see Figure 34(b)).

A similar situation would be expected with respect to food service.

In food production there may be more reason to believe that diminishing returns may occur as there is a fixed factor of kitchen equipment with which the kitchen brigade operates. There will be some appropriate combination of staff and equipment for any desired level of meal sales and if additional staff are employed, diminishing returns are likely.

But in most kitchens equipment is divisible (one ring on a multiring cooker) and there are usually available in any one kitchen a wide range of sizes of equipment (small pans as well as large steamers). Consequently, the proportions in which the factors are combined need not vary greatly; variable costs can vary in proportion to output. Not all of the kitchen equipment need be operated all of the time and thus constant *AVC* is likely.

Fixed costs

So far the discussion of costs has been concerned with variable costs and has noted a difference in the accounting and economic models. There is no difference, however, with respect to the behaviour of fixed costs.

These costs are constant regardless of the level of output. The greater the level of output then the lower the fixed cost per unit of output (or average fixed cost: *AFC*). The fixed costs are spread over a larger volume of output and thus the *AFC* curve will be a continuously falling one, as in Figure 35.

The combination of *AVC* and *AFC* in the economic model would give curves such as those in Figure 36, where *ATC* is average total costs.

These curves have been traditionally used in economic analysis and remain prominent in economic textbooks today despite evidence to the contrary in

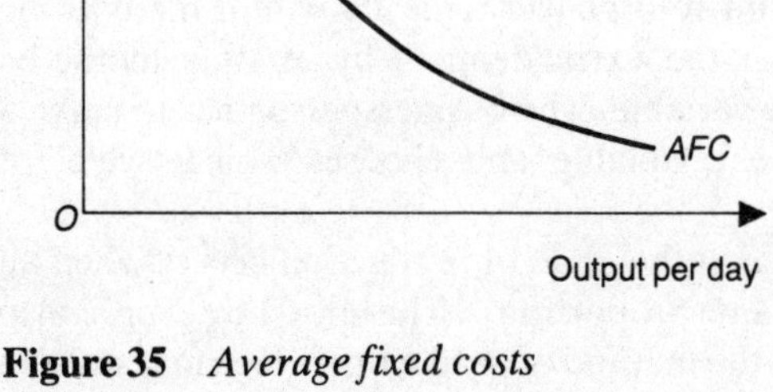

Figure 35 *Average fixed costs*

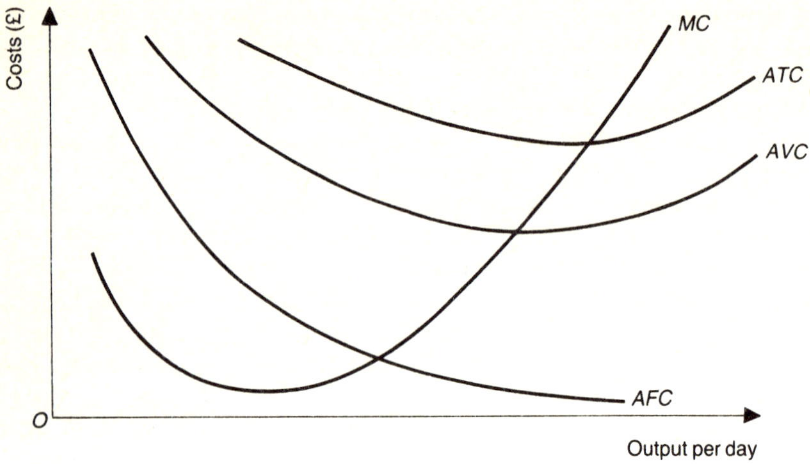

Figure 36 *ATC, AFC and AVC (economic model)*

respect of *AVC* (and thus *MC*). As was seen in Chapter 2, the shape of the supply curve in economic models of price determination is very much determined by an underlying assumption of a U-shaped marginal cost curve in particular.

Long-run costs

If, instead of being 'locked-in' to a situation where only some inputs are variable and others are fixed, all inputs can be varied then the firm is in a long-run situation. In the short-run there is only one way of producing a given output and that is by adjusting the variable inputs. In the long-run, however, a choice is open to the firm of all the many technically possible methods available. Which method is chosen (e.g. much labour and little capital or little labour and much capital) will, it is assumed, be decided by reference to cost-minimization (profit-maximization implies cost-minimization).

By reference to Table 41 it is evident that short-run *AVC* are rising at an output of 264 meals (eight persons employed); given a potential increase in business beyond this, it might be considered appropriate to build a new restaurant or kitchen, or re-fit and re-organize radically within the existing building, rather than try to meet the extra demand by existing methods. Potentially, all the inputs are now variable. The businessperson has to make a choice from all the opportunities available and chooses which 'scale' of production to operate at.

In its strictest sense, an increase in the scale of production occurs when all factor inputs are increased in the same proportion.[13] The term, however, is also generally used to cover changes in the method of production which may involve

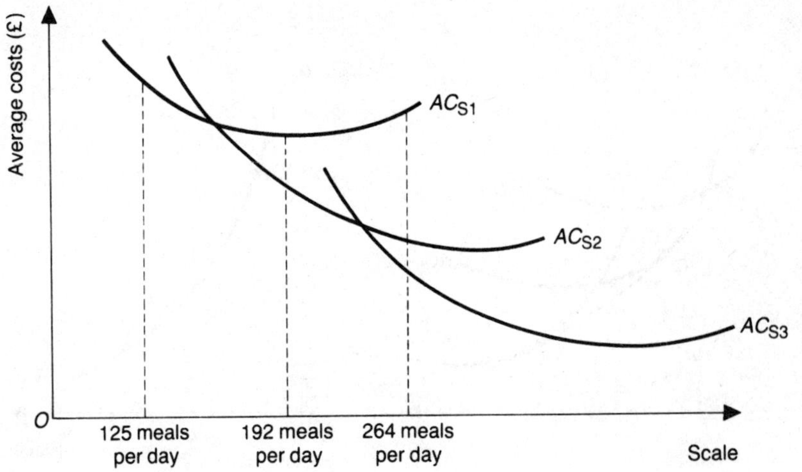

Figure 37 *Relationship of short-run average cost curves in the long-run*

changes in all or some of the factors, and also, perhaps more confusingly, to cover changes in the rate of output using the most efficient known methods at each scale.[14]

Once a particular method of production or type and size of establishment is chosen and operative, then the business once more becomes 'locked-in' to a situation where only some of the factor inputs can be altered and the short-run cost curve will be applicable. Each potential new method or establishment will thus have its own short-run curve. The long-run cost curve is derived from the short-run cost curves in the following way.

Each short-run (*SR*) cost curve will stand in relationship to the others as depicted in Figure 37. There will be one *SR* cost curve for each potential new method or establishment.

In the short-run any variation of output between 125 and 264 meals per day would have to be within the given capacity of the existing establishment (establishment 1 with *AC* curve of AC_{S1}). However, given a completely free choice of methods or establishments, then an output of 192 meals is best produced with a new establishment and/or different techniques such that AC_{S2} prevails; 192 meals can be produced at a lower cost here than in establishment 1. Similarly, 264 meals are best produced in a new establishment such that AC_{S3} prevails, where average costs are lower than either of the techniques or establishments 1 and 2 are able to achieve.

The long-run cost curve will show the lowest cost of producing any particular level of output and will be made up of one point from each of the short-run cost curves (see Figure 38).

The long-run average costs are considered to fall continuously, i.e. there are economies of scale. Like other cost curves, the long-run curve indicates the

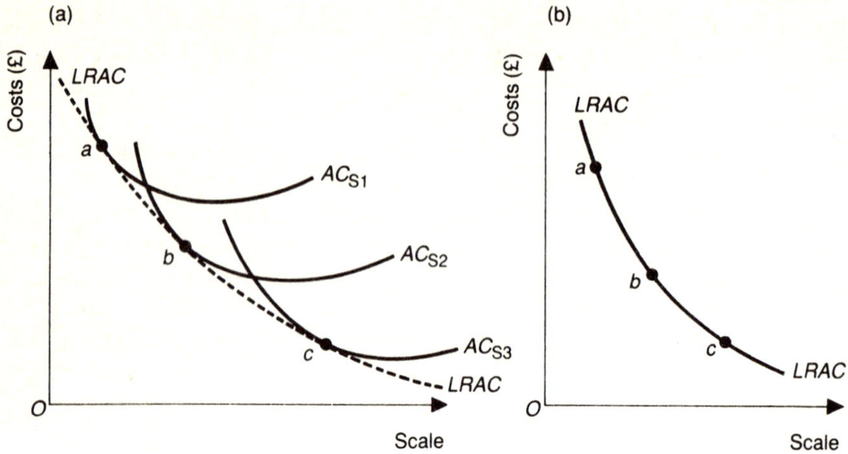

Figure 38 *Long-run average costs*

average costs *at a particular point of time,* of a number of alternative situations, rather than what would happen over time.[15] These economies occur, in the strictest sense, when all factor inputs are increased in the same proportion and the output increases by a greater proportion (thus AC falls). However, as noted earlier, 'scale' may also be more loosely interpreted and economies may be said to occur whenever average costs fall as the outcome of any long-run decision; thus not all factor inputs may increase in the same proportion, some may not increase at all and there may be a re-organization of the existing inputs.

The four sources of the economies are:[16]

Specialization of function

As scale increases there is an increased opportunity for the factors of production to specialize and concentrate on one or a limited set of activities. Both labour and machines can specialize and this in itself can make factors more productive and reduce average costs. A number of chefs each concentrating on work in one 'corner' of the kitchen are likely to be more productive than if they each worked in all corners. Each chef can be employed in the job in which his/her superiority is greater; constant and undivided attention to a limited range of tasks leads to greater skill, and time is saved in not switching from one operation to another.

It is only at high levels of output that specialization becomes economic and at lower levels the concentration of labour and machines on particular tasks would be wasteful.

Indivisibilities

Machines and equipment can often only be purchased or hired in fixed amounts and each one of these amounts may be too large for a particularly low level of sales or output. Certain equipment will thus be underutilized at low levels of output.

More capital-intensive methods of production, automated and mechanized production, become possible and economic at high levels of output. The high capital costs can be spread over a large volume of output and the nature of the processes is usually such that the average costs of production are thereby lower than costs associated with more labour-intensive methods, e.g. cook-freeze systems.

The firm has the ability to spread high costs over a large output making possible the use of sophisticated production techniques. A high level of output is necessary for the most efficient machines to be used.

Specialization of function and indivisibilities are evidently connected; the inability to specialize on tasks at low levels of production is associated with the indivisibility of labour in particular; the advantage of large-scale capital-intensive production is associated with the specialization of machinery and labour in certain tasks.

Physical relationships

It is evident that costs of constructing certain capital equipment/buildings do not always rise in the same proportion to the increase in capacity of that equipment. The surface area of a three-dimensional object, whether it be an oil tanker, gasometer, aeroplane, hotel or saucepan, does not increase as fast as its volume. Thus the amount of material required to construct any one of these will not necessarily double as the required carrying capacity doubles.

Economies of massed resources

If firms wish to keep spare machinery to cover breakdowns or keep stocks of raw materials should supplies be interrupted, then the level of these 'reserves' increases less than proportionately to output.

The four economies discussed above are a consequence of large-scale production and are known as technical or production economies of scale. As such, they influence the size and nature of the productive unit (establishment) whether it be factory, hotel, restaurant or kitchen.

Additionally, there are advantages of large firms which are quite distinct from the technical or production economies described above. Large firms may, for instance, be able to obtain raw materials more cheaply than small firms because of discounts and their bargaining power. They may be able to attract and afford to hire better quality staff; they may gain easier and cheaper access to finance for investment purposes. There are also advantages derived from marketing on a large scale. Large firms are often diversified and are thus better able to spread their risks than are small, less diversified firms.

Thus there are advantages which accrue to large firms independently of the rate of output or size of establishments owned by these firms. A firm may be large and achieve these non-technical advantages despite owning a number of small establishments.

Related to economies of scale are 'experience efficiencies'; these are 'cost advantages gained *over time* as a firm's knowledge grows and the cumulative number of units produced increases'.[17] A source of these efficiencies is the learning curve: employees and management gain expertise in their tasks over time. They learn by experience, avoid repetition of mistakes and the costly search for the best way of achieving objectives. If each worker specializes in a particular task, each worker can accumulate experience faster. Also, over time, a firm can benefit from past experience in designing new production processes, designing products and discovering the most economic combination of factor inputs.

Economies of scale in practice

1 Those studies there have been of the extent of economies of scale have usually concentrated on manufacturing industry; the most well-known studies are those of Pratten who was mostly concerned with technical economies of scale.[18] Table 42 indicates some of the findings; the minimum efficient scale of production (MES) is that level of output which is necessary to achieve

Table 42 *Economies of scale in certain UK manufacturing industries (1969)*

Industry/product	*MES as proportion of UK output*	*Percentage increase in average costs at 50% of MES*
Aircraft	>100	>20
Computers	100	10
Domestic electrical appliances	50	8
Car assembly (1200 cc)	50	6
Detergents	20	2.5
Oil refining	10 [40 (regional market)]	5
Beer	3 [6 (regional market)]	9

Source: C. F. Pratten, *Economies of Scale in Manufacturing Industry* (Cambridge University Press 1971).

Table 43 *Hotel construction costs (New York) 1975 Gross cost per square foot medium rise, average quality hotel*

Number of rooms	80	120	150	180	225	275	350
	$41.23	$39.86	$38.48	$36.83	$35.50	$34.02	$32.70

Source: J. J. Clark and R. H. Penner, 'Hotels and Life-Cycle Costing', *Cornell HRA Quarterly*, 16 (4) (February 1976).

economies of scale and lowest average cost. If the MES in a particular industry is 25 per cent of that industry's output, then only four establishments can survive and achieve lowest AC; if the MES is over 100 per cent, then the industry's output is not great enough for establishments to achieve lowest AC. The overall conclusion of the studies was that there do exist economies of scale in many industries but that there are probably too many establishments operating at too small a scale.

Significantly, even if operating at less than the optimal level of output, average costs were not necessarily a great deal higher than the lowest average cost (at MES). In the case of car assembly, average costs at half the MES are only 6 per cent higher than they are at MES (see Table 42).

The existence of these economies of scale may account in part for the level of market concentration in certain UK industries. It was noted earlier that levels of market concentration in the UK are probably higher than in several other countries and this may be partly explained by the smaller size of the UK market compared, for instance, with the USA.

However, firm concentration is often higher than is plant/establishment concentration and it is at the plant/establishment level that the technical economies operate. Thus, firms may well be exploiting the non-technical advantages of large firms but not the technical economies of scale.

2 With regard to the hotel and catering industry and most personal service industries, it would appear that the scope for achieving technical economies of scale is limited. There are, undoubtedly, benefits from having a 'large' establishment or from producing on a large scale in hotels and catering, e.g. the construction costs of hotels or restaurants do not rise in the same proportion as capacity (see Table 43). Central cooking facilities may be established where units are concentrated geographically and one central kitchen can prove more economical than several smaller ones; the size of the kitchen and amount and size of equipment do not increase proportionately with output. Large steamers in kitchens can prove cheaper to buy and operate per unit of output, than a number of smaller saucepans. With respect to hotels, the larger units can

ensure maximum utilization of corridor space, lifts, public areas, and so on. A hotel twice as large as another will not necessarily require twice the floor area for reception, kitchen or bar purposes, nor double the staffing requirements. Cook-freeze and chill systems are expensive to install but become economical at large volumes of output.[19]

The 'Pickering' research report,[20] when considering economies of scale in the industry, concluded that 'a size of between 40 and 60 bedspaces is a particularly difficult one (for a hotel) and that larger size can be accommodated with no increases in staffing'. Further, the research team considered that while existing small hotels could survive, 'it is now strongly argued that a new hotel of less than 100 bedrooms would not be viable'. The team also considered that 'normally a minimum viable size of 30 to 50 seats may be necessary' for a high-class restaurant. While this is not evidence of substantial economies of scale, it suggests there are cost advantages of operating at high levels of output.

None the less, compared with other industries, especially in manufacturing, the ability to achieve significant average cost reductions is not great. The largest source of economies in any industry probably lies in the ability to automate and mechanize. In personal service industries, the opportunity to do this is restricted and thus any economies that can be achieved will be relatively minor.

'Menu items cannot be produced en masse and held in inventory but must be prepared on demand; demand is characterized by severe peaks and valleys and the product line is diverse and marked by frequent changes...Large scale, highly automated, assembly-line production methods – the major avenue for achieving operating-cost scale economies – are, with some important exceptions...generally not feasible for restaurants'.[21] Fast food operations do, however, offer some significant opportunities for achieving economies of scale and experience efficiencies.

Even where there might be substantial potential economies for hotels and catering the very nature of the market and demand may restrict the ability to achieve them. The market is so diverse and segmented and geographically stratified, that physically large establishments and establishments producing large volumes of output are often not justifiable.

However, technical changes, increases in costs and the awareness of possibilities for standardizing the market are making technical economies more important and increasingly influential on establishment size and production volume. Currently, however, large establishments in hotels and catering do not have a significant advantage over small establishments.[22]

With respect to non-technical advantages, there do appear to be significant benefits in marketing, training, purchasing, etc., derived from being a large hotel and catering firm compared with being a small one.[23]

The growth of individual firms in the hotel and catering industry is thus more likely to take the form of acquiring additional establishments rather than by increasing the size of individual establishments. The scope for achieving production economies within an existing geographical market may also be limited by the physical restrictions of the building and on the ability to expand on the site.

Before leaving the topic of long-run costs and economies of scale, it is necessary to note that the advantages of being 'large' may be outweighed by 'diseconomies' such as the difficulties of managing and co-ordinating a large enterprise and the worsening of labour relations. There is little evidence to suggest that this is very significant, in practice, and it would seem that the long-run average cost curve falls continuously.[24]

Opportunity cost

As noted at the beginning of the chapter, the economic definition of cost can differ from other definitions. As the fundamental economic problem is that of 'scarcity' of resources, the economic definition of 'costs' seeks to reflect this. It seeks to signify the real cost of production of a product in the sense of the sacrifice incurred by society in devoting limited resources to one particular activity rather than another. In this way a judgement may be made about whether or not the 'optimal' allocation of resources is being approached. Because of scarcity, a choice of alternative uses has to be made and once resources are committed to one particular use then an opportunity to produce the alternatives is lost. The real cost of an increase in government spending on the health and educational services will be the output of cars and television sets that might otherwise have been produced.

The real, or opportunity, cost is thus 'the benefits foregone by not using it (a resource) in its best alternative use'.[25]

If a restaurant makes, according to its accountants, a profit of £10,000 in a particular year, then the owner may feel well satisfied. However, it might be that the same restaurateur could have gained employment as manager of some other firm's restaurant at a salary of £10,500 a year. The restaurateur has thus effectively sacrificed £500 and from an economic point of view, his/her business would be operating at a 'loss' of £500, rather than the £10,000 profit recorded by the accountant (see Figures 39(a) and (b)).

A person who sought to maximize his/her own economic welfare would in such circumstances move from self-employment to employee status as a salaried manager. There is clearly a certain monetary return which would be necessary to induce a producer to enter and remain in a particular industry; at least £10,500 in the above example. If it is not forthcoming then production will not occur; the producer will not set up or continue with his/her own restaurant. There is a cost which needs to be met if restaurants are to be provided.

Whatever is generally considered to be an appropriate monetary incentive to encourage producers to enter and stay in the restaurant business is as much a cost of production as are the wages paid to employees and the invoices payable for supplies received. Only when all these costs are covered can profit *in the economic sense* be earned.

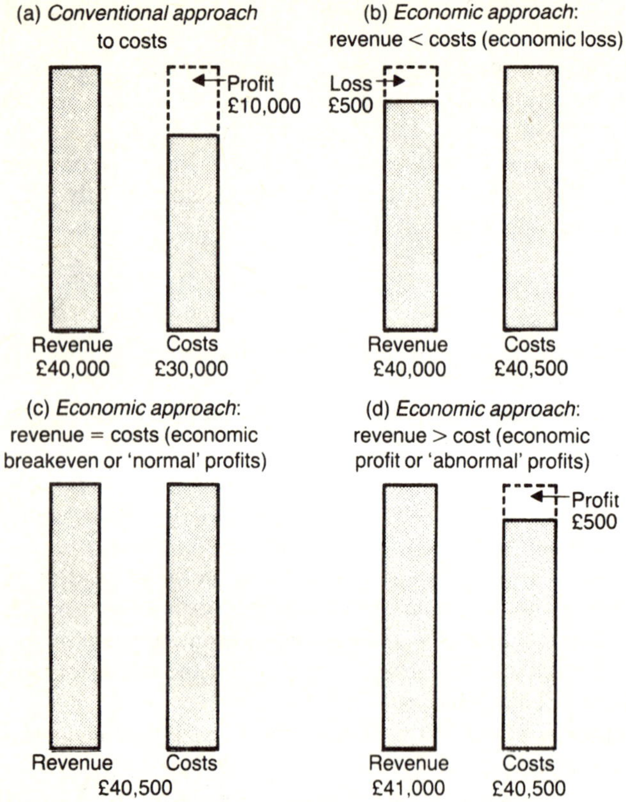

Figure 39 *Opportunity costs*

This specific opportunity cost is also (rather confusingly) termed 'normal profit' and any return over and above that is an 'abnormal' or 'supernormal' profit, i.e. is more than is necessary to attract and retain a producer in an industry (see Figures 39(c) and (d)).

Consequently when economic models show the costs of and revenue from production as equal (see Chapter 2), this signifies that the opportunity costs are being met (or normal profits earned).

Questions for essays and seminar papers

1 Discuss the meaning and significance of economies of scale in the hotel and catering industry.

2 How far are diminishing returns likely to be evident in hotel and catering activities?

3 Analyse the cost structures of hotel and catering establishments. Assess the implications for the industry of a high proportion of fixed costs.
4 How far can the growth of hotel and catering firms be explained by a desire to achieve economies of scale (with Chapter 4)?
5 Why, despite the existence of economies of scale, do so many small firms continue to exist in the hotel and catering industry (with Chapter 3)?

Practical assignment

Taking an existing local hotel or catering unit as an example, find out what benefits, if any, there might be in constructing and operating a unit with twice the number of rooms or meal-production capacity. You should make use of your expertise in other subject areas and may need to call upon the assistance of other subject lecturers.

CHAPTER 6

Labour

The topic of labour, or the workforce, is singled out for particular attention because of its special significance in the service industries in general and the hotel and catering industry in particular. Services employ a large and growing proportion of the country's labour force and they are particularly reliant upon a labour input in order to produce their output. Many of the services have a 'large' labour content in relation to their output. In Table 44 it can be seen that the service industries have a significantly high number of employees for every £1m worth of output produced (and have a low value of output per employee).

From an economy perspective the service industries (including hotels and catering) would appear to have considerable potential for creating jobs. In Chapter 1 it was noted how the service sector has become an increasingly important employer (from 47 per cent of employment in 1961 to 67 per cent in 1986). Within the service sector, which industries are the most important employers and which have shown the most rapid growth?

Working population

From Table 45 it can be seen that employment in the service industries as a whole has increased by 24.7 per cent between 1971 and 1986 whereas all other sectors of the economy have experienced a reduction in the number of employees.

The numbers employed in the service industries have increased but this increase has not been enough to compensate for the loss of employment in the rest of the economy. Overall, despite there also having been an increase in the number of self-employed throughout the economy, there has been a fall in the number of persons in employment (see Table 47).

In addition to the number of employees in the labour force there are also 'employers' and the 'self-employed' (see Table 46).

The 'labour force' or 'working population' will include employees, employers and self-employed with the addition of those in HM Forces and those registered as unemployed (see Table 46). It may seem curious to include the unemployed in estimates of the 'working population' or 'labour force', but this is a measure of those persons who are in work or who are available for and willing to work.

The size of the working population will therefore be influenced not solely by

Table 44 *Labour intensity of production 1986*

	Employees per £1m worth of output	*Output per employee (£000)*
Agriculture, forestry and fishing	55.7	17.9
Production (manufacturing and energy and water supply)	55.8	17.9
Construction	49.4	20.2
Services	67.7	14.8
(Distribution, hotels and catering; repairs)	(96.2)	(10.4)

Sources: Calculated from data in *Annual Abstract of Statistics, 1988* (HMSO 1988) and *Social Trends*, No. 18 (HMSO 1988).

Table 45 *Changes in employment by industry (GB) 1971–86*

	Total number of employees June 1986 (000s)	*% change 1971–86*
Agriculture, forestry and fishing	329	−26.9
Energy and water supply	539	−32.4
Construction	992	−17.2
Manufacturing	5239	−35.0
Services	14495	24.7
(Distribution; hotels and catering; repairs)	(4403)	(19.4)
(Banking, insurance, finance, business services and leasing)	(2203)	(64.9)

Source: Central Statistical Office, *Social Trends*, No. 18 (HMSO 1988).

the number of jobs available but also by the number of persons who choose to register as unemployed. A decision by some of the unemployed not to register as such could cause the size of the working population to fall. For instance, in the two years after September 1979, the number of females in work fell by 0.6m but female unemployment rose by only 0.4m; 0.2m did not register as unemployed and the female working population fell.[1]

Many women may enter or leave the working population several times over in their lifetimes – at some time they may be searching for or in employment and at others, out of or not searching for employment (see later in this chapter). Those who have a long-term tendency to stay in the labour force may be

Table 46 *Composition of the working population (UK) June 1987*

	000s
Employees in employment	
Males	11881
Females	9930
	21810
Self-employed	2861
HM forces	319
Work-related government training	311
Workforce in employment	25301
Unemployed	2905
Working population (workforce)	28206

Source: Department of Employment, *Employment Gazette*, August 1988.

Table 47 *Employed labour force, unemployed and working population (workforce) (UK) 1976–86 (June)*

	Employed labour force	*Unemployed*	*Working population*
1976	24844	1266	26110
1986	24542	3229	27771
Change 1976–86	−302	+1963	+1661

Source: *Employment Gazette*, Historical Supplement No. 2, 'Employment Statistics' (October 1987).

classified as 'primary' workers, whereas those whose attachment is much less permanent and who move in and out are classified as 'secondary' workers.

Over the period 1976–86 the working population has increased but the employed labour force has fallen (see Table 47). As a consequence, the number of persons unemployed has risen.

The fall in employment was largely confined to the private sector rather than the public (government) sector (see Table 48). This has reversed in recent years, however, with public sector employment falling from a peak of 7.4m during 1979–80 to 6.5m in 1986.

Table 48 *Employment by private and public sector (UK) 1961–86*

	Public sector		*Private sector*
		(millions)	
1961	5.9		18.6
1981	7.2		17.2
1986	6.5		18.0

Source: Central Statistical Office, *Social Trends*, No. 18 (HMSO 1988).

Many of the public sector jobs are 'services' – education, health, central and local government, etc., plus employment in the public corporations, not all of which are services (coal, rail, gas, electricity, etc.).

Service sector employment[2]

Within the service sector as a whole, it is public sector employment that showed the more rapid rate of growth during the 1960s and early 1970s. That growth has, since the mid-1970s, slowed down to be overtaken by growth in private sector service employment.[3]

Political decisions about what is a desirable role of government in the economy and society have contributed to these variations in the growth of public sector service employment. Conservative Governments since 1979 have particularly sought to reduce the role of government, partly because of a belief that 'too much government restricts initiative and enterprise' and also as part of general deflationary policies designed to cure inflation. A large part of public sector output is 'non-marketable', e.g. health and education services, armed forces, civil service, etc., which are not sold.[4] Employees and other resources in these sectors are not available for employment in sectors the products of which can be sold. A bottleneck could thus arise should the 'market' sector wish to expand.

Additionally, the non-market sector has to be financed through taxation (the products are not sold) and an expansion of the sector would mean an increased tax burden for the rest of the economy. These views have contributed to the slow-down in the growth of public sector employment.

Apart from this growth another major category of service employment growth has been banking, insurance, financial and business services. The number of employees has grown by 64.9 per cent between 1971 and 1986 (see Table 45).

Considerable faith has increasingly been placed in the service sector as the main creator of new jobs in the economy. However, it is clear that much of the service sector is becoming as amenable to productivity improvements through the introduction of technology, as is manufacturing.[5] Professional and

Table 49 *Employees in employment in hotels and catering (GB) 1981–7 (June)*

	000s
1981	930
1982	959
1983	949
1984	995
1985	1046
1986	1070
1987	1095

Source: Department of Employment, *Employment Gazette*, July 1988.

scientific services (education and health) and public administration and defence perhaps offer the most opportunity for increases in output to create jobs, with hotel and catering services in an intermediate position.

See Chapter 1 for discussion of causes of growth of service employment.

Hotel and catering employment

Robinson and Wallace[6] estimate that hotel and catering employment grew by 36 per cent over the period 1971–81 compared with a total service employment growth of 15 per cent and a growth in all industries of −2 per cent. By 1987, hotels and catering (1980 SIC definition) accounted for 5.0 per cent of all employees in employment in GB (from 3.1 per cent in 1971).[7] Since 1971 the number of employees in the industry has risen from 0.69m to 1.09m in 1987 (see Table 49).

The numbers employed have fluctuated, falling in both 1981 and 1983, but the long-term trend has been upwards. These fluctuations in growth of employment will be related to the underlying state of the economy and demand for accommodation and catering (see Chapter 2). Other factors will be considered later in this chapter.

In 1987 employees were employed in sectors of the hotel and catering industry as shown in Table 50.

The Hotel and Catering Industry Training Board (HCITB) has estimated hotel and catering employment at 2.3m in 1984[8] which is considerably in excess of the Department of Employment's SIC figures (see Table 49). The HCITB figures are derived from a much wider base than are the Department of Employment's estimates. They include an estimate for the self-employed and for those in industrial, educational and welfare catering (excluded from SIC unless provided by contractor). The fact that there may be many persons employed on a part-time, seasonal, temporary or casual basis means that

Table 50 *Employees in hotels and catering by sector (GB) 1987*

	June 1987 (000s)
Restaurants, snack bars, etc.	238.1
Public houses and bars	281.2
Night clubs and licensed clubs	146.6
Canteens and messes	135.7
Hotel trade	260.9
	1094.7

Source: Department of Employment, *Employment Gazette*, November 1987.

Table 51 *Employment in hotel and catering occupations by sector 1981–84*

		1981 (000s)	*1984*
1	Hotels, guest houses and other tourist accommodation	324	375
	Restaurants, snack bars and cafés	307	304
	Public houses and bars	351	373
	Nightclubs and licensed clubs	150	155
	Contract catering	114	117
2	Self-employed	9	9
3	Subsidiary activity sectors	996	998
		2.25m	2.33m

Source: *Hotel and Catering Manpower in Britain, 1984* (HCITB 1985).

there are problems in estimating the numbers employed in hotel and catering occupations. A figure of 2.3m would mean that those in hotel and catering occupations were about 10.9 per cent of the employed labour force (1984).

About 40 per cent of those in hotel and catering jobs are believed to work in 'subsidiary activity sectors', i.e. where the main business of the enterprise is something other than hotels and catering (see Table 51).

The number of self-employed in the industry's labour force is likely to be high as there is a high proportion of small owner-managed firms. In the UK the self-employed represent 9.8 per cent of the employed labour force (1985)[9] whereas the proportion in hotels and catering has been estimated at between 13.6 per cent (1985) and 20 per cent.[10]

Employment in the industry is estimated to grow by 19.0 per cent between 1985 and 1995 compared with an estimated growth of total service employment of 12.9 per cent.[11]

Supply of labour

The supply of labour to the economy as a whole and therefore to particular industries will be determined by three factors: participation in the labour force, hours worked by the labour force and the quality of the labour force.

Participation

The size of the working population (those willing and able to work) will, in the long term, be influenced by the degree to which various sectors of the population wish to participate in the labour force. This shows itself as differences in 'activity rates', i.e. the proportion of any age or sex group that is working or seeking work.

Male activity rates in the UK show a long-term tendency to decline (80.5 per cent in 1971 and 73.4 per cent in 1986).[12] This is probably associated with increased economic prosperity leading younger males to stay on in education and older males to retire earlier. Increases in real pay, associated with economic prosperity, will have the effect of making each extra unit of time *not* worked more costly but that effect has been outweighed by a desire to take part of the increased prosperity in the form of non-work (see the section titled 'Hours' later in this chapter). There are short-term fluctuations which may operate in the opposite direction, such that male activity rates fall during periods of slow or negative economic growth and rise when growth is high. This is known as the 'discouraged worker' effect with some males (secondary workers) dropping out of the working population completely in economically depressed times.

In contrast, female activity rates have shown an upward trend. The activity rate for married women, for instance, has risen from 22 per cent in 1951 to 50 per cent in 1979.[13] This rate has stabilized since the mid-1970s, however. It may be that women are more likely to be 'secondary' than 'primary' workers, i.e. to move into and out of the working population over their working lives and thus their activity rates may show greater short-term fluctuations than for males. During periods of slow economic growth (recession) married women (and other secondary workers) may seek to augment household income by joining the working population, i.e. the 'added worker' effect.

Why have long-term female activity rates increased?

1 It could be that women have been 'pulled' into the working population by the

inability of employers to obtain other employees, especially during periods of economic expansion.

2 It is more likely that the cause has been a general expansion of 'female' jobs rather than a general shortage of manpower. Many of the jobs created in the economy have been in service industries where female labour is particularly in demand.[14]

In hotels and catering many of the jobs are of a 'domestic' nature in the sense of being an extension of activities that occur in most households. Females may be willing to take the jobs because there is often no necessary pre-entry qualification; employers are eager to employ females because there is often no need for extensive training. Additionally males may not be attracted into what might traditionally be considered to be 'women's' jobs.

Growing opportunities for part-time or seasonal work may also have attracted females into the working population since these may be patterns of work that offer minimum disruption to any domestic commitments. The supply of labour to the hotel and catering industry has been increased by extending the number of part-time jobs.

3 From the supply side, many more females may be able and willing to join the working population. Family size and household 'drudgery' have reduced, thus increasing the opportunities for employment. Society is, too, more tolerant of 'working mothers'.

4 As with males, increased real pay will have made non-work a more costly use of time for females. It may be, also, that employers could employ females at lower rates of pay than males, at least before equal pay and opportunities legislation.

Female employment

Female employees outnumber male employees in the hotel and catering industry by nearly 2 to 1. Most women are, in fact, employed in the service industries and those industries are, in turn, dependent on female labour. Over three-quarters of all female employees are in the service industries and in those industries they amount to over half the labour force.[15] (In manufacturing, by contrast, women are less than a third of the labour force and their numbers and relative importance are declining.)

Certain service industries are heavily dominated by female employees. Retail distribution, hotels and catering and 'other services' (including education and health) each has a labour force which is over 60 per cent female and together they employ 63 per cent of all female employees in GB.[16]

Table 52 confirms that females are concentrated in certain occupations which are largely service occupations whether in service or manufacturing industries.[17]

Table 52 *Occupational analysis of persons in employment by sex (GB) 1985 (Spring)*

Occupation group		*Males* %	*Females* %
I	Professional and related supporting management and administration	9.1	3.8
II	Professional and related in education, welfare and health	5.5	14.5
III	Literary, artistic, sports	1.2	1.0
IV	Professional and related in science, engineering, technology and similar fields	6.9	0.7
V	Management	11.7	5.5
VI	Clerical and related	6.4	30.1
VII	Selling	4.8	10.1
VIII	Security and protective service	2.6	0.4
IX	Catering, cleaning, hairdressing and other personal services	4.2	22.6
X	Farming, fishing and related	2.3	0.7
XI	Processing, making, repairing, and related (excluding metal and electrical)	8.2	4.8
XII	Processing, making, repairing and related (metal and electrical)	15.9	0.8
XIII	Painting, repetitive assembling, product inspecting, packaging and related	3.9	4.1
XIV	Construction and mining NEI	5.7	0.0
XV	Transport operating, materials moving and storing	9.0	0.5
XVI	Miscellaneous	2.1	0.3
Inadequately described/not stated		0.3	0.1

Source: Department of Employment, *Employment Gazette*, May 1986.

Of the growth in service sector employment that was noted earlier in the chapter, most was employment for females. Just over three million of the 4.4 million jobs created in the service industries (1951–81) were for females.

This expansion of female employment has been associated with a growth of part-time job opportunities, especially in hotels and catering (see later in this chapter). It has also been associated in hotels and catering with a growth of low paid jobs.

The supply of labour to an economy or industry will also be influenced by the availability of foreign labour. Despite the relative freedom of labour

Table 53 *Average weekly hours worked by full-time manual workers (UK) in manufacturing and 'certain other industries' 1962–86*

	Males aged 21 and over or on adult rates	*Females aged 18 and over or on adult rates*
1962	47.0	39.4
1972	45.0	37.9
1986*	42.7	38.1

*1986 figures relate to manufacturing only.

Sources: *Facts in Focus*, 3rd Edition (Penguin Books with HMSO 1975); Central Statistical Office, *Annual Abstract of Statistics, 1988* (HMSO 1988).

movement within the European Economic Community, only about 8 per cent of the hotel and catering labour force is non-British.[18]

Hours

The supply of labour to the economy and to particular industries and firms is not only influenced by activity rates but also by the number of hours worked by the labour force.

Over the long term the average weekly hours worked by full-time manual workers has reduced (see Table 53).

Despite short-term variations in hours worked as the economic climate alters, there is a clear tendency for actual hours worked to fall. As incomes rise over time, the relative price of leisure (non-work) rises in that each hour not worked is costly in terms of potential income lost. This would bring about a 'substitution effect', whereby hours of work would be increased at the expense of leisure. Against that is the 'income effect' such that workers can decide to consume more of all goods and services, including leisure which, of course, is desirable in its own right.

It is apparent that the labour force has chosen to increase its leisure time as real wages have risen. The supply of labour to any one industry or firm could fall as pay rises if the income effect outweighs the substitution effect; less overtime could be worked, absenteeism might increase, and so on.

Changes in income tax rates may have similar effects upon hours worked. A rise in income tax means that leisure is now less costly (less income is foregone by non-work). Hours of work may fall and activity rates may fall. Alternatively, the income effect could be dominant and workers work more hours in order to maintain consumption of goods and services.

Part-time employment

It was noted earlier that the increase in female employment has been related to

Table 54 *Growth in full- and part-time employment in all industries and in hotels and catering 1971–81*

	Male		Female	
	Full-time	Part-time	Full-time	Part-time
	% change in employees over the period			
All industries	−11	21	−4	36
Hotels and catering	10	52	−2	87

Source: O. Robinson and J. Wallace, *Employment Trends in the Hotel and Catering Industry in Great Britain*, Service Industries Journal 3 (3) (1983).

an increase in part-time employment (widely considered to be employment for less than 30 hours per week). There has, in fact, been a general increase in part-time employment throughout the economy for both males and females (see Table 54).

Part-time employees male and female are concentrated in the service industries (91 per cent of all part-timers).[19] A high proportion of hotel and catering employees are part-time (67.0 per cent of females and 38.7 per cent of males). In this industry, female part-time employment has been the most rapid growth sector (see Table 54) and was also the major form of hotel and catering job growth during 1981–86. The trend towards part-time employment has been evident in all sectors of hotels and catering so that female part-timers outnumber female full-timers in all sectors except for 'hotel trade' (SIC). Their relative importance is considerable in the commercial catering and public house sectors. Male part-time employees outnumber male full-timers only in 'public houses' and 'clubs'. According to the HCITB, part-time employment in hotels and catering is typically concentrated in the 8–15 and 16–20 hour per week bands.[20]

Part-time employment in hotels and catering is largely the result of the nature of the demand for the product. There are fluctuations in demand during the day and week, and part-time employment to meet these peaks in demand is particularly appropriate. Unlike many manufacturing activities, it is not as easy to produce the 'product' and store it, releasing from stocks at peak demand time.

Increased part-time employment may also be a response to the difficulties encountered by employers in obtaining full-time labour. This may be true even during periods of high unemployment since the unemployed may not be suitable for the hotel and catering vacancies. They may also have appropriate qualifications but be located in the wrong part of the country or they may be unaware of the existing vacancies.

During the 1970s, the extension of statutory employment rights and benefits to staff working 16 hours or more per week probably contributed to a noticeable increase in the proportion of female employees in hotels and catering who worked fewer than 16 hours per week. Individual employers may also grant certain rights and benefits to full-time employees, thus increasing the incentive to have part-timers. (Also avoid paying employer's contribution to National Insurance.) Robinson and Wallace[21] confirm, however, that employers are more influenced by 'operational requirements' in their increased demand for part-time employees. The advantage to hotel and catering firms of part-time employment lies in the ability to adjust labour input to fluctuations in demand and thus make wage savings.

The expansion of part-time jobs in hotels and catering means that employers have been able to draw on an additional (cheap) source of labour without having to attract labour away from other employments by offering higher rates of pay.

Quality

The supply of labour is also determined by the 'quality' of each member of the working population. The value of output from each worker will differ because of variations in 'natural' abilities and in the amount of education and training received. (Additional factors will include amount and quality of machinery used and the efficiency with which production is organized.)

Education and training of the labour force may be regarded as an 'investment' in human capital.[22] The return to that investment will be in the form of increased earnings for the individual and increased output for society. (Education might also have 'external' effects in the form of a more 'fulfilled' and 'stable' society, etc.)

Against these benefits must be set the costs incurred by the individual and society. Any person staying on in education beyond the compulsory leaving age will lose earnings from the employment that he/she might have undertaken during that period of education. There will be a loss to the economy in the form of the output that could have been produced. In addition there will be direct costs in the form of teachers' and lecturers' salaries, cost of buildings, textbooks, etc. Most studies have pointed to a positive return to education. Much of the cost in the UK is, in fact, borne by the state, thus effectively raising the return to the individual.

Any investment that is made in 'human capital' in this sense will be 'embodied' in the worker. When a worker seeks employment then he/she is clearly only hiring out his/her services and is not transferring the 'capital' itself. This is unlike the situation where the employer can buy a machine or retain control over its use. Thus if an employer (actual or potential) were to contribute to or undertake to bear all of the costs of education/training of individuals, there would be no certainty about the return to his/her investment. A person who was trained and/or educated at a firm's expense could move to another firm and the return would be lost.

In the same way some firms can benefit by doing no training and simply recruiting labour trained by other firms. Training that is specific to a particular firm will be more likely to be supported financially by a firm than is 'general' training that can be of use to many firms.

Unless firms were very generous or benevolent, there may be a tendency for 'underinvestment' in education and training to occur. Individuals or their families can finance the investment but a lack of foresight, of knowledge about the benefits or a lack of money may restrict such action. There may, therefore, be a role for the Government to play; in the UK governments have borne most of the direct costs of primary and secondary education. Costs of further and higher education are directed more towards the individual but even here there remains a large government financial input.

With regard to training, a number of Industry Training Boards were set up by the Government after the Industry Training Act 1964; a Hotel and Catering Industry Training Board (HCITB) was established in 1966. These bodies were to improve the quantity and quality of training in industry and were also to operate a system of training levies and grants. Broadly, money (levies) was to be paid to the ITBs by firms in an industry (though not necessarily all firms) in order to share the cost of industry's training. No firm (except the smallest) would therefore avoid contributing to costs and would gain an unfair advantage over the firms that did train their employees. This latter category of firm would receive grants from the training boards to cover some of the cost of training. All firms were, in this way, encouraged to train since those that did not experienced a net outgoing (the levy). Firms that could demonstrate that an appropriate programme of training already existed could be exempt from the levy-grant system.

Most of the ITBs were abolished by government in 1981 but the HCITB and a number of others remain. Some have re-established themselves on a voluntary basis to ensure that the objectives of encouraging more training and sharing the costs fairly are fulfilled.

There now exists a wide range of education and training courses for entrants to and employees in the hotel and catering industry, including craft courses and management degree courses. Estimates of those in the industry without formal qualifications (including CSEs and O-levels) range from 50 per cent to 85 per cent![23] Some on-job training, which does not result in a formal qualification, may have been given to that 50 to 85 per cent, of course. Just over half of an employee sample in hotel and catering claimed to have had any kind of internal training; about 60 per cent of establishments claimed to offer some kind of internal training.[24]

The apparent lack of qualified manpower in the hotel and catering industry was reinforced by the HCITB report for the Education and Training Advisory Council.[25] It concluded that the output of students from colleges, polytechnics and universities would not be able to meet the increased demand for qualified manpower in the industry up to 1987.

Supply of labour to particular 'uses'

If the owner of the factor 'labour', i.e. the worker him/herself, is assumed to be a 'rational economic being', seeking the maximum return on his/her investment, then labour will enter those 'uses' – occupations, industries and firms – where the return is greatest. A positive relationship between pay and quantity of labour supplied might, therefore, be expected. (It was noticed earlier how, over time, increases in pay may actually lead to reductions in activity rates and hours worked.)

The return for particular uses will, however, include non-monetary elements as well as a monetary reward. Some jobs will be particularly dirty or dangerous or of a low social standing. Other jobs may be pleasant, give considerable prestige and carry little risk of unemployment. Owners of the labour inputs will therefore seek to achieve the greatest 'net advantage', i.e. combination of monetary and non-monetary elements. Labour will flow into different uses until the net advantage from each is equalized (see the section titled 'Wage differentials' later in this chapter).

Demand for labour

Long-run[26]

All factors of production, whether labour, raw materials or capital, are required by firms not for their own sake but for the contribution they make to the production of goods and services, i.e. their demand is a 'derived' demand, derived from the demand for goods and services.

In the long-run, all the factors of production can be varied; the firm can choose from any one of several techniques for producing its output from very labour-intensive techniques to very capital-intensive techniques (i.e. using machinery and equipment rather than manpower). If it is assumed that the firm is a profit-maximizer, it will choose that technique which minimizes costs.

As the relative prices of labour and capital alter, so the least-cost combination of the two inputs will change. If the price of labour relative to capital increases, the firm will attempt to substitute capital for labour. The ability to substitute one input for another will depend on the nature of the product and the state of technology; it is likely that the ability to substitute capital for labour in hotels and catering is limited compared with many manufacturing processes. Labour-saving machinery and production processes have, of course, been introduced especially as technology has advanced to produce appropriate equipment. Labour that performs repetitious and unskilled tasks will have been most affected since it is easiest to introduce machinery to carry out such tasks. Food production processes have been re-designed to contain more repetitious tasks and to require less skill, in order to allow appropriate capital to be introduced.

It would seem attractive to attempt to resolve any national unemployment problem by reducing the pay of labour or restricting the rate of pay increase. This could have the effect of making labour a relatively cheap input and labour-intensive products cheaper. However, it is possible that such a general restriction of pay would cause the purchasing power of employees to fall and thus the demand for goods and services would fall – causing more unemploy-

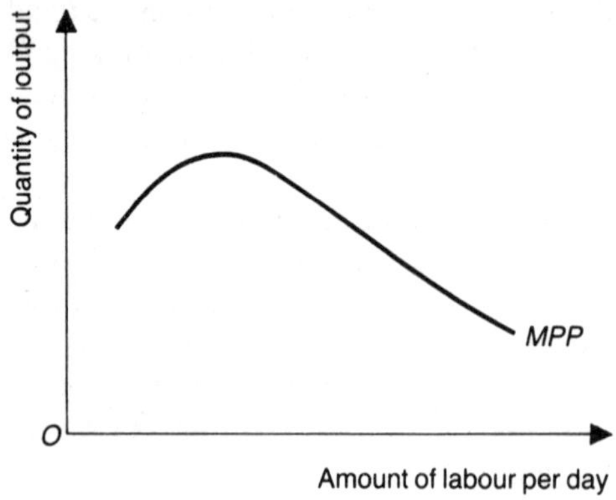

Figure 40 *Marginal (physical) productivity of labour*

ment. In practice, it is not clear what might happen since it is also possible that the expenditure of firms and savers might rise and stimulate demand and employment – the former because of increased profits and the latter because of reduced inflation. More goods and services might also be bought by overseas buyers.

Short-run

1 In Chapter 5 it was noted that in the short-run the firm is limited to adjusting the quantity of only some of the factors and not all of them. (Some factor or factors is limited in supply.) As a consequence, as the number of units of any particular factor, such as labour, was increased, diminishing returns would result. This is shown in Figure 40 as the marginal (physical) productivity of labour, i.e. the extra output resulting from employment of one more person.

This extra output (say, twenty meals) will sell for a price and the extra revenue received from that output will be marginal revenue. The *value* to the firm of each unit of labour will therefore be given by marginal physical product of the labour (twenty meals) × marginal revenue of the output (say, 30p). This is known as the marginal revenue product (£6 = 20 × 30p), and its curve will have a similar shape to that in Figure 40. (See Figure 41.)

As a profit-maximizer a firm would not employ extra units of labour if the extra cost of hiring that labour (i.e. marginal cost) exceeded the extra revenue it brings in (its marginal revenue product). Conversely, if the marginal revenue product exceeded the marginal cost, it would be of benefit to the firm to hire extra labour. The firm could earn more profit for as long as the extra revenue brought in by labour (*MRP*) exceeded its extra cost (*MC*).

In the same way as it could be demonstrated that the profit-maximizing firm would produce at a level of output where marginal revenue (of output) = marginal cost (of output) (see Chapter 2), so such a firm would hire labour

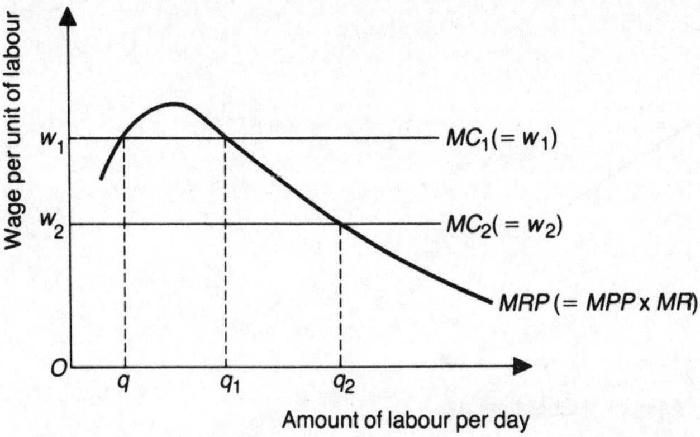

Figure 41 *Profit-maximizing level of employment*

until marginal revenue product (of labour) = marginal cost (of labour). Profits are maximized when $MRP = MC$.

If it is assumed that the firm pays the current market wage for its labour and has no direct influence on that wage, then the extra (marginal) cost of hiring labour will equal its wage. Every additional worker hired will cost the same. Thus $MC = w$. Since $MRP = MC$, the condition for profit-maximizing becomes $MRP = w$ (see Figure 41).

In Figure 41 at a wage rate of ow_2 the amount of labour demanded by the firm would be oq_2 since at any other amount profits would not be maximized. At levels of employment less than oq_2 it would pay the firm to increase employment: *MRP* exceeds *MC* and thus profits could be added to. At levels of employment above oq_2 the firm would find that the extra cost of hiring labour (MC_2) would exceed the extra value of output (*MRP*) and thus profits would be reduced.

If the wage rate was ow_1 then the profit-maximizing condition $MRP = MC$ is satisfied at levels of employment oq and oq_1. Employment of oq_1 units of labour will give more profits than will employment level oq; by moving from oq to oq_1 more will be added to revenue (*MRP*) than will be added to costs and profits will therefore rise.

The amount of labour demanded by the firm is shown by the *MRP* curve and thus the *MRP* curve (its downward-sloping part only) is the firm's demand curve for labour (see Figure 42).

It would seem reasonable to assume that, *if all else remains unchanged,* a firm would only hire more labour if its price (wage) was reduced and if the price rose the firm would reduce its demand. The amount that a firm pays for labour may well be greater than the wage, in practice, as firms in the UK have to pay contributions to National Insurance for each employee.

2 In the same way as the demand curve for any good or service can shift (see

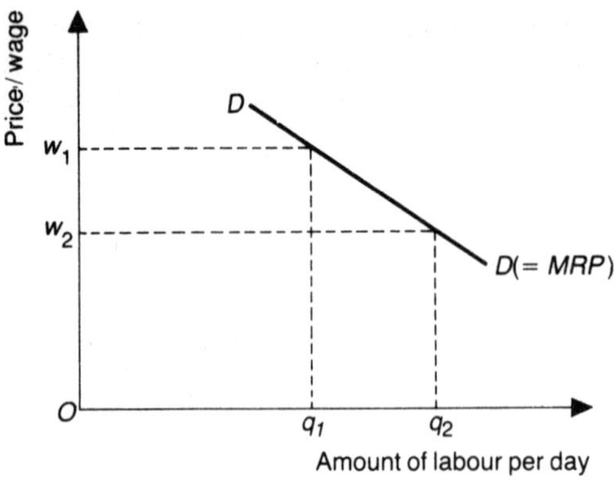

Figure 42 *Demand curve for labour*

Chapter 2), so too can the demand curve for labour. Given that the demand for any factor is a derived demand, then a change in the demand for the good or service that labour helps produce will shift labour's demand curve. An increase in consumers' disposable income, or a fall in the relative price of eating out could cause the demand for hotel and catering services to rise and shift the demand for labour employed in the industry.[27]

The demand curve for labour could shift outwards (away from zero) as the relative price of some other factor of production rises. Conversely, the substitution of cheaper capital for labour would cause the demand curve to shift inwards (towards zero).

If the productivity of labour increased, then there would be a shift of the demand curve outwards. Each unit of labour would be worth more than previously because of its greater efficiency or because of a higher revenue received from its output.

3 The elasticity of demand for labour will depend, in part, on the ease with which other factors can be substituted for it. The more essential labour is in a particular process and the more difficult it is to replace by other factors, the more inelastic will be the demand for labour.

Additionally, if the good or service which labour is producing faces an inelastic demand, the demand for labour will be inelastic.

The demand for labour will be inelastic, also, the lower labour costs are as percentage of total costs of production. If labour costs are only 10 per cent of total costs, then a 50 per cent rise in wages would cause the price of the product to rise by only 5 per cent. The effect on the demand for labour would obviously be greater if labour costs were, say, 60 per cent of total costs; a wage rise of 50 per cent now would cause price to rise by 30 per cent. This illustrates the 'importance of being unimportant' and how employees in capital-intensive industries may be able to achieve higher rates of pay than those in labour-intensive industries. Since labour costs are such a high proportion of costs in hotel and catering, it is difficult for employees and their representatives to raise pay significantly without eating into profits or causing price of the finished product to rise.

4 An industry's demand curve for labour will have a similar shape to the demand curves of the individual firms. The slope of the industry demand curve is likely to be steeper, however, since a rise in wages could cause a reduction in employment and output. As output falls the price of the product may rise causing the MRP of labour to shift outwards. There will be less of a fall in the demand for labour than initially envisaged.

5 The demand for hotel and catering labour exhibits considerable short-term fluctuations for certain categories of employee. It has already been noted how, therefore, part-time labour is a feature of hotel and catering employment, but there is often a pool of labour which is called upon at irregular intervals for specific purposes and functions, i.e. casual labour. In the Scarborough accommodation industry this pool was equivalent to a third of total employees. Clearly, seasonal fluctuations in demand are reflected in seasonal employment: about 71 per cent of total non-casual employees in Scarborough were seasonal.

Price of labour[28]

The wage rate (taken to include salary rates also) may be interpreted as the price of the factor 'labour'. Like all prices, the wage rate will be determined, according to economic theory, by the demand for and supply of labour. In addition to markets for consumer goods and services, there exists a set of 'factor or resource markets' in which buyers and sellers of resources/factors are brought together. By means of these markets, resources/factors are allocated to meet consumer needs and if perfect competition prevails in factor as well as goods and service markets, then optimal allocation of those resources occurs. As the demand for consumer goods and services alters, so will the derived demand for labour and labour will move between employments accordingly. Imperfections in the *factor* markets will therefore restrict the ability of any economy to satisfy consumer wants in the most economic manner.

If there is perfect competition in the labour market such that no one buyer or seller of labour has control over the price of labour, the labour is homogeneous (all are identical in ability) and is perfectly mobile, then labour will move freely from low wage to high wage employment until any pay differentials are eliminated. A single price for labour will be established by market demand and supply – a price that will be accepted as given by any individual firm seeking to employ labour (see Figure 43).

In Figure 43(a) it is assumed that the supply of labour is positively related to

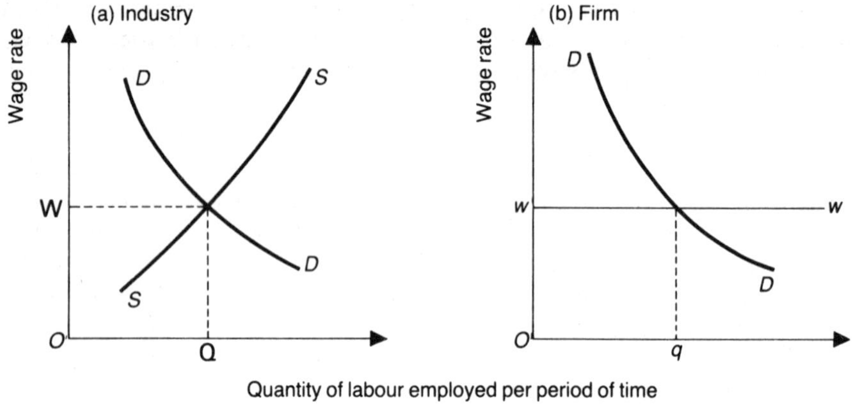

Figure 43 *Wage determination in perfectly competitive labour market*

pay and demand inversely related. In the industry *oQ* labour will be employed at a wage of *oW*. That wage is accepted as 'given' by the individual firms in the industry and in Figure 43(b) the firm employs *oq* labour.

As the demand for any one consumer product rises, then the demand for the labour to produce it will shift to the right. The wage rate will rise and labour will be attracted into that particular use. The demand for labour in other uses may be declining and as an excess of supply over demand develops, the wage rate will fall and labour will move out.

Wage differentials

Why is it that certain individuals and groups of labour receive higher pay than others?

In Table 55 it can be seen that non-manual employees, on average, earn more than manual, and males earn more than females.

Table 56 gives further detail of category X which relates to hotels and catering.[29]

Comparison of these earnings with those in Table 55 would suggest that earnings of hotel and catering employees are among the lowest of all occupations. Of nearly ninety male manual occupations only eight (including caretakers and gardeners) have lower earnings than chefs/cooks. In the case of females just over fifty manual and non-manual occupations are listed, and only six have earnings lower than those of chefs/cooks. They include shop assistants, check-out operators and sewing machinists. There has been, however, some improvement in the relative pay of hotel and catering employees over time, e.g. hourly earnings for men in full-time manual employment in hotels and catering rose from 66.9 per cent of the all-industry average in 1972, to 71.5 per cent in 1982. Similar rises were experienced for women (full- and part-time).[30]

Table 55 *Average gross weekly earnings (employees on adult rates) April 1987*

		Full-time males £	*Full-time females* £
Non-manual			
II	Professional and related supporting management and administration	327.2	236.5
III	Professional and related in education, welfare and health	258.9	181.6
IV	Literary, artistic and sports	281.6	210.3
V	Professional and related in science, engineering, technology, etc.	265.4	176.4
VI	Managerial	264.3	173.6
VII	Clerical and related	180.2	135.6
VIII	Selling	197.9	112.1
IX	Security and protective services	236.6	208.1
Average (non-manual)		263.9	155.4
Manual			
X	Catering, cleaning, hairdressing and other personal service	145.1	106.2
XI	Farming, fishing and related	132.8	—
XII	Materials processing	184.9	113.6
XIII	Making and repairing	188.6	105.6
XIV	Processing, making, repairing and related (metal and electrical)	200.4	125.9
XV	Painting, repetitive assembling, product inspecting, packaging and related	175.8	116.4
XVI	Construction, mining and related	180.1	—
XVII	Transport operating, materials moving and storing and related	179.0	124.5
XVIII	Miscellaneous	164.7	—
Average (manual)		182.0	111.4

Source: Department of Employment, *New Earnings Survey 1987, Part D: Analyses by Occupation* (HMSO 1987).

The hotel and catering industry is unusual in that some part of earnings often comes directly from customers rather than from the employer, i.e. in the form of 'tips' and 'service charge'. Not all hotel and catering employees receive such a payment, of course, and it can only be a partial explanation of the low level of earnings.

Table 56 *Average gross weekly earnings of hotel and catering occupations (full-time employees on adult rates) April 1987*

Males	*£*	*Females*	*£*
Chefs/cooks	142.6	Catering supervisors	124.4
Barmen	132.4	Chefs/cooks	112.1
		Barmaids	94.4
		Counter hands	100.2
		Kitchen hands	92.7

Source: Department of Employment, *New Earnings Survey 1987, Part D: Analyses by Occupation* (HMSO 1987).

The differences between occupational earnings may be explained by a large number of complex influences, some of which would be expected in perfectly competitive markets for labour and some of which are 'imperfections'. Some of these influences are discussed below.

Non-monetary influences

Even in a perfectly competitive market where the quality of labour is identical from person to person, there will exist differences in job requirements and conditions of work. The less attractive or the more demanding are the non-monetary features of a job, then the greater may be the need for compensatory monetary payments. Dangerous or dirty work, and jobs requiring a great deal of responsibility and/or skill, may receive more monetary 'compensation' than jobs which are in pleasant conditions and which require little responsibility.

The provision of free or cheap meals, uniform, laundry, or transport to hotel and catering employees may help explain their low pay. In reality, such fringe benefits are no greater in value than the benefits provided in other industries (except for those employees who receive free accommodation), and thus cannot be considered an important explanation of low pay.[31]

Some jobs are risky in that there are regular lay-offs (entertainment professions) or the total working life is short (airline pilots) and compensatory monetary payments account for part of the pay of labour in these jobs.

Labour, in deciding which occupation/industry to enter, will seek to maximize the 'net advantage' to be gained, i.e. the sum of the wage and non-wage elements. In a perfectly competitive labour market it will be 'net advantages' of different jobs that will be equalized (and not the wage). Thus wage differentials will persist.

Table 57 *Distribution of hotel and catering employees by 'skill level' 1981*

	%
Managers and professional staff[a]	14.5
Supervisors	3.4
Craft and semi-skilled[b]	14.6
Operatives and others[c]	67.4

Note: Includes those in 'main activity' sectors and in 'subsidiary activity' sectors.

[a] Includes self-employed working proprietors.
[b] Chefs/cooks, waiting staff, receptionists, etc.
[c] Bar staff, kitchen/counter hands, domestic staff, hall porters/stewards, etc.

Source: *Hotel and Catering Manpower in Britain 1984* (HCITB 1985).

Labour differences

The labour force is, of course, not homogeneous and individuals have many different skills and abilities. For those jobs which require considerable manual skill, organizational ability, or commercial initiative, for instance, the number of persons able to fill them may be limited. Jobs which are unskilled and intellectually undemanding could potentially be done by a much larger number of persons. The interaction of supply and demand is likely to result in a higher pay for the former group than for the latter.

Many occupations in hotels and catering may be classified as semi- or unskilled. The HCITB classification of hotel and catering occupations puts about two-thirds of employees in relatively unskilled occupations (see Table 57).

Entry is relatively easy into the less skilled jobs and there is a large supply relative to the demand. Moving down the table from category 1, the nature of the jobs becomes less industry-specific. Potentially, individuals in the 'lower' categories may be able to find employment in a relatively large number of semi- or unskilled occupations in several industries and, conversely, there may be a large potential supply of labour to hotels and catering.

At the managerial, supervisory and craft levels, abilities may be less easily transferred to other industries and persons from other industries will similarly be restricted in their ability to move to hotel and catering occupations.

Natural abilities, such as physical strength, may be in plentiful supply and workers with only these abilities will be able to earn a relatively low wage only.

The price (wage) paid to labour will, of course, be the outcome of both demand and supply. If the demand for unskilled labour increases, then the wage of such labour will rise and may come to exceed the wage paid to more skilled labour. In the same way, there have been many instances in the past of highly-paid skilled workers falling down the earnings league table as the demand for their services has fallen. Similarly, pay for unskilled work may rise if people are unwilling to take up such employment.

Certain abilities (natural or otherwise) may be so scarce relative to demand that pay is almost entirely demand-determined, i.e. 'economic rent'.[32] This is defined as a payment over and above that which is necessary to keep labour in its present use. Professional entertainers, sportspeople and very talented haute cuisine chefs may be able to earn much in excess of the pay they could have received in other occupations. As the demand for top-quality chefs or managers rises, there will be little impact on supply (because the talent is so limited) and pay will rise. In normal circumstances, the supply of labour would be expected to rise and the pay rise would be less.

Human capital

The quality of labour differs not only because of differing natural abilities but also because of varying amounts of investment in 'human capital', i.e. education and training. Pay is partly a return on this investment and differences in the amount of education received can lead to pay differentials. Table 58 shows the extra pay that is likely to result from various educational investments.

However, high pay is only paid for as long as the abilities given by education and training are demanded. If the abilities remain scarce relative to demand, the return on investment will be forthcoming. A fall in the demand for such labour will reduce the 'return' regardless of the amount of investment made.

There is a direct impact that education and training may have on the quality of labour, but it could be that investment in education is valuable even if the investment adds nothing directly to workers' productivity. It may be that by going on with further and higher education, students are 'signalling' to prospective employers that they have certain 'high-level' abilities, regardless of the subject(s) they study.[33] The educational system would thus be 'screening out' the 'more able' people.

Pay differentials explained by non-monetary influences, labour differences and human capital would be expected to arise in perfectly competitive markets. Other influences may, however, restrict the competitive process and give rise to pay differentials which would not otherwise occur. They have the effect of splitting up the labour force into a number of separate, non-competing markets between which labour finds it difficult to move.

Different groups of individuals exist in relatively distinct labour markets and form 'non-competing' groups.

Immobility

The free movement of labour between uses is limited by social, occupational

Table 58 *Some sources of pay differentials for men (UK)*

	Manual	*Non-manual*
Percentage extra pay for:		
Extra year at school	+ 4	+ 5
University degree	+ 5	+38
Other post-school qualification	+30	+35
A-level exams	+13	+22
O-level exams	+10	+14

Source: R. Layard, D. Metcalf and S. Nickell, *The Effect of Collective Bargaining on Wages* (British Journal of Industrial Relations 1978).

and geographical immobility. Despite improvements in social mobility that have occurred in the UK during the post-war period (associated with universal free education), entry into many occupations and professions is effectively restricted to particular social groups. Similarly, education 'take-up' rates are lower for 'working class' children than for other groups.

Labour is often geographically immobile and may be reluctant to move from one part of the country to another. This might be because of personal ties, financial difficulties, or prejudice etc.

Occupational immobility exists in the sense that the labour in excess supply in certain job markets will not necessarily be able to fill other job vacancies. Different jobs have different requirements and movement to other occupations may require further education and training.

Thus pay differentials may arise from competitive pressures and persist because of the immobility of labour to move in response to those differentials.

Trade unions[34]

Labour organizes itself into trade unions in order to negotiate with employers over pay and other conditions of employment. Wage differentials can arise from the differing abilities of trade unions to raise pay above the 'competitive' level. The ability of a trade union to influence pay in this way will depend, in part, on the elasticity of demand for the type of labour concerned (see earlier in this chapter) and on its ability to control the supply of labour to particular occupations and firms.

1 If the demand for labour is inelastic then pay rises may be obtained with little or no impact upon employment of union members (see the section titled 'Demand for labour'). If, however, demand for labour is elastic, a pay rise

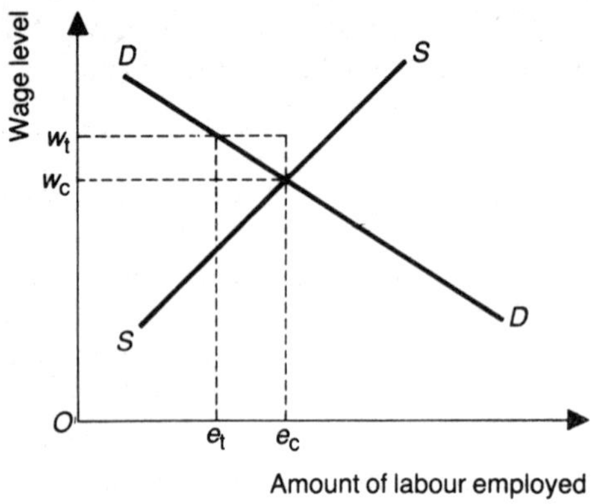

Figure 44 *Effects of trade unions*

could lead to firms reducing employment. A trade union may, therefore, be faced with a choice between achieving high pay or security of employment (see Figure 44). Trade unions may be more concerned about 'job security' than pay rises, in some situations.

If it assumed (in Figure 44) that the competitive wage and employment levels are ow_c and oe_c respectively, a successful trade union effort to raise wages to ow_t would result in a fall in employment from oe_c to oe_t. A powerful trade union might be able to negotiate *both* a wage rise to ow_t and an employment level at oe_c. The ability to do this will depend, among other things, on the degree to which firms are prepared to accept a fall in their profits. The outcome will be the net effect of the relative strengths of the employers and the union in the negotiating process.

If, on the demand side, employers are organized into a negotiating group as well, it may be possible to raise pay without creating a surplus of labour.[35] Before the entry of a trade union into such a labour market, the employers' organization may have been able to pay its labour force a wage rate which was less than the 'competitive' one. A trade union could therefore negotiate pay rises up to the competitive wage level without fear of losing employment.

2 Trade unions can also raise the pay of their members by restricting the supply of labour to an occupation or firm. The effect is to shift the supply curve inwards and the equilibrium pay is thereby raised. Certain minimum requirements for duration of apprenticeships and training and control over the number of apprentices and trainees can restrict supply of labour to certain uses and remove the impact of competition from other groups of workers. In addition, trade unions could be successful in operating a system whereby only union members can be employed (workers are either members before employment or become members after employment).

The ability to raise pay through negotiations with employers is influenced by the ability to control supply. The achievement of a high wage level for union members will be of little benefit to those members if the employer is then able to employ non-union members at lower rates of pay.

3 Overall, trade unions appear to have been successful in raising the pay of their members. It has been estimated that trade union members in the UK manufacturing industries earn about 8 per cent more than non-union members (after adjusting for other possible differences in pay).[36] It is more likely that this is a 'once and for all' effect, giving such workers a higher rank in the pay league than a progressive effect such that union/non-union differentials widen over time. For many years, the share of labour in national income has remained stable, implying that unions have benefited at the expense of the non-unionized and the unemployed. Over the last twenty years, however, labour's share has risen apparently at the expense of profits.[37]

Trade unions have had little direct impact on pay in hotels and catering, largely because union membership is so very low. Somewhere between 6 and 10 per cent of the hotel and catering labour force is believed to belong to a union[38] compared with 38 per cent of the working population as a whole (1985).[39]

4 Professional associations may be able to achieve similar results to those achieved by trade unions. These associations are organizations of individuals, whether self-employed, employers or employees, which seek to 'control standards' in certain occupations. This usually requires controlling entry to the profession: by setting examinations. This restriction on supply may have the effect of raising pay and of reducing competition from other workers. Some professional associations may be able to achieve government support such that, by law, only members of their associations are allowed to practise certain occupations; the most obvious examples occur in the medical profession.

Within hotels and catering, the most significant professional association is the Hotel, Catering and Institutional Management Association (HCIMA).[40] It does set its own examinations and exempts those with appropriate equivalent educational qualifications. It is not yet so that only members of the HCIMA can operate as hoteliers and caterers, however, and entry as an operator/manager into the industry is relatively easy.

Wages Councils[41]

Where trade union representation is weak in an industry, governments in the UK have introduced Wages Councils to determine wage levels; these wage levels have the force of legal minimum payments. Such councils have employer and employee representatives on them. These statutory councils were intended to be in existence only so long as it took for unions to establish themselves in particular industries and be able to represent employees.

They have existed in various parts of the UK economy since the early part of this century but were not introduced in the hotel and catering industry until the 1940s. Not all of the hotel and catering industry is covered by the council system – the unlicensed accommodation sector, in particular, has never really been covered. The council covering Industrial and Staff Catering was abolished in 1976, as it was considered to be no longer necessary.[42]

As minimum rates of pay, the council rates can be and are exceeded, but in recent years the importance of council rates in total earnings in the industry has increased, e.g. between 1972 and 1982 statutory minimum rates rose from 60 per cent of the earnings of men (full-time) under the Licensed Residential and Restaurant Council (LRRC) to over 75 per cent.[43] Employers have been less inclined to exceed the legal minimum. There has also been an increase over the same period in the number of employees being paid less than the minimum, e.g. from 6 per cent of men (full-time) under the LRRC in 1972 to 21 per cent in 1982. Over this period, the authors of one study believe that hotel and catering employers have reduced the impact of paying equal pay to women by tending to keep pay for men and women closer to the statutory minimum.[44]

It is arguable whether Wages Councils contribute to the persistence of low pay or whether they have kept pay from falling even further. It is possible that minimum wage rates are set at levels below those which might occur in 'normal' circumstances, or where there was collective bargaining between trades unions and employers. On the other hand, there is a view that such minimum wage legislation causes labour to be overpriced;[45] the abolition of the councils would therefore lead to lower wages (and increased employment?). The 1986 Wages Act removed employees aged under twenty-one from the protection of wages councils.

Discrimination

Discrimination may mean that certain groups in the community find it difficult to enter certain occupations. To some extent the pay differential between women and non-whites on the one hand and males and whites on the other is a reflection of the different jobs they hold. A high proportion of women are in clerical and service jobs and a higher proportion of non-whites than whites are likely to be in unskilled jobs. The supply of labour relative to demand in any one of these jobs is likely to be high, especially if such labour is limited in the jobs it can choose to enter; pay is likely to be low.

It is, though, possible that females and non-whites have been and may still be paid less than others for doing the same job, i.e. outright discrimination in pay. A major cause of sex differentials, however, probably lies in the reluctance of employers to train and promote females; females are perceived to have only a limited and interrupted stay in the labour force. Females are less able to reach senior jobs since they do not accumulate seniority and experience.

Females and non-whites may have limited access to educational opportunity, they may receive an 'inferior' education, or they may be reluctant to take up the available opportunities. Employers may therefore perceive the worth of such workers to be limited and job-choice for such workers remains limited.

Other explanations for low female pay may include the view that their working conditions are often more pleasant than those of male occupations. Female labour tends to be drawn from a limited geographical area and thus any element of pay that is necessary to induce labour to travel to a particular firm will be low. (In the Scarborough accommodation industry, two-thirds of the resident workforce took less than 15 minutes to travel to work.)

Fewer females may be organized into trade unions and thus they may not be able to achieve the results discussed under trade unions. Females may also be confined to 'secondary labour markets' (see the next section).

Market segmentation[46]

1 The labour market may be considered as being segmented into two broad categories – that segment which is characterized by 'good jobs' and that which is characterized by 'bad jobs'. The relative wage structure between the two segments is influenced by the relative size of employment in each. A large supply of jobs in the 'bad job' segment (or secondary labour market) and a small supply of jobs in the 'good job' (or primary labour market) segment will lead to low pay in the former and higher pay in the latter.

The pay differential is, then, according to this view, broadly one between types of job, regardless of the efficiency or ability of any individual in the two segments. Able and efficient labour may be confined to the secondary labour segment because of the lack of opportunities elsewhere and thus earn low pay. A person's human capital affects not his/her pay but only his/her relative chance of entering the primary labour sector.

2 The number of good and bad jobs is, in turn, influenced by industrial characteristics.

The 'good job' segment is associated with the more highly concentrated industries and the 'bad job' segment with the less concentrated industries. In those industries with the higher market concentrations employment relationships may be more formalized and wage and salary grades institutionalized. There are usually well-developed 'internal labour markets' within firms such that promotion and filling of vacancies is from within the firm; entry to the firm usually occurs at the bottom of the job hierarchy. Job stability may be high and labour turnover low; firms give fringe benefits and unionization is likely to be high. Negotiations between employees and employers take place within a formalized framework.

In the lower-concentration industries, employment relationships may be more casual, employment may be more unstable and labour force attachment to particular firms may be low. Unionization may be low and employer–employee relationships may be on an individual basis rather than on the formalized collective basis of union–firm negotiations. Internal training and promotion may be limited and employers may exercise 'coercive' methods of control. (The expansion of part-time employment at the expense of full-time may be viewed as a form of occupational segregation designed to exercise closer control over the labour and wage costs.)[47]

3 The characteristics of these two segments may in themselves explain pay differences though much of the analysis has been conducted in terms of the *relative sizes* of the two segments and thus of 'good' and 'bad' jobs (see above). However, employers in the primary labour market may be able to employ higher-quality labour because of the attractions of the jobs, whereas the secondary labour market employers may only be able to attract 'inferior' quality labour. This in itself could be a cause of the pay differences.

The differences in unionization can also explain the pay differences as can the differing abilities of firms to pay high wages. Firms in the more highly concentrated industries may be distributing some of their higher profits (if they exist) in the form of increased pay to employees. Firms in the less concentrated industries are less likely to earn such profits. The relative intensity of product competition in the 'bad jobs' segment may restrict the ability of firms to pay high wages.

Certain groups in society may find themselves channelled into the primary or secondary labour markets, with males and whites dominating the former and females, immigrants and non-whites the latter.

4 The hotel and catering industry has been identified as one which falls within the 'bad job' segment (or the secondary labour market).[48] Witz and Wilson suggest that the 'competitive and unconcentrated' nature of the industry leads the industry to operate within the secondary or 'bad jobs' labour market. Jobs are semi- or unskilled, and employment is characterized by part-time and casual work. There are 'exceptionally high rates of labour turnover' and a lack of formalized employment structure. The 'individual contract between employer and employee' dominates, along with 'the discretionary allocation of rewards by management'.

Conclusion

Despite the existence of institutions in the labour market and the clear interest of the participants (employees and employers) in many non-economic aspects of employment, studies do emphasize the significance of economic forces in explaining pay and pay differentials.[49] The demand for and supply of labour are factors that cannot be ignored in pay no matter how much the human participants may wish to do so. In the short term there is evidence of a positive relationship between earnings changes in industry and employment changes.

Expanding industries tend to raise their relative earnings to obtain the labour they require. The connection between wage changes and employment changes becomes less evident the longer the time period considered, since elasticities of labour supply fall over time. The existence of vacancies in expanding industries and the absence of vacancies elsewhere may be sufficient to re-allocate labour without a long-term change in relative earnings.

Labour markets are a mixture of economic and non-economic elements and perhaps because of the human dimension, the non-economic element can often seem to dominate. The concept of the 'just wage' has had a long history. The earnings of labour do, however, respond to market forces whether these markets are competitive or not.[50]

Despite the apparent immobility of labour, the resource does move in response to changes in pay. There is a fairly mobile component in the population (the young and the school- and college-leavers in particular) which is usually sufficient to re-allocate labour in appropriate ways throughout the economy.

Questions for essays and seminar papers

1 What factors are likely to affect the supply of labour to the hotel and catering industry as a whole?

2 High wages are sometimes justified as compensation for unpleasant work. How therefore can the fact that kitchen porters earn less than hotel managers be explained?

3 Discuss the view that low pay in the hotel and catering industry is solely a reflection of labour's marginal productivity.

4 How far is the 'segmented labour market' model a useful explanation of pay in the hotel and catering industry?

5 Identify the factors that have influenced the number of persons employed and the types of jobs offered in the hotel and catering industry over the last twenty years.

Practical assignment

By visiting local job centres and employment agencies, and looking through job advertisements in the press, judge whether there are differences in the way in which local hoteliers and caterers try to obtain staff. What ranges of pay can you discover?

CHAPTER 7

Capital

In Chapter 1 capital was referred to as man-made resources in the form of physical assets, i.e. the previously-produced means of production. It is the stock of produced goods that contributes to the production of other goods and services. As such, it includes factories, hotels and restaurants, the machinery, furniture and fittings within them, as well as vehicles, 'social capital' such as schools, hospitals and roads, and dwellings that provide housing services (see Table 59). Even consumer durable goods such as washing machines and cookers which provide household laundry and catering services, may bé considered as capital, though they are normally classed as items of consumer expenditure.

Stocks and work in progress are a further component of capital and are made up of unsold finished goods, semi-finished goods and raw materials held by firms which have yet to be used up in production. Such stocks and work in progress usually form only a small part of the gross domestic product (GDP) of this country (equivalent to national output) but are subject to considerable fluctuations compared with other components of GDP, including the formation of 'fixed' capital, i.e. gross domestic fixed capital formation (see Table 60). These fluctuations can have a significant effect on fluctuations in national output.[1]

The production of capital (whether fixed or stocks and work in progress) is known as investment. (Again, this is different from the usual definition of investment.) Some part of total investment will go towards replacing that part of the capital stock which wears out and becomes less productive over time, i.e. depreciation. If total (gross) investment is just equal to depreciation in the economy, then the capital stock is not being added to. Net investment is of significance since it shows whether the capital stock is growing or not (see Table 60). There is no ready way of determining, however, the proportion of gross investment that is 'superior' to existing or worn-out equipment. Even if net investment was nil, the capacity of the economy to produce goods and services could rise if the gross investment was in new superior machinery and techniques.

Spending on gross investment has shown real growth between 1982 and 1986, but less than a quarter of that spending is 'net'. As a proportion of GDP, investment is about 20 per cent.[2]

Table 59 *Stock of capital (UK) 1986*

	£b at 1980 replacement costs
Road vehicles	35.2
Railway rolling stock, ships and aircraft	12.7
Plant and machinery	328.3
Dwellings	381.8
Other buildings and works	481.9
	1239.8

Source: Central Statistical Office, *UK National Accounts, 1987* (HMSO 1987).

Table 60 *Investment in fixed capital and stocks and work in progress (UK) 1982–6*

	Gross domestic fixed capital formation	*Net domestic fixed capital formation* (£b in 1980 prices)	*Value of physical increase in stocks and work in progress*
1982	39.5	9.8	−1.0
1983	41.6	11.0	0.7
1984	45.0	13.6	0.3
1985	46.4	14.3	0.6
1986	46.6	13.6	0.7

Source: Central Statistical Office, *UK National Accounts, 1987* (HMSO 1987).

Of the gross domestic fixed capital formation in 1986 (£64.2 billion in current prices),[3] approximately 1.7 per cent was accounted for by investment in the hotel and catering industry (see Table 61). Investment in the service sector as a whole has increased as a proportion of GDP, whereas manufacturing investment has fallen in importance. Investment in hotels and catering has fluctuated from year to year as has investment in general (see Table 62). Some of the causes of fluctuations are discussed on pages 157–8.

Significance

If the economy's resources were devoted entirely to the production of consumer goods and services, the stock of capital goods would not be added to,

Table 61 *Investment in hotels and catering (by type of asset) 1986*

	£m
Gross domestic fixed capital formation:	
Vehicles, ships and aircraft	66
Plant and machinery	522
New buildings and works	502
	1090

Source: Central Statistical Office, *UK National Accounts, 1987* (HMSO 1987).

Table 62 *Fixed capital expenditure of hotels and catering 1983–7*

	£m in 1980 prices
1983	641
1984	670
1985	782
1986	846
1987	831

Source: *British Business* (27 May 1988).

and would be reduced by the failure to replace capital which wears out or becomes obsolete. The result would be no increase in output of consumer goods and services in the first instance and a reduction of that output in the second. Production of consumer goods and services depends on the prior production of capital goods.

It is not impossible to produce consumer goods and services without capital goods but it is clearly difficult, more laborious, lengthy and often expensive. The use of capital can make the production process more efficient.

The using up of resources of manpower and raw materials to make capital goods does mean, however, that these resources are not currently available to make consumer goods and services, e.g. steel can be used to make a machine to manufacture cars or can be incorporated directly into a car by existing machines. A person can be employed as a waiter or could be employed to build a hotel. There is therefore a conflict between consumer and capital goods production. Increased capital production *now* means a production *now* of fewer consumer goods than might otherwise have been possible. An increased production of consumer goods and services *in the future*, however, depends on that investment in capital goods. There is therefore a sacrifice of current consumption for increased future consumption.

In the same way investment by a firm entails expenditure currently in anticipation of future gains and streams of benefits.

The concept of 'productive capacity' was introduced in Chapter 1; investment can add to that capacity by increasing the quantity or quality of the capital stock. The relatively poor economic performance of the UK economy since the end of the Second World War may be attributed in part to an inadequate level of investment. There is certainly some evidence that high growth countries devote a higher proportion of their GDP to investment than does the UK, but it is not clear whether the investment is necessarily the cause of the growth.[4] The causes of economic growth are so many and complex that it is impossible to isolate investment as the most important one.

Demand for capital

In the same way that the marginal productivity of labour was the basis of the demand for labour, so the 'marginal efficiency of capital' (MEC) is the basis of the demand for capital. If capital is subject to 'diminishing returns', then every addition to the capital stock gives a lower return than the previous units of capital; the *MEC* curve will be as represented in Figure 45. The financial benefits from investment will accrue over time and are usually expressed as a percentage of the original sum of money invested, e.g. in Figure 45 the *ok* unit of capital will give a return of *or* per cent per year, whereas the ok_1 unit will give only or_1 per cent per year.

A profit-maximizing firm will continue to add to its capital stock for as long as the value of the extra output from each extra unit of capital exceeds the cost of obtaining that extra unit. The cost of the capital may be represented by the 'rate of interest' (expressed as a percentage per year). If funds are borrowed in

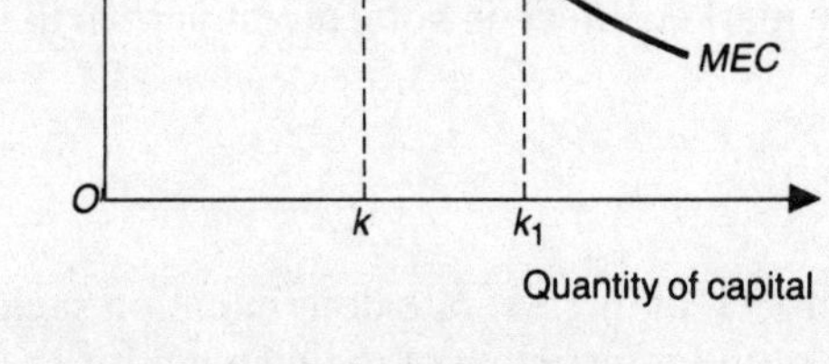

Figure 45 *Marginal efficiency of capital*

order to purchase or hire the capital, interest will usually be payable on the sum borrowed. This reflects the fact that most people have a 'positive time preference' and lenders will require the incentive of earning interest in order to lend their funds to others, thus sacrificing current use of those funds.

Even if funds are not borrowed, it will still be necessary to recognize the opportunity cost of the internal funds used (see Chapter 5), i.e. what the funds invested in particular capital stock could have earned in their next best alternative use. This may be represented by a current rate of interest that could have been received, for instance, by leaving funds in a bank account; known as the 'imputed' internal interest rate.

The return from investment in capital stock will therefore need to be no less than the interest rate payable on any borrowed funds or the 'imputed' internal interest rate. The firm will reach an equilibrium with regard to the quantity of capital stock when *MEC* = rate of interest. In Figure 45, if the current rate of interest is *or* the firm will invest up to *ok*. Any addition to the capital stock beyond that when the interest rate is at *or* would reduce profits since the extra efficiency/productivity of capital would be less than the extra cost. A change in the interest rate will therefore be expected to affect investment.

In practice interest rates have not had a decisive effect on the level of investment in the economy. The relatively narrow variations in interest rates in the past may have meant that the impact of interest rates has been limited.[5] Additionally, many firms may be less concerned with estimating returns on capital employed and relating them to rates of interest than with estimating how long it will take to recover the initial financial outlay (see later in this chapter). Some investment may be of a long-term nature and be unaffected by short-term movements in interest rates. Also, interest charges may be a small element in the overall cost of a project.

Changes in the level of demand probably have an important role to play in determining investment. Investment is sensitive to changes in the level of income in the economy; as incomes and demand rise it may be necessary to increase the capital stock to meet the demand.[6]

It is also sensitive to the climate of opinion concerning likely future profits and demand. During periods of economic recession, businesspeople may feel pessimistic about the future and not be inclined to invest even if interest rates were low. Conversely, high interest rates need not restrict investment when businesspeople are optimistic about future trading prospects.

Whatever the 'usual' causes of investment, there is little doubt that a scheme of government grants and loans had a marked effect on hotel investment in the early 1970s, as shown in Table 63.

Interest

It is possible to construct a 'simple model' of interest rate determination such that the interest rate is the outcome of the joint action of the demand for the supply of capital. This is similar to the determination of the wage rate or any

Table 63 *Number of hotel bedrooms completed (England) 1968–76*

1968	1199
1969	2741
1970	4934
1971	6543
1972	12658
1973	31885
1974	2267
1975	2455
1976	740

Source: R. Tiltscher, *An Investment Review of the UK Hotel Industry* (Sector Investments 1983).

other price. In reality, though, the determination of the interest rate is rather more complex than this simple model would suggest, and is not something that need be discussed here.

To some, the charging of interest for loans is unfair, immoral or unnecessary, but it is difficult to avoid the conclusion that the use of funds in a particular capital project has an opportunity cost. In order to attract funds and resources into any one particular use, it is necessary to attract them away from competing uses. If resources are to be allocated to their most 'economic' or 'productive' use then it will be necessary to ensure that resources in each use at least cover their opportunity cost, as represented by the rate of interest.

Without such a 'price' of capital it would be difficult to allocate resources among the competing demands. This does not necessarily mean that interest rates have to be charged, only that they should be assigned in a 'shadow' form and investment should occur only if that (opportunity) cost is met.

There is, of course, more than just one interest rate existing in any economy but it is sometimes convenient to conduct the analysis in terms of only one. There will be a number of interest rates reflecting different degrees of risk attached to different types of investment.[7] Certain industries may be subject to greater fluctuations in demand than others and the return on such an investment may be uncertain. Rates of interest asked for by lenders of funds to such projects are likely to be higher than for less risky activities.

The longer the duration of the loan, the higher is likely to be the interest rate – as compensation to the lender for doing without funds for such a lengthy period. Shorter-duration loans may not attract such a high rate of interest.

Uncertainty about inflation, i.e. the rate of change of prices, may also influence the structure and level of interest rates. If the interest rate is, say, 10 per cent per year, but there is a general price rise of 12 per cent per year, then the burden to the borrower is reduced in real terms; payments are raised by 10 per cent by the interest rate but in real terms these repayments are reduced by 12 per cent by inflation. Each pound is worth less and is less of a loss to the

Table 64 *Hotel development costs 1983*

	60 room budget motel		*100 room 3-star motor hotel*	
	(% of total)			
Land	14.1	77.5	11.4	74.2
Construction costs and fees	63.4		62.8	
Furniture, furnishings and equipment	16.9		17.1	
Other	5.6		8.6	

Source: R. Tiltscher, *An Investment Review of the UK Hotel Industry* (Sector Investments 1983).

borrower when he/she makes repayments. In effect, the borrower will be paying and the lender receiving a 'negative' interest rate. An inflation rate of 7 per cent would leave the borrower to pay and the lender to receive a 'positive' interest rate but the 'real' interest rate (3 per cent) would be less than the 'money' interest rate (10 per cent). Differing money interest rates may therefore occur reflecting differing views of businesses and lenders about future inflation rates.

Investment in hotels and catering

Of the total investment an unusually high proportion, especially in hotels, is in the form of fixed assets. Compared with many other industries, only a small proportion of capital is in the form of stocks and work in progress. This reflects the fact that, in the case of hotels in particular, the product is the fixed asset.

The fixed assets themselves are in the form of:

1 Land and buildings.

2 Interior assets of furniture, fittings and equipment.

The land and buildings are often a high proportion of fixed assets; in Table 64 they constitute at least 74 per cent of total development costs.

Land and construction costs vary according to site and type of unit (among other factors) but the land cost is likely to be of considerable importance in luxury hotel development in city centres.[8] The profitability of hotel and catering establishments often depends upon being in a 'prime' site. Competition for such sites may be intense, however, resulting in high costs; the sites are limited and may be subject to planning controls and conditions (regarding maximum height and minimum car parking) which could increase cost further.

Such sites could constitute between 30 and 40 per cent of total development costs,[9] compared with between 11 and 14 per cent in the examples in Table 64. If, as the ETB suggests, a tariff of at least £1.27 per room for every £1,000 of development costs is necessary to cover all costs, then development costs in central London, for instance, are prohibitively high (1982). The necessary tariff would be far in excess of those the market was currently able to bear.

Investment in hotels is characterized by the large sums of money required for individual projects and the low amount of turnover generated in relation to sums invested.[10] The low returns on the capital invested (see later) can result in a long pay-back period; part of the cause of the low returns is the high absolute cost of the investment. It is not unusual for hotels to make losses in the first 3–6 years of operation before achieving a steady level of operation. A hotel is, therefore, essentially a long-term investment and firms need to raise long-term finance. There is relatively little demand for medium-term finance (for plant and machinery) or for short-term finance (stocks and work in progress).

In the case of catering the absolute sums involved are usually smaller but fixed assets are still a high proportion of the investment. Pay-back periods are relatively short and the need for long-term finance is less than in the case of hotels.

Returns to hotel and catering investment

The benefits from (or returns to) investment in hotel and catering projects will vary according to the nature of the individual project and the expertise with which it is planned and operated. The report *Hotel Prospects to 1985* demonstrated how different categories of hotel appeared to have different performances in terms of returns on capital invested.[11] These varied according to location, sales bias (accommodation, food or liquor), type of ownership (group or independent) and tariff.

There have not been regular comprehensive surveys of returns throughout the industry and it is therefore difficult to make generalizations on a recent database.The conclusion of a survey carried out in the 1960s on behalf of the Economic Development Committee for Hotels and Catering (HCEDC) was that 'rates of return on capital invested (in hotels)...appear to be low in comparison with...average rates of return earned by manufacturing industries'.[12] This was not necessarily true of all firms and projects in the industry, of course, but similar opinions still prevail.

A study of financial performance in the hotel industry (published 1979)[13] found that its average return on capital was one of the lowest (forty-third) out of forty-five industries.

A more recent report on hotel investment suggests that returns do not exceed 'a loosely defined "norm" or "average"'.[14]

Whatever the reasons for the unexceptional returns, many people still find it an attractive industry to enter and are reluctant to leave because of its non-monetary advantages. Some companies may look more towards a rise in

Table 65 *Sources of funds for UK industrial and commercial companies 1983*

	%
Internal funds	73
Bank borrowing	7
Other loans	2
Capital issues (UK)	7
Overseas	10
Credit	2

Source: P. Johnson, *British Industry: An Economic Introduction* (Basil Blackwell 1985).

the value of the capital assets (property and land) than towards profit as a reason for being in the industry.[15]

Extension and modernization investments are less often assessed by reference to a percentage return of the sum invested. These projects are more often seen as a necessary way of safeguarding or increasing profits and as a necessary response to keep up with changing public tastes.

Sources of finance

In Table 65 it can be seen that company savings or undistributed profits ('internal funds') have been the single most important source of funds for companies. (For government as a source of finance, see Chapter 8.)

It is significant that 'capital issues' provide only a small proportion of funds. This category includes the issue by companies of shares (ordinary and preference) and of debentures. Shares are permanent 'equity-capital', and not loans and therefore the funds do not have to be repaid; the shareholders are the owners of the company. There is usually no obligation on companies to distribute profits to shareholders and thus pay a return on the funds.

Much of the finance for firms, whether from the purchase of shares or otherwise, will be channelled from savers (individuals and companies) through 'financial intermediaries' such as banks, insurance companies, pension funds and unit and investment trusts. Funding of companies directly by persons through ownership of 'ordinary' shares has become increasingly less important over time and 'indirect' funding has become more important. Between 1963 and 1981 the percentage of ordinary shares held by individuals fell from 54 to 28 per cent, whereas the percentage held by insurance companies doubled and by pension funds increased four-fold (see Table 66). These institutions are now very important shareholders, and thus owners, of companies in the UK, though much of their funds will, of course, have come from individuals.

Table 66 *Pattern of share ownership (UK equity) 1963–81*

	1963	*1981*
	(% of total)	
Persons	54.0	28.2
Insurance companies	10.0	20.5
Pension funds	6.4	26.7
Unit trusts	1.3	3.6
Investment trusts	11.3	6.8
Banks	1.3	0.3
Overseas	7.0	3.6
Other	8.7	10.3
	100.0	100.0

Source: *Economic Progress Report*, No 181, Nov.–Dec. 1985, (HM Treasury).

Table 67 *Legal forms of business (GB) 1983*

	Hotels and catering		*Production*	
	(% of total businesses in each category)			
Sole proprietors	40.4	75.3	17.9	31.3
Partnerships	34.9		13.4	
Corporate businesses	24.7		68.6	

Notes:
1 The figures probably understate the importance of the smallest firms and therefore of sole proprietors and partnerships.
2 Production: mining and quarrying, manufacturing, and public utilities.

Source: *British Business* (13 April 1984).

Debentures, however, are 'loan capital' and companies will normally incur a liability to make repayments to the lenders (who are not owners of the company, but creditors).

'Capital issues' are not usually available to the small firm which is often a 'sole proprietor' or 'partnership'. This form of organization, i.e. not a company, is common in the hotel and catering industry (see Table 67). There is a heavy reliance in such firms on bank loans, trade credit, hire purchase and own savings. Obtaining longer-term finance often means obtaining a loan

Table 68 *Sources of finance for accommodation businesses (Scarborough) 1975*

	% of businesses
Building society only	34
Mostly savings and own capital	22
Private loan or mortgage	2
Building society and bank	17
Finance house and bank	25

Source: C. Stallibrass, 'Seaside Resorts and the Holiday Accommodation Industry; a case study of Scarborough, *Progress in Planning*, 13(3) (1980).

(mortgage) on the security (or collateral) of the assets of the business. Default on repayment would mean that the assets could be forfeited to the lender.

Data for the Scarborough accommodation industry (see Table 68) illustrates the importance of banks and building societies in financing the smaller firms in the industry. (98 per cent of the owners of 'traditional' accommodation and 80 per cent of the owners of self-catering owned only one establishment.) Building societies were the only source of finance for a third of the operators in this particular survey.

For industrial and commercial companies one of the most important sources of external finance is banks (see Table 65) in the form of loans and overdrafts. Equipment leasing is also becoming increasingly important. 'Sale and leaseback' was popular in the hotel and catering industry during the 1970s but has since declined (i.e. sale of all or part of the fixed assets, especially land, to an organization which then leases them back to the seller).

An investment problem?[16]

It is occasionally observed that there is an investment problem in the hotel and catering industry – a problem identified as a shortage of finance for funding investment.[17] Essentially this is believed to relate to a reluctance on the part of financial intermediaries and other lenders to provide funds for projects in this industry.

It is likely that lenders are always cautious about lending to small firms (see later in this chapter).[18] Additionally there may be certain characteristics of hotels and catering which result in even more caution being shown by lenders to both large and small firms. (Many of the largest, well-established hotels and catering firms will, however, face little difficulty raising finance.) Why might the problem exist?

1 It has already been noted that hotels are a long-term investment, initial

Table 69 *Bankruptcies and company liquidations 1982 (England and Wales)*

	Bankruptcies (individuals and partnerships)	*Company liquidations*
	(% of total)	
Agriculture and horticulture	1.5	0.5
Manufacturing	3.9	33.6
Construction	18.4	11.8
Road haulage	7.2	5.4
Wholesaling	3.7	7.7
Retailing	16.3	11.5
Financial and professional services	6.1	10.1
Hotels	0.8	0.5
Restaurants	7.9	2.3
Garages	6.2	3.8
Other consumer services	3.4	4.7
Other industries	2.7	8.2
Other individuals	22.1	–
	100.0	100.0

Source: *British Business* (29 April 1983).

returns are negative and life-time returns may be low. Many financial institutions are reluctant to lend on a long-term basis because of the risk compared with other shorter-term investment. Banks have usually shown a preference for short-term lending but are showing an increasing tendency to lend long-term (ten years or more). If only short-term loans can be obtained, then the obligation to repay over that short period makes the annual burden of already high costs even greater.

2 The industry may also be considered to be inherently risky. Table 69 suggests that this is probably truer for catering than for hotels, since the percentage of 'failures' that are in the restaurant sector would appear to be disproportionately high.

Hotels and catering generally have had a poor reputation (whether well-founded or not) and even the HCEDC commented that 'catering establishments are generally speculative as an investment'.[19] Catering, in particular, is highly competitive and certain areas may experience overprovision of services. Rapid changes in market taste add to the difficulties facing catering management.

Part of the poor reputation of hotel investment may arise from the overcapacity that existed in the 1970s. The increase in the hotel stock that was largely due to a government grant scheme (see Table 63 and Chapter 8) coincided with a reduced growth of demand and rise in costs. As a consequence, many hotel firms faced considerable difficulty in repaying their loans. The inflexibility of hotel supply means that it is very difficult to adjust to changed market conditions.

Because of the risks believed to be associated with hotel and catering investment, finance may only be available from lenders in the form of 'mortgages' or 'debentures' and not in the form of permanent 'equity-capital'. The firm therefore has the burden of making payments to lenders at a time when it may be particularly difficult to do so, i.e. in the earliest years of operation.

3 Additionally, because many hotel and catering operations are small owner-manager operations, they may be considered to be more risky. Management may lack managerial and financial expertise and have relatively few resources to fall back on. The importance of the 'personal' element in the success of a hotel and catering business can make the investment less attractive because success or failure can be too dependent on one person.

The demand for hotel and catering services is subject to considerable fluctuation and like many other industries, is susceptible to the general economic climate. Rapidly changing fashions and tastes in eating out and the limited season and low occupancy rates in many resort areas, all contribute to make the skills necessary to ensure success that much more demanding.

4 Both hotel and catering buildings and interior fittings have a limited value as security for loans. Financial institutions may be reluctant to accept hotels, in particular, as security because they have a limited 'alternative-use'; they are generally purpose-built and can be used for few other forms of business. The value of the building is therefore heavily dependent upon the profitability of the hotel business rather than having an intrinsic value which many factory buildings might have – they can often be used for the manufacture of many different products. A falling-off of profit will therefore affect the value of the building. Before the building is built, there is not even this to offer as security; firms may therefore face particular problems raising finance in this period.

Furniture and fittings will have value only for so long as their style conforms with contemporary market standards and there may be a constant need to modernize and maintain standards.

Because the capital assets provide little security, loans from any one source are often limited to a proportion of the total. Until units are complete, some security in addition to the unit may have to be offered.

5 Financial institutions may have little or no knowledge of or sympathy with the nature of the hotel and catering business and its 'peculiar' problems.[20] They may therefore feel unable to judge effectively the potential of a business or to monitor its operation.

6 Most firms in hotels and catering are small and small firms in any industry 'suffer... by comparison with larger firms, in seeking finance from external sources'.[21] Small firms may find that sources of finance such as the issue of shares are not available to them because of their size and the cost involved.

Small firms may also be required to pay more for their finance than large firms do.[22] This could be in an absolute sense reflecting the higher risk but also in a relative sense. Small amounts of finance can cost proportionately more to raise than can larger amounts; the administrative costs associated with a loan (or issue of shares) do not rise in proportion to the amount of money raised and thus the burden can rest more heavily on the smaller firm.

Banks and other lenders may be inclined to treat small firms with more caution because of their lack of past 'track-record', especially if the firm is unable to provide much finance of its own for the venture.

Many small firms lack information about the full range of lenders that might be prepared to provide finance. Such firms may have little idea either, about the most appropriate and effective way in which data should be presented and the case for support made to financial institutions.[23]

As a consequence many small firms are reliant upon retained profits, personal funds and bank and trade credit. In the early years of operation, though, small firms may find particular difficulty in financing themselves from retained profits (if they exist at all). At the same time, such firms face difficulties raising finance from external sources and security much in excess of any loan may be required by lenders.[24]

7 It may be that government policies have also seemed to inhibit investment in this industry. UK governments have been rather more encouraging of investment in manufacturing than in service industries generally (see Chapter 8 for details of government policies).

8 Despite the range of financial institutions that exists, it is occasionally argued that some form of specialist lending agency might be necessary.[25] There are already a number of agencies that are sympathetic to the industry but they are perhaps not 'specialist' enough.

It has already been noted how building societies play a significant role in financing the smaller owner-managers of the industry. Breweries are also an important source of finance for hoteliers and caterers.

The Industrial and Commercial Finance Corporation (ICFC) has been 'an important source of funding for a considerable number of hotel projects and must be seen as a growing and continuous source of finance for the industry'.[26] This corporation is funded largely by the banks and by the Bank of England to assist new, smaller and more risky enterprises. In 1982–3 nearly 6 per cent (£5.2m) of its loans were to hotel and catering firms (a similar proportion to that given to electrical and electronic engineering).[27] Other 'sympathetic' organizations include the Highlands and Islands Development Board and the Council for Small Industries in Rural Areas (CoSIRA). Financial assistance is also available from the tourist boards in the UK though, in total, the amount is not particularly high. In 1987–8 the English Tourist Board paid £11.8m in grants and loans;[28] a new city centre 4-star hotel (200 rooms) would cost at least £8m to develop (1983).[29]

Given the particular problems that hotel and catering investment faces and a possible inherent bias on the part of many institutions in favour of manufacturing, the creation of Leisure Development Ltd in 1984 may be particularly appropriate.[30] This is an 'equity fund' (it purchases shares) which is funded from non-government sources (banks and pension funds) and is specifically aimed at financing investment projects in the wider leisure and tourism sphere.

Whether such a fund or a similar proposal for a 'Hotel Investment Trust' should be government-financed (in part, at least) is arguable.[31] There is, probably, a continuing need for some government involvement in helping the industry raise finance, if only as an indication of government interest, confidence and support.

Investment appraisal

It was observed earlier that small firms may not be able to present a 'good case' to lenders of finance. In particular firms may adopt what might be considered to be 'inappropriate' methods of investment appraisal.

In deciding whether or not to undertake a particular investment project, firms may use any one of several techniques to assess its net worth (future stream of benefits less costs). These techniques may be grouped into (1) conventional methods and (2) discounting methods. The conventional methods do not take account of the *timing* of future income and expenditure, whereas the discounting ones do. It is often suggested that these discounting techniques are, therefore, in some way superior.[32]

Conventional methods

Necessity or postponability

A degree of urgency or lack of postponability is often used as a reason for arguing that a scheme is so important or essential that any kind of objective evaluation is unnecessary. Much of the work that hotels and boarding houses were obliged to carry out under the Fire Precautions Act 1971 could be considered to be of this form. Refurbishment of hotel and catering premises may be considered necessary if other competitors have undertaken similar investments.

Pay-back method

The pay-back period is the time required for an investment to generate sufficient profits to recover initial expenditure. The shorter the period then the more attractive the investment is considered to be. A variation of this is to ask whether an investment does 'pay-back' within a certain fixed period of, say, three years.

Table 70 *Investment techniques used by hotel and catering firms (USA) 1980*

	% of firms using a particular technique
Pay-back	73
Return on investment	62
Rate of return	29
Net present value	29
Internal rate of return	23

Source: J. J. Eyster and A. N. Geller, 'The Capital-Investment Decision: Techniques used in the Hospitality Industry', *Cornell Hotel and Restaurant Administration Quarterly* (May 1981).

These are simple methods and as such are likely to be popular (see Table 70) but they take little or no account of income earned after the pay-back period. As such, they may favour shorter-term projects.

Rate of return

There are a number of variations of this technique and a common one is to express expected profit over the lifetime of a project as a percentage of original capital cost ('return on investment' in Table 70). There may be different approaches between firms to the valuation of capital and the calculation of depreciation (profit may be estimated after an allowance for depreciation); profits may also be estimated before or after tax. Thus comparison of firms' returns would need to be treated with caution. Profits may also be related to the total assets of the firm rather than the project cost ('rate of return' in Table 70).

The calculation of the return on capital that is expected in the third year of operation has been a common standard by which investment has been judged in the UK hotel and catering industry.[33]

Whatever the individual advantages and disadvantages of these techniques, none of them reflects the 'time-value of money'.[34] It is not just the total profitability of a project that is important but also the timing of cash inflows and outflows. Cash that is available now is worth more than an equal sum in the future. Early cash inflows from investment projects can be re-invested in other profit-generating projects, whereas there is an opportunity cost associated with more distant cash inflows: the opportunities for additional investment projects that are foregone by not having funds available.

Two investment projects may have the same pay-back period and same return but one may earn most of its returns early in its life, whereas the other may not receive them until later on. Conventional methods will not recognize that the former project would be preferable to the second.

Further problems relating to the 'time-value of money' will arise as inflation reduces the value of future income; also the risks of achieving certain expected income will increase the further into the future that income is expected.

There is a need, therefore, for a method of evaluating investment projects which takes into account the time-value of money.

Discounting methods

These allow for the timing of cash flows so that early cash flows are given more *weight* than those arising later.

Net present value (NPV)

This is a calculation of the value of the annual cash flow *discounted* back to the present minus the cash outlay. The cash flows are discounted (or weighted) by using a predetermined discount rate, e.g. at a discount rate of 10 per cent, a cash return of £100 a year from today will have a 'present value' of £90.90 (approximately). This is easily seen by considering the value of £90.90 invested today at 10 per cent interest – in a year's time it would have a value of about £100.

The discount rate is derived from the current cost of raising money or the opportunity cost of not lending the money elsewhere.

Thus the £100 expected in the future is discounted or weighted to give a present value and the further into the future cash inflows are expected to be, the lower will be their present value. In this example, a project with a present value of £90.90 will be a satisfactory one provided the project cost is less than that, i.e. if the NPV is greater than zero. If the NPV is negative, then the project would normally be considered to be unsatisfactory.

Internal rate of return (IRR)

Instead of starting from a predetermined discount rate, a discount rate (the IRR) for a project is estimated that will result in an NPV of zero, i.e. a discount rate (IRR) that equates cash inflows with cash outflows.

If this IRR is greater than the current interest rate then the project is worthwhile (i.e. the application of the current interest rate as a discount rate to the project would have yielded a positive NPV). Conversely, an IRR below current interest rates would suggest the project is not a desirable one.

The two methods were used by less than a third of the USA firms represented in Table 70. The authors of the article from which that table is taken considered that the techniques that were favoured by the majority of firms were 'naive and misleading'. The HCEDC report on investment concluded that existing well-used techniques were 'not sophisticated enough' and it recommended that discounting methods 'should be more widely used'. Whatever the merits of these techniques, the majority of firms still use conventional methods and in this they are not very different from firms in many other industries.[35] The conventional methods do have the advantage of simplicity whereas the discounting methods are more complex and time-consuming.

Cost-benefit analysis[36]

In some parts of the public sector of the economy, covering local and central government and the nationalized industries, investment appraisal may take a different form. It might be appropriate for public bodies to take a broader and longer-term view of their investment projects than commercial companies might take of theirs.

All benefits and costs could be included, of whatever nature (financial or otherwise) and to whomsoever they accrue (firms, consumers and non-consumers of a product). Such a wide approach is the basis of cost-benefit analysis (CBA) as investment appraisal. A commercial firm building a factory is likely to consider only those costs it would bear, such as labour and raw material costs. Other costs could be imposed on the community, however, in the form of air and water pollution. A hotel or restaurant may cause noise disturbance to local residents. These wider 'costs' would ideally be considered in a CBA.

Benefits which were felt by 'non-users' of a road-improvement scheme might include the increase in revenue of a roadside café resulting from a higher traffic flow. Benefits to the actual users of the road would include 'time-savings' on journeys; these should be included in the investment appraisal but considerable difficulties arise in practice in giving such benefits a monetary value.

A study of Norfolk beaches which attempted to assess the value of coastal protection schemes, sought to assess the recreational value of beaches.[37] That value could not be assessed directly but several indirect methods were used to assess the value of beaches to holidaymakers and day-trippers. In particular, use of the 'Clawson' method involved determining the distances users travelled to reach the beach, converting these into 'cost' incurred and constructing a 'demand' curve from that information. The recreational benefit was considered to be the area under the demand curve.

Many of the effects, although difficult to value, are critical in terms of the investment decision, e.g. time savings often amount to 60–70 per cent of benefits accruing to transport improvements. The value assigned to them can have a decisive effect upon the final appraisal. The effects may be less objective than the direct monetary returns to and costs of an investment but they may, in the CBA, be given equal credence and weight.

A further problem may arise over choice of a discount rate. The actual rate chosen can be important in deciding whether a project is worthwhile or not.

CBA has also been criticized on 'distributional' grounds. Although a project may be judged to be desirable by a CBA, it may affect different individuals and groups in different ways. If it can be assumed that every £1 worth of benefit or cost will be of greater significance to lower-income families than to higher-income families, then some weighting along these lines might be appropriate. It is unusual for CBA to weight costs and benefits in such a way as to recognize the distribution effects.

CBA does seek to make decision-making by the public sector more objective and investment appraisal more all-embracing. Ultimately though, as with all investment appraisal techniques, CBA can only *assist* in decision-taking and cannot provide the complete answer.

Questions for essays and seminar papers

1 Discuss why conventional investment appraisal may not be suitable for projects such as improvements to roads in and to holiday areas. What appraisal techniques might be appropriate?

2 Small hotel and catering firms often lack managerial expertise. To what extent is this the cause of difficulties that such firms face in raising finance?

3 What effect would a reduction of government tax allowances for investment have on hotel and catering firms (with Chapter 8)?

4 Discuss whether there is a need in the UK for a financial institution which specializes in lending money to the hotel industry.

5 Examine the likely effects on the hotel and catering industry and the economy generally of a fall in interest rates (with Chapter 8).

Practical assignment

Find out what information you would need to present to a local bank manager in order to obtain finance to set up a restaurant. Compare the rates of interest and other conditions of borrowing that different financial institutions would impose on financial assistance to you.

CHAPTER 8

Government

The influence of government policies on firms and industries has been discussed briefly in previous chapters. That influence may, however, be considerable and it is appropriate to bring together those aspects of government economic activity that might bear upon the hotel and catering industry.

In the widest sense governments may have an influence on the general economic environment, i.e. through macro-economic policy which will have an influence on the economy as a whole. Additionally, governments have been concerned to influence firms and industries directly by means of micro-economic policies: competition, industrial and regional policies.

Macro-economic policies[1]

Governments have had certain objectives which cause them to try and influence the level and direction of economic activity in the economy as a whole. Those objectives are usually considered to be:

1 Full employment. This does not necessarily mean zero per cent unemployed but some generally acceptable 'low' level where the amount and duration is minimized (where vacancies exceed unemployment?). Associated with this may be a desire to reduce regional differences in unemployment.

2 Reducing inflation, i.e. the rate at which the general price level increases.

3 A balance of payment surplus. The balance of payments records all financial transactions between consumers, firms and government in this country and those in other countries.

The sale of goods and services to foreigners creates a flow of currency into this country; conversely the purchase of foreign goods and services by British residents creates a flow of currency out of this country. Additionally, there will be inflows and outflows of currency that arise for investment and other capital reasons (see later in this chapter).

If the net result of these currency flows, for goods and services, for instance, is such that the outflow exceeds the inflow, there is a 'deficit' on that part of the balance of payments. A 'surplus' exists where the inflow exceeds the outflow.

In a situation where an overall deficit arises in respect of the purchases and sale of goods and services and because of the investment and similar flows, governments would need to borrow to finance the 'gap'. Alternatively they could use the country's reserves of gold and foreign currency for the same purpose. Neither of these options is particularly desirable nor even possible over a long period of time. A surplus would obviously be a more desirable long-term situation, avoiding the need to borrow or use up reserves and enabling the country to pay off 'old' debts and/or add to the gold and foreign currency reserves.

4 Growth, i.e. to increase the output of consumer goods and services, in particular. In this way the standard of living of the population will rise.[2] The output of goods and services (whether for consumer use or not) is measured by the 'national income'. The terms gross domestic product (GDP) and gross national product (GNP) are closely related to national income but are not exactly equivalent.

Some of the terms explained:

GDP at factor cost = output of goods and services produced in this country, valued in terms of the cost of inputs used in producing them (including profit). The value of expenditure taxes (such as VAT) and any subsidies is removed from market prices to get to this 'true' cost.

GNP = GDP plus or minus 'net property income from abroad' i.e. rent, interest, profits and dividends received by UK residents from abroad minus the corresponding payments made abroad.

National income = GNP minus 'capital consumption', i.e. that part of output which is used to replace the capital stock that has worn out and which is therefore used to maintain productive capacity.

A rise in national income may come about as a consequence of increased total demand and thus increased economic activity within the existing productive capacity of the economy. Increasing the capacity itself is more of a long-term policy matter (see Chapter 1). Government economic policies will be directed at both capacity and total demand.

The achievement of any one of these objectives may well be incompatible with the achievement of the others. It has proved difficult to achieve full employment and low inflation at the same time, in recent years. A balance of payments surplus has often been achieved only at the cost of low rates of growth and high unemployment. The nature of such relationships is beyond the scope of this book but this brief mention does illustrate the complexity of the tasks facing any government. If all objectives are not compatible then government policy-makers will need to 'trade-off' one objective against another and may settle for 'less-than-ideal' solutions in each case.

Table 71 *Britain during the 'Great Depression'*

	% unemployed	*Index of industrial activity*	*Wholesale prices index*
1929	10.4	118.7	100.0
1930	16.1	107.4	87.5
1931	21.3	86.8	76.8
1932	22.1	81.1	74.9

Source: S. Pollard, *The Development of the British Economy, 1914–1967*, 2nd Edition (Edward Arnold 1969) Chapter 4.

Macro-economic developments

Since the end of the Second World War most UK governments have taken an increased responsibility for intervening in the workings of the economy. This is largely due to the work of economists such as J. M. Keynes (1883–1946)[3] who recognized that the fluctuations in economic activity that had characterized most industrialized economies could be influenced by government action. In particular, it was felt that the experiences of the world depression of the late 1920s and early 1930s were to be avoided in post-war Britain. During 1929–32 industrial production fell substantially and unemployment rose considerably (see Table 71).

For most of the post-war period such experiences have been avoided in Britain with, until recently, output increasing and unemployment at a low level. Much of the responsibility for this may lie with the more active approach taken by governments towards 'management' of the economy. There have been, however, years when production has fallen, e.g. between 1973 and 1975 (see Table 72).

Unemployment during most of the post-war period was considerably lower than that experienced in 1929–32 and between 1959 and 1969 it fluctuated between 1.4 and 2.5 per cent of the labour force. Rather higher unemployment rates have been experienced since, however (Table 72), reaching 12.4 per cent in 1983.[4]

Whereas 1929–32 saw a fall in (wholesale) prices, the major economic problem of the 1970s and 1980s has been that of price rises (see Table 72). Inflation has become identified as the 'new economic problem' in the same way as large-scale unemployment of pre-war Britain had been a major problem previously. Between 1960 and 1970 retail price increases fluctuated between 1.1 and 6 per cent but there was a clear acceleration during the 1970s (see Table 72). By 1986, however, the rate of increase of retail prices had been reduced to 3.4 per cent.[5]

Table 72 *UK economic indicators 1973–87*

	% unemployed	*Index of industrial production*	*Inflation (%) (retail prices)*
1973	2.4	99.4	8.7
1975	3.7	92.2	23.6
1980	6.1	100.0	18.1
1985	11.2	108.1	6.1
1986	11.4	109.6	3.4
1987	10.2	113.1	4.2

Sources: *British Business* (26 August 1988); *Economic Progress Report No. 179*, August 1985 (HM Treasury).

Table 73 *UK balance of payments 1965–85 (£m)*

	1965–67	*1968–71*	*1972–78*	*1979–84*	*1985*
Current account					
Visible balance	−322	−191	−2825	− 270	−2068
Invisible balance	+266	+743	+2086	+3049	+5020
Current balance	− 56	+552	− 739	+2779	+2952
Investment and other capital transactions	−506	+350	+ 412	−3676	−2860

Source: M. J. Artis (Ed.), *Prest and Coppock's The UK Economy*, 11th Edition (Weidenfeld & Nicolson 1986).

With regard to the balance of payments, the UK has shown a tendency to have a deficit on the import and export of 'visibles' i.e. goods (see Table 73). The balance from the import and export of 'invisibles' (services such as banking, insurance, hotels and catering, air transport, shipping services, plus interest, dividends and profits, and transfers of funds) has, however, tended to be positive, i.e. a surplus. The surplus would be much larger but for the outflow in respect of government invisible items exceeding the inflow (military spending, economic aid, payments to and from the EEC). In some periods (e.g. 1968–71) this invisible surplus has covered the deficit on visibles and has thus reduced the need for 'official financing', i.e. the need for government to borrow or use up gold and foreign currency reserves. The visible deficit remains a matter of concern to governments and it is at this aspect of the balance of payments that most attention has been directed.

The investment and other capital transactions represent the transfer of funds for direct investment (e.g. buying or building a factory or hotel abroad) or portfolio investment (e.g. buying shares in a foreign company). Additionally, it represents movements of funds to banks and other financial institutions for future trading purposes, to earn high rates of interest or to take advantage of exchange rate movements. These funds can move rapidly from one country to another for short-term gain.

How have governments tried to achieve their objectives? They have done so in a variety of ways which may be categorized simply into two: monetary policy and fiscal policy.

Fiscal policy[6]

This is the management of economic activity through altering government revenue and expenditure. Government revenue and expenditure are shown in Table 74; taxes are the major sources of revenue and the main items of expenditure are education, health, defence and social security (unemployment, retirement and health benefits, etc.).

Table 74 *Public sector income and expenditure 1987–8 forecast*

Income	%	*Expenditure*	%
Central government tax		Social security	27
Income tax	23	Defence	11
VAT	13	Health and personal	
Corporation tax	8	social services	11
N. Sea revenue	2	Education and science	10
Road, fuel, alcohol		Home Office	4
and tobacco duties	10	Employment	2
Taxes on capital	2	Other depts	22
	58		
National insurance and		Interest payments	10
other contributions	16	Other	3
Local authority rates	10		
Interest and dividends	3		
Other sources	10		
	97		
Public sector borrowing			
requirement	3		
	100		100

Total of income and expenditure = £173 billion

Source: *Economic Progress Report Supplement*, No. 189, March/April 1987 (HM Treasury).

If the public sector account (local and central government) is in deficit then there will be a net 'injection' of demand into the economy. The withdrawal of purchasing power from the economy in the form of taxation, local authority rates, etc., will be less than the addition (injection) through public sector spending. The deficit is financed by borrowing, i.e. the Public Sector Borrowing Requirement (PSBR). As its magnitude alters so too will the net effect on the economy, either adding to or reducing the total level of demand (or aggregate expenditure) in the economy.

The total demand, or aggregate expenditure, in the economy may be defined as the total of expenditure by government, consumers, firms (in the form of investment) and by foreigners on British goods and services, less any expenditure by the first three on goods and services produced abroad. As this aggregate expenditure on domestically-produced goods and services alters, for whatever reason, so too will the level of output and employment (provided there is unused capacity in the economy). A rise in aggregate expenditure should cause output and employment to rise.

It is essentially in the Keynesian spirit to adopt such a policy since it was a deficiency of aggregate expenditure that was identified as being responsible for pre-war unemployment. If other agents in the economy are unwilling to raise expenditure – e.g. investment by firms – then Keynesians advocated a government boost to demand through a public sector deficit. Post-war public sector deficits have been common in the UK. Governments since 1979, however, have sought to reduce the PSBR (at least as a proportion of GDP); a surplus was achieved in 1987–88.

Through altering the form and level of revenue and expenditure and the balance between them, governments may be able to reduce unemployment by increasing aggregate expenditure. They may be able to encourage growth by tax relief for investment, and to remedy balance of payments problems by reducing aggregate expenditure, which may have the effect of reducing import growth. Inflation may be reduced by restricting growth of aggregate expenditure.

There are practical problems involved in fiscal policy, especially the difficulty of altering expenditure quickly. Part of the expenditure may be long-term investment (road-building) which it is difficult to increase or reduce at short notice. Some may be more influenced by demographic than economic factors (retirement pensions).

Additionally, fiscal policy may be too 'clumsy' an instrument to adjust the economy by the 'fine' amounts required; the magnitudes can only be adjusted by relatively large amounts. Fiscal policy may be highly suitable for curing large-scale unemployment through large boosts to aggregate expenditure, but not particularly suitable for adjusting inflation, say, from 6 to 4 per cent.

The PSBR that has arisen has itself been branded as a partial cause of the high inflation experienced during the 1970s. To the extent that the PSBR is met by borrowing from the banking system, rather than from individuals or firms, then an addition to the supply of money is likely to result.[7] This could be significant in stimulating inflation.[8]

The Conservative Governments since 1979 have sought to increase economic activity by reducing taxes and relying on this to provide incentives for businesses and individuals. This 'supply-side' economics is in contrast to the 'demand management' of fiscal policy, operating through the effects of direct government expenditure.

Monetary policy[9]

The apparent failure of fiscal policy to cope with inflation in the post-war years led governments to move the emphasis towards monetary policy. This involves altering the supply of money and rates of interest. The whole concept of the money supply is a very difficult one and it is enough to recognize that there are several definitions of what constitutes 'money'.[10]

The monetarist view[11] is that the economy is basically self-regulating and no government intervention is required. Fluctuations in economic activity that do occur are believed to be caused by changes in the money supply; in particular, monetarists claim evidence of a strong positive but lagged relationship between inflation and changes in the money supply, e.g. the increase in the measure of the money supply (M3) by 26.6 per cent in 1972 and 27.2 per cent in 1973 was believed to be at least partly responsible for the rise in inflation during the 1970s.

Fiscal policy is ruled out because it is believed to only substitute public expenditure for private-sector expenditure. Some monetarists claim that an active monetary policy would lead to more instability in the economy. Altering the supply of money in order to influence short-term fluctuations in the economy would be worse than doing nothing at all. The lack of information about what is actually happening in the economy and the time-lags associated with obtaining that information lead to government action being more destabilizing than stabilizing. The appropriate monetary policy would be, therefore, merely one of increasing the money supply at a rate equal to the rate of growth of output. Controlling the growth of the money supply is seen as a vital element of the policies and may be undertaken in a number of ways, most of which involve the Bank of England, as the Government's agent, in influencing the ability of the banking system to create money.[12]

The medium term financial strategy (MTFS) introduced in 1980 was based on the assumption that monetary control is a necessary and sufficient element of anti-inflation strategy.[13] The targets of MTFS were to reduce growth of the money supply (M3) from between 7 and 11 per cent in 1980–1 to between 4 and 8 per cent by 1983–4. PSBR is regarded as a major contributor to growth of money supply and this was to be reduced from 3.75 per cent of GDP in 1980–1 to 1.5 per cent by 1983–4. These targets have not been met but inflation has been reduced; in practice, the money supply and PSBR have proved difficult to control.

Since 1981 there has been, in practice, less emphasis on direct control of the money supply in the UK and more on indirect control through interest rates. The Government has chosen not to use the instruments available to it directly to influence money supply. Pre-1971, governments exercised some influence over interest rates in the economy through the officially-determined Bank Rate. Movements in this were followed by movements in all UK interest rates. Between 1971 and 1981 this was replaced by the minimum lending rate (MLR) which was designed to be less a leader of other interest rates and more a follower of market-determined rates. In practice, changes in MLR were later seen as strong 'hints' that government wished to see interest rates move in a particular direction. Since 1981 the Government has chosen not to publish MLR. This would make the banking system more uncertain about the terms on which the Bank of England would provide liquidity to it and, it was hoped, would make the banks more cautious about expanding credit.

In 1985 the Government returned to a policy of more active determination of interest rates in the UK by announcing occasional changes in MLR; bank base rates have moved swiftly in the same direction.

There is an influence on interest rates that is exerted in other ways. As governments borrow, they may offer higher interest rates to attract loans to them. Also the volume of government borrowing is such that interest rates in general would be affected. Furthermore, restrictions in money supply growth may have the effect of causing interest rates to rise.[14]

Investment and consumer spending may be responsive to these changes in interest rates and thus economic activity would be affected. Short-term inflows of money from abroad could also be encouraged by high interest rates and would alleviate a balance of payments problem.

An aspect of government policy which is less relevant now than it was in the period up to 1972 is 'management' of the exchange rate. Before 1972 the UK, like most other countries, was under an obligation (to the International Monetary Fund (IMF)) to maintain a fixed rate of exchange between sterling and other foreign currencies.[15] Variations in the rate (such as the devaluation of 1967) were allowed only in exceptional circumstances, but could have significant effects on the balance of payments. Since 1972 the exchange rate has 'floated' and found its own level as determined by demand and supply. Some influence can still be, and has been, exerted upon the exchange rate by government intervention though it tends to be much less obvious or direct. By buying and selling pounds sterling and other foreign currencies it is possible for the Bank of England to influence the price of sterling (exchange rate) in the same way as any price may be influenced through variations in demand and supply. A rise in interest rates in the UK might encourage an inflow of foreign currency; this would increase the demand for sterling as foreign currency was exchanged for it and the exchange rate would rise.

Effects on industry

Whatever form government macro-economic policies take, the consequent development of the economy will itself influence the hotel and catering industry. By increasing or reducing unemployment, or altering the rate of economic growth, the incomes of consumers will be affected and so will the demand for goods and services (see Chapter 2). One of the most important determinants of consumer demand is real disposable income and this may be affected in a number of ways. If inflation declines, then the real value of money incomes will rise; a rise in inflation faster than the rate of increase in money incomes would reduce real incomes. Alterations in income tax and National Insurance contributions can leave more or less income for consumers to 'dispose' of.

Policies which succeed in reducing inflation may have the effect of reducing costs of industry generally. However, the use of high interest rates to achieve certain objectives may cause costs to rise for firms that have already borrowed and find it necessary to increase their repayments. Reductions in money supply growth can make it more difficult for firms to find finance to cover temporary financial difficulties and survive as well as to obtain finance for expansion.

If governments influence exchange rates this too can affect costs for as exchange rates fall, import prices rise. The demand for hotel and catering services will be influenced since it would also be cheaper for foreigners to visit the UK.

With respect to the public-sector element of hotels and catering, health and education catering in particular, there may well be indirect effects of government macro-economic policies. There may be specific 'micro' policies relating to these services (such as 'privatization') but government macro policies may seek to contain the growth of the public sector generally.[16] This may have the effect of forcing financial restrictions on the health and education services and therefore on their catering sections.

Micro-economic policy

The various forms of this policy are less concerned with the manipulation of economic aggregates such as the level of total expenditure in the economy or growth of the money supply, and are more concerned with individual parts of the economy. This concern for the 'parts' will, of course, be governed by a desire to achieve the macro-economic objectives discussed earlier. Industrial and competition policies may encourage 'efficiency' in firms so that increased exports and a more rapid growth of output can be achieved. Regional policy may attempt to reduce unemployment but may also assist in reducing inflation.

Competition policy[17]

The previous discussions of the structure, conduct and performance model (Chapters 2–4) illustrated how market structure was believed to influence the performance of firms. The 'ideal' market structure in terms of achieving a performance of allocative and productive efficiency was considered to be perfect competition. Other market structures could be viewed as leading to a 'misallocation' and waste of resources.

Competition policy is concerned with the performance of firms and will therefore also be concerned with market structure and conduct.

Governments have, broadly, three options:

1 To alter market structures so that they become closer to the competitive 'ideal'.
2 Directly influence the conduct of firms within their existing market structures. Policies along these lines would reflect the practical difficulties of modifying market structures – altering concentration levels and barriers to entry – and also the fact that imperfect market structures have advantages. High concentration levels may be necessary to achieve economies of scale or to ensure adequate competition against foreign firms.
3 Influence performance through prices or profits controls.

Competition policy in the UK has tended to favour option 2, whereas USA policy has made more use of option 1 in that existing dominant firms may be broken up into smaller firms.

1 Monopolies and mergers have been targets of UK competition policy, with monopolies being defined in a less restrictive way than the economic definition. Policy has also concerned itself with restrictive trade practices which are actions by firms collectively designed to restrict competition. (In the late 1950s before appropriate legislation was introduced, over half of manufacturing output was believed to be subject to some form of collective restriction.)[18] Resale price maintenance (RPM) is the practice of manufacturers legally enforcing a price at which a product will be sold by retailers and in this way restricting competition between retailers; this has been a focus of competition policy also.

2 There have been a number of statutes relating to these matters[19] and a number of bodies established to carry out the policy. Monopolies and mergers that meet certain criteria may be referred to the Monopolies and Mergers Commission (MMC). Monopolies are defined as those situations where one firm supplies 25 per cent or more of a market. Recently (1984–88) the criterion for merger referral has mainly been how competition is or would be affected.

Cases are judged on their merits as to whether they are detrimental to the 'public interest'. This is a rather loosely defined concept and, in practice, policy has been to balance any reduction in competition against gains in efficiency. Such a pragmatic, *ad hoc* approach to monopolies and mergers reflects the difficulty of achieving perfect competition and a recognition of the potential advantages arising from high concentration. There has been a presumption in favour of competition but to a model more akin to 'workable competition' than to perfect competition (see Chapter 4). Workable competition is less concerned with structure than with performance. It may be defined in terms of a set of ideals or norms relating to the important dimensions of performance; to matters such as technical progressiveness, price, foreign trade record, etc. There is little agreement, though, about what 'ideal' performance is, once perfect competition is abandoned; nor is it clear what structure or conduct will bring it about.

Monopolies and mergers policy has, therefore, been ambiguous and inconsistent. The Government does have powers to stop mergers, regulate prices, break-up merged firms, allow mergers subject to conditions and impose conditions on existing monopolies. These powers have been used on relatively few occasions, with government preferring to seek voluntary assurances from firms.

Given the market structure of the hotel and catering industry, it is not surprising that there are few instances of hotel and catering firms being subject to investigation by the MMC. (Breweries and the supply of beer have been investigated in the past[20] and are currently the subject of an inquiry initiated in 1986). There was, at one stage, a possibility of the Trusthouse Forte bid for the Savoy Group (1981) being referred to the MMC. (Operation in the casino market did involve Grand Metropolitan in a MMC investigation in 1983.) An unsuccessful takeover bid by the Australian firm Elders IXL for Allied Lyons (including Embassy hotels) was referred to and cleared by the MMC in 1986. The referral was because of the unusual method proposed for financing the bid, rather than because of effects on competition. In the same year a Hanson Trust bid for Imperial (brewers, tobacco, pubs, hotels, popular catering, food processing) was not referred to the MMC though a concurrent attempt by Imperial and United Biscuits (food processing, popular catering) to merge voluntarily was referred. The Hanson bid was successful and subsequently parts of Imperial were sold off. Trusthouse Forte bought Happy Eater, Welcome Break motorway catering, Imperial Inns and Anchor Hotels from Hanson but this was referred to the MMC in 1986 because of the possible effects on competition in the roadside restaurant market that might arise from the common ownership of the Happy Eater and Little Chef chains. The Commission concluded that there were sufficient pressures, existing and potential, to ensure effective competition for Trusthouse Forte, and thus the purchase had not been against the public interest.[21] (The MMC found it necessary to address itself to defining the market within which these catering units operated and was confronted with a number of possible definitions).

Concentration levels in British industry remain high despite the existence of competition policy. Whether or not these high levels should give rise to concern though is not immediately obvious given their mixed effects. European Community monopolies and mergers policy is, as yet, not as clearly developed as UK policy and applies only when trade between member states is affected. The takeover of British Caledonian airline by British Airways (to give BA over 90 per cent of scheduled airline capacity in Great Britain) was cleared by the MMC in 1987, but subsequently concessions had to be made by BA in order to avoid a blocking of the merger by the EEC.

3 In contrast, policy with respect to restrictive trade practices and RPM has been more decisive. Both have been prohibited unless a case could be made before the Restrictive Practices Court that they were in the public interest. This is judged by reference to a number of 'escape clauses' but very few cases have succeeded in obtaining a judgement for continuation. Despite the prohibition of these activities, the underlying market structure remains and it may be that mutually-beneficial conduct continues in less open ways. RPM has been replaced by manufacturers' 'recommended' prices and an occasional attempt to enforce retail prices. Unregistered agreements probably continue to exist as evidenced by the occasional discovery by the Office of Fair Trading (see below). European Community policy towards restrictive trade practices is well developed and is similar to that of the UK.

Since the legislation was applied to services (1976) a number of hotel agreements were registered which *may* have amounted to restrictions on competition, e.g. collective price-fixing, mutual referrals, etc. In 1982 the Restrictive Practices Court gave its judgement on the ABTA 'Stabilizer' System.[22] The Association of British Travel Agents (ABTA) is a trade association of tour operators and travel agents and a main component of Stabilizer is 'exclusive dealing', i.e. member travel agents agree to sell member tour operators' products only and member tour operators to sell only through member agents. The Stabilizer System was supported by the Court because of the protection it gave the consumer, though some modifications to the system were recommended. In particular, it was recommended that travel agents should be permitted to discount the published tour prices.

4 In the years since 1973 the exercise of some of the powers relating to competition policy has been transferred to the Office of Fair Trading (OFT). The OFT can itself investigate certain 'anti-competitive' practices including those carried out by individual firms rather than collectively, e.g. giving discounts to retail customers for 'loyalty', selling below cost, requiring retailers to buy whole ranges of products from suppliers, even if only one particular product is required, supplying to only one outlet in an area, and requiring retailers to hold stocks of only one manufacturer, etc. The OFT can seek voluntary assurances from firms or can refer cases to the MMC, to the relevant Minister, or to the Consumer Protection Advisory Committee. The OFT may investigate 'any price' and has general responsibility for reviewing activities relating to the supply of goods and services that might adversely affect the economic interests of consumers. Attention is therefore directed more to conduct than to structure or performance. The activities of the OFT in respect of consumer protection have resulted in a number of instances where firms' behaviour has been modified. In particular, voluntary codes of practice have been adopted in a number of markets including package holidays.

Restrictive practices legislation now covers services and monopoly legislation has been extended to cover most nationalized industries.

5 Control over performance (efficiency) has usually been imposed as part of anti-inflationary policies. The activities of the Price Commission (1973–80) and its predecessor, the Prices and Incomes Board, did encourage a search for efficiency in firms by permitting price rises only in 'unavoidable' circumstances. Firms wishing to alter prices often underwent thorough 'efficiency-audits' by these government bodies. Price Commission reports relating to hotels and catering have been mentioned earlier in this book: Trusthouse Forte Hotels Ltd and Butlins Ltd.[23] Breweries have also been subject to Price Commission reports.[24]

Industrial policy[25]

It is quite consistent with the general, *ad hoc,* pragmatic nature of much of competition policy for government industrial policy to, for instance, encourage mergers.

Industrial policy includes a broad range of activities that have occurred with the general objective of improving 'efficiency' and to improve Britain's industrial performance and international competitiveness. Unlike competition policy which may be viewed as creating a framework within which market forces can operate, industrial policy seeks to supplement or replace those forces. It therefore includes financial support and incentives, advice, encouragement and guidance designed to 'seek either the achievement of particular production targets or individual structures or to promote growth, investment and technical progress in individual firms and industries'.[26]

Most of this government intervention has been justified by reference to the existence of imperfections and externalities, i.e. 'market failure' (see Chapters 2 and 4). Imperfections may be such as to lead governments to replace the market system by some other mechanism such as centralized planning. Supporters of government intervention might claim that the pursuit of profit cannot be equated with the maximization of social benefits.[27] The existence of imperfections gives rise to welfare losses and inefficient production. Firms will use up resources to preserve the imperfections and, thus, their positions. This tendency for oligopolistic structures to perpetuate themselves, combined with an inherent tendency for market economies to be unstable (subject to cyclical fluctuations in economic activity), can lead at one extreme to demands for outright government ownership of industry.

1 In the UK a number of firms and industries are government-owned. Most, such as British Rail and the National Coal Board, were 'nationalized' as a deliberate policy soon after the Second World War, but a number of individual firms in particular have passed into (and out of) government hands almost by accident. Rolls–Royce (aero-engines) and British Leyland were in such a dire financial position that nothing short of a government injection of funds (and therefore public ownership?) would have ensured their survival. Governments have also, at various times, had financial interests in

organizations as diverse as Ferranti (electronic equipment), British Petroleum (BP), ICL (computers), the British Sugar Corporation and Thomas Cook.

By owning firms or industries, governments may be able to exert more control over the economy and achieve their macro-economic objectives. Ownership of key sectors such as power, transport and telecommunications can ensure an adequate 'infrastructure' for the development of other industries. Some nationalized industries may be 'natural monopolies' in that one firm in an industry is the most efficient method of organization; a larger number of small firms could lead to wasteful duplication and an inability to achieve economies of scale.

Political and social motivations have dominated the desire for public ownership, in practice. A desire to transfer profits from the pockets of the 'capitalist' to the pockets of 'all' and concepts of 'industrial democracy' have been important reasons for nationalization.

The pursuit of non-commercial objectives can be considered as an appropriate policy for nationalized industries. Some goods and services may not be produced by private firms because they are not profitable, but are so important, in some sense, that they 'ought' to be produced. Railway lines and bus services in rural areas can be regarded as essential for the preservation of rural communities. A domestic aircraft-manufacturing industry might be considered necessary on national security grounds. On political, national security or balance of payments grounds, it may be preferable to produce coal from 'uneconomic' mines rather than import oil from abroad.

Similarly, employment could be safeguarded by public ownership. The apparently inevitable decline of some industries could be delayed or halted to avoid creation of an unacceptably high level of unemployment, especially if concentrated in particular areas.

The difficulty associated with these social or 'external' benefits is that they are often difficult to identify and measure. They also incur an opportunity cost and due regard would have to be taken of what other alternative productive opportunities would be lost by channelling resources into firms for balance of payments, employment, national security or 'social' reasons.

For a number of reasons (see below) individual firms have been considered worthy of support and public ownership (partial or otherwise) was a way of exercising some control over the use of funds invested in them.

2 There have been varying forms and degrees of government intervention but it has not been welcomed by all. At the opposite extreme from the supporters of public ownership are those who see no role of any significance for government in this respect and see the intervention that has occurred as being partly responsible for Britain's economic problem (compare monetarists).

This view has been expressed by Hayek: 'Businessmen seeking their own profit will inevitably lead to decisions in the best interests of consumers. If government intervenes, its decisions will not be made in accordance with free market criteria of prices and profits and it will make mistakes. Such wrong judgements by a national authority injure everybody'.[28]

The appropriate industrial policy is therefore to remove government intervention and leave the market mechanism to operate freely. Government intervention has in this view only propped up an archaic industrial structure to the detriment of performance. In setting out to reduce government financial intervention in industry a government minister commented (1970): 'National decadence is a consequence of treating the whole country as though they were lame ducks. The vast majority lives and thrives in a bracing climate, not in a soft, sodden morass of subsidized incompetence.'

The Conservative Governments since 1979 have adopted a similar view and have attempted to impose the 'discipline of the market' on industry. Financial support for private industry is being reduced (see below) and nationalized industries are being encouraged to be less reliant upon government assistance. 'Privatization' may take several forms:[29] selling-off of nationalized industries and firms in public ownership to the private sector (British Telecom, British Airways, BP, British Aerospace, etc.); permitting private firms to carry out certain activities in government services (health service cleaning or catering); encouraging nationalized industries and government agencies to adopt a more 'commercial' approach by, for instance, charging more economic prices or achieving commercial rates of return, rather than operating on a subsidized basis.

Privatization is part of this return to *laissez-faire* and its implicit faith in the ability of the market mechanism to achieve efficiency.

The present UK Government has pursued a policy of disengagement from industry and has sought to relieve business of burdens that, it believes, have been placed upon it by previous governments. To this end, planning procedures have been speeded up, government requests for information reduced, requirements relating to health and safety at work modified, and so on.

In 1988 the Government announced a policy, through the Department of Trade and Industry, of encouraging a spirit of 'enterprise' throughout British industry and education. This was based on the view that part of the reason for Britain's economic problems was an 'anti-enterprise' culture where risk taking, initiative and the pursuit of profit had not been encouraged. In particular, a set of initiatives has now been launched to encourage the development of management skills through the use of outside consultancy services by small and medium businesses. The cost is partially met by the Government.

Industrial policy is more than the financial consideration of the subsidization of private (or public) enterprise and extends to government direction, persuasion and guidance.

Investment incentives

These have been a particularly important aspect of industrial policy and their form has been as tax relief or cash grants for investment. (Most recently cash grants have featured in regional policy (see below) rather than industrial policy.) Tax relief has been available throughout the UK in the form of 'capital allowances' to offset investment expenditure against corporation tax. Until 1984 manufacturing firms were eligible for 100 per cent initial (first year) capital allowance on plant and machinery and 75 per cent on buildings, i.e. 100 per cent of machinery cost and 75 per cent of buildings cost could be set against tax liability if the firm decides it is in its interests to do so. In the service industries, only expenditure on plant and machinery qualified for this allowance. Since 1978, hotels were eligible for the initial capital allowance on building costs and structural alterations, though at a lower rate (20 per cent) than that given to manufacturing. This allowance was regarded as particularly important given the high proportion of hotel investment in buildings rather than in machinery.

Such allowances could be of considerable significance in the initial difficult stages of an investment project but it is not clear just how effective such allowances have been in stimulating investment.

Over the period 1984–88 all initial (first year) capital allowances have been phased out leaving normal standard allowances for plant, machinery and buildings (including hotels). It was felt that they had encouraged 'uneconomic' and poor quality investment, and were not particularly conducive to the creation of jobs as such.

Specific firms and industries

Industrial policy has also focused on the restructuring and support of particular firms and industries. Industries such as cotton and shipbuilding have long been subject to government intervention in order to concentrate production in fewer but more efficient units. Governments have tried to ease their decline by encouraging investment in new processes and rationalization of the industries.

Certain other firms and industries with good long-term profit and growth prospects have been singled out for support. They have been industries which have faced short-term difficulties in being unable to acquire the necessary heavy capital investment or long-term investment for technologically-based developments (aero-engines, microelectronics, etc.). Additionally firms and industries which could be significant exporters or employers have been supported (vehicle assembly and tourism).

Many of these firms which came, as a result, into full or partial government ownership, were transferred to the National Enterprise Board (NEB), now part of the British Technology Group. The NEB was established by a Labour Government in 1975 with the object of promoting industrial efficiency and competitiveness. Initially it was intended that it should acquire financial interests in some of the largest manufacturing firms and thus exert considerable influence over the whole economy. Its role in practice was much less dramatic and it has acted as a catalyst in providing investment finance and managerial help to new and existing firms in the forefront of the development of new technologies in particular. The NEB has now divested itself of most of the assets it has owned, including in 1984, the sale of Inmos (microchip manufacture). It is now concentrating on providing finance and expertise for small innovative firms. The NEB's predecessor, the Industrial Reorganisation Corporation (IRC) 1967–71, acted in a similar catalytic way and encouraged the re-structuring of industry through merger. In particular the IRC was largely reponsible for the merger of separate companies to become British Leyland.

Under the Industrial Development Act of 1982 (Section 8) the Government has wide discretion to give financial assistance anywhere in the UK to 'major (manufacturing) projects which are in the national interest'. Section 8 grant assistance may be especially useful in encouraging investment in the UK by firms which might otherwise locate abroad.

Development of Tourism Act 1969[30]

The hotel industry in the UK has been given considerable financial assistance in the past; financial assistance continues on a limited scale. The Development of Tourism Act 1969, which applied to England, Scotland and Wales, established a network of tourist organizations. These were the British Tourist Authority (BTA) which has responsibility for promoting Britain to overseas visitors, the English Tourist Board (ETB), the Wales Tourist Board (WTB) and the Scottish Tourist Board (STB), which had responsibility for promoting their own countries to British tourists. Some re-organization and clarification of roles occurred during 1983–4 but the broad structure remains.[31] The organizations are statutory bodies and are funded by government; the hotel and catering industry (at least in part) will have benefited from any success the organizations have had in encouraging tourism in Britain.

Part II of the Act introduced the Hotel Development Incentive Scheme (HDIS).[32] The scheme was designed to rapidly improve the stock of hotel accommodation in Britain and gave grants and loans to meet part of the cost of building new hotels and extensions and the installation of fixed equipment such as lifts, bathrooms and central heating. To qualify for assistance, hotels had to meet certain minimum requirements such as having at least ten bedrooms, provide breakfasts and evening meals, and provide evening meals every day of the week. Projects were to be started between 1968 and 1971 and completed by March 1973.

The scheme was administered by the three national tourist boards and over £52m in grants was paid out (loan payments were relatively small). Over 70,000 new hotel bedrooms were added to the stock in Britain (over 50,000 in England and nearly 20,000 in London) and many of the largest London 'flagship' hotels were built under this scheme.[33] (See Table 63 in Chapter 7 for effects on annual rate of hotel building.) Considerable improvements were made to a number of existing hotels, especially in the form of private bathrooms.

The initial result of the scheme was to create a surplus of hotel accommodation in particular locations such as London and Liverpool. The restricted growth in the number of visitors 1974–6, coincided with the availability of the new hotel stock. The excess supply led to price-cutting and 'tariff wars' to raise occupancy levels.

A number of 'new' firms were attracted into the hotel industry by the government grants. Some were property developers and some may have had little sympathy with or understanding of the hotel business. Some of the finished projects were therefore not particularly good hotels.

Breweries such as Vaux (Swallow Hotels) were attracted into the industry by the scheme and existing hotel companies such as Centre and Strand (J Lyons) accelerated their existing hotel building programme.

Because of the time limit on the scheme, construction and equipment costs were forced up. Some development plans were hastily conceived and executed. Substandard work may therefore have resulted and some hotel projects were completed which, in retrospect, might have had better layouts or ranges of facilities. Some hotels were built on secondary rather than prime sites because of the cost pressures; it proved difficult to make a financial success in such locations.

The tourist boards had no discretion under the grant scheme as to which locations or markets to favour. Grants were given regardless of location, type of customer aimed at, viability of project or level of managerial expertise. Perhaps too many hotels were built in London and too many satisfied the 'upper end' of the market, rather than the cheaper, low-cost accommodation market. Like all cash grant schemes, there was no incentive or necessity to be profitable (unlike a capital allowance scheme).

In many ways this 'crash programme' of hotel development created problems but the long-term effects have probably been beneficial. The overcapacity has disappeared, the hotel industry and the standards of hotels have been transformed. The scheme led to the entry of large professional groups into the industry, groups which have done much to introduce new management approaches to the industry and raise the standard of facilities. The overcapacity in itself proved a considerable spur to the introduction of marketing techniques in the industry.

A 'less-urgent' scheme and one designed around capital allowances may have achieved the benefits of the HDIS without the short-term problems that did emerge.

Despite the ending of the HDIS, limited financial assistance continues under Section 4 of the 1969 Act. The assistance is in the form of grants (and to a lesser extent, loans) for capital expenditure on 'tourism' projects. Initially the scheme was confined to the 'assisted areas' (see below) but since 1982 it has been extended to the whole of Britain. Unfortunately this extension of geographical coverage was not accompanied by a corresponding rise in the amount of finance available. The scheme is, once more, administered by the three national tourist boards. In England during 1971–88, loans of just over £1m and grants of £67.3m were paid.[34] The distribution of grants during 1987–8 is shown in Table 75.

Small firms[35]

The importance of this sector of industry has been recognized by all

Table 75 *Grants approved by English Tourist Board by type of project 1987–8*

	£m
Leisure attractions	3.3
Health and recreation	4.5
Self-catering	1.3
Rural tourism	2.3
Tourism infrastructure	0.1
Serviced accommodation	3.3

Source: *Annual Report for the Year 1987–8* (English Tourist Board 1988).

governments since the Bolton Committee (see Chapter 3). Particular attention has been paid to encouraging small firms through, for instance, the 'Small Firms Service' of the Department of Employment. This gives advice to owners and managers of small firms and to those about to start such businesses. Governments in the UK have not felt it necessary to provide finance at favourable rates of interest to small firms, unlike the USA government agency, the Small Business Administration. There has been some response to the small firm's financial difficulties in recent years. A lower rate of corporation tax applies to small companies (25 per cent compared with 35 per cent for other companies; Budget, 1988). There is a VAT threshold (currently £22,100 turnover per year) which relieves firms below it of some of the administrative burdens associated with the tax. In 1987 traders with turnover below £¼m were permitted to delay payment of VAT until paid by the customer.

A 'Venture Capital Scheme' is designed to encourage investors to take equity-stakes in small companies. A loss on such an investment is allowable for tax purposes against income of the investor; the risk to the investor is, in this way, reduced.

The 'Business Expansion Scheme' permits in certain instances 'outside' investors in small companies to claim tax relief on their equity holdings. In 1986 companies with land and buildings forming more than 50 per cent of net assets were disqualified from the scheme on the grounds that with such asset backing they should find it relatively easy to raise money. It is feared that this might adversely affect some hotel development. A government-funded survey during 1983–4, relating to BES, had concluded, however, that hotels and restaurants had been among those facing the greatest difficulties raising alternative finance. The 'Loan Guarantee Scheme' for small businesses is designed to assist small businesses obtain loans from a number of banks and other financial institutions. The Government guarantees repayment of 70 per cent of such loans (85 per cent in some inner city areas) made to eligible small businesses; the loans are subject to relatively high interest rates, however.

There are complaints that many of these schemes are limited, cumbersome and complicated.[36] At its simplest it may be sufficient to increase the opportunities for industry and individuals to accumulate and retain funds in order to finance small enterprises. Reductions in income tax and capital gains tax are often regarded as desirable in order to allow the availability of funds to establish and grow and also to provide the incentives necessary for business-people to take the necessary risks.

Whatever the appropriate form of assistance, the rate of growth of the small firm sector would need to be much increased if a significant impact on unemployment was to be achieved.

Planning

The British experience of planning is such that it has usually been 'indicative' rather than 'imperative', i.e. it has suggested ways in which industry should develop rather than imposing targets. Important in this respect has been the National Economic Development Council (NEDC) established in 1962 as a forum for representatives of employers, employees and government to meet to discuss conditions for maximizing economic growth. A number of economic development committees for individual industries were also established in order to identify problems and opportunities at that level (e.g. the Economic Development Committee for Hotels and Catering 1966–79). Through these EDCs and subsequent Sector Working Parties, all sides of industry and government would try to identify ways to improve industrial efficiency.

NEDC has been a useful forum for dialogue between industry and government but dialogue has not been a sufficient condition for improvement. The system has been good at diagnosing the causes of poor performance but has been less able to reach agreement on remedies and go on to implement them.

Undoubtedly there is a case for some forum where a long-term view of industry and its problems is taken and which tries to provide a consistency in government attitudes and actions. A closer and deeper understanding between government and industry of needs and problems on both sides is a necessary first step to improving industrial performance.

Innovation

Given the uncertainty surrounding innovation and the high social return (compared with private return) to most successful innovations, government support for research and development is widely considered to be of great importance. Private industry may not undertake the work in view of the risk and the calculation of private returns only. It has already been noted how important government finance of research and development actually is in the UK, both through its own research establishments and through finance to private industry and other organizations.

A high proportion of this expenditure is on defence and it may be considered desirable to shift the balance towards other activities more closely related to Britain's industrial performance. The British Technology Group (NEB and the National Research Development Corporation) is a government agency that has been particularly active in encouraging and supporting private sector investment in technological innovation.

The 1988 enterprise initiatives ended most innovation grant support to individual firms and encouraged more collaborative R&D within industry itself and with education and encouraged the use of technology by firms. The start-up of small firms in high technology activities is to be encouraged through the expansion of an award scheme for research and technology. Additionally, small firms (less than twenty-five employees) in development areas will be eligible for innovation grants of up to 50 per cent of costs.

Industrial policy in the UK has been limited and piecemeal. It has changed rapidly as governments have changed and this in itself may have been destabilizing. Firms may be reluctant to make long-term decisions about investment, for instance, because of fears about changes in government policy. There has rarely been a coherent, all-embracing industrial strategy identifying those activities to be encouraged and the best manner in which that encouragement should happen. Policy has tended to be reactive in that it has been developed in response to particular crises. Industrial policy has been termed 'supportive' rather than 'innovative'.[37] It has tended to work within the existing industrial framework rather than seeking to promote significant changes in the framework itself. Such an industrial strategy which emphasizes the balance of payments and employment as the criteria for support 'is likely to give rise to a succession of dubious or wasteful projects'.

For a long time, policy has appeared to focus on 'the problems of contracting industries and some large failing firms rather than on promoting new industries'.[38] The emphasis is shifting, however, and attention is being directed to small firms and those firms involved with the 'new technologies'.

The Conservative Governments since 1979 have preferred to be less involved directly with industry than have other governments. It is acknowledged, however, that there may well be imperfections in the market which present small and technologically-based firms with special problems that may justify some government intervention.

Regional policy[39]

Since the 1930s successive governments have attempted to redress the economic imbalance between the regions of the UK. This imbalance is usually seen in the form of different rates of unemployment as shown in Table 76. Unemployment is not the only manifestation of the regional problem. Areas of above-average unemployment also usually experience net emigration, low activity rates (below-average tendency for adults to join the labour force) and low income per head.

The decline of 'old' industries such as coal, textiles and shipbuilding, on which certain regions have been dependent has undoubtedly been a cause of the problem. The decline in agricultural employment has had a similar effect.

According to this 'structural' hypothesis there is no reason to believe that new industries would be at a disadvantage if they located in the high-unemployment regions. They have not done so in numbers sufficient to reduce the regional imbalance. This failure of new firms to locate in the high-unemployment regions may be due to a lack of information about available sites, labour force skills and transport facilities or it may be because of sheer inertia – some form of government intervention may therefore be appropriate.

If, however, new firms have not located in the high-unemployment regions because they are inherently 'unsuitable' for some reason, then greater levels of government intervention may be necessary.

Form

Policy has usually taken the form of designating certain geographical areas as qualifying for government assistance. There have been various categories of such assisted areas including 'special development areas', 'development areas' and 'intermediate areas'. It was announced in 1984 that there are to be only two tiers of assisted areas – the development and the intermediate areas covering about 35 per cent of the working population.

The most important form of assistance in the assisted areas has been automatic cash grants to manufacturing for expenditure on new building works, machinery and plant. The chemical and allied industries have received nearly a quarter of these grants (1972–84). In 1988 this regional development grants scheme was ended, though selective assistance will continue. Firms in the assisted areas and inner cities will receive a higher level of assistance than firms elsewhere if they participate in the consultancy-related business initiatives announced in 1988. Small firms (less than twenty-five employees) in those areas will also be eligible for grants of up to 15 per cent towards the cost of fixed assets.

'Some service industries but not hotels or tourism'[40] did in 1984 for the first time become eligible for regional development grants. (Hotels and tourism were excluded apparently because of the availability of Section 4 grants.)
excluded apparently because of the availability of Section 4 grants.) Automatic grants will be confined to development areas and only selective financial assistance will be given in the intermediate areas (including parts of the West Midlands for the first time).

Selective financial assistance is available throughout the assisted areas under Section 7 of the Industrial Development Act 1982. Industrial activities, whether in manufacturing or services, may qualify for discretionary grants related to capital costs, job creation and training costs, provided they meet certain criteria. During 1982–3 selective assistance amounted to £131.6m compared with regional development grants of £689.5m,[41] but selective assistance has tended to assume more importance in recent years. Government departments and agencies also build premises (factories, warehouses) and provide land for sale or lease.

The creation of Enterprise Zones (since 1980) in several urban areas has meant that firms locating in them (including hotels and catering) qualified for

Table 76 *Rates of unemployment by region (UK) 1974–86*

	1974 %	*1986* %
England	4.6*	15.7*
North	2.5	12.7*
Yorkshire and Humberside	2.2	10.3
East Midlands	1.9	8.8
East Anglia	1.5	8.4
South-East	2.6	9.7
South-West	2.1	12.9*
West Midlands	3.4*	14.4*
North-West	3.7*	14.3*
Wales	3.8*	13.8*
Scotland	5.4*	18.3*
Northern Ireland	2.6	11.5
United Kingdom		

*Regions with above-average unemployment.

Source: Central Statistical Office, *Annual Abstract of Statistics, 1988* (HMSO 1988).

tax relief and were exempt from local authority rates and land development tax.[42] They are also subject to less rigorous planning procedures, and less 'interference' from government generally.

The European Community has contributed to regional policy in the form of the European Regional Development Fund, in particular. Financial assistance has been directed particularly at the assisted areas. Loans have also been available through the European Investment Bank and the European Coal and Steel Community. All the sources have helped finance tourism projects.

Rationale

Government policies have tended to support the 'work to the workers' approach rather than of encouraging labour to move to firms and industries located outside the high-unemployment regions. This is an implicit recognition of the immobility of labour and of the undesirability of 'stripping' regions of their population (especially the young and able). Such a depopulation would lead to underutilization of social capital such as roads, hospitals and schools and add to congestion in the areas to which the labour moved. Therefore it might be 'socially' more desirable to encourage work to the workers.

The existence of differences in average incomes between the regions has not attracted firms in sufficient numbers to the 'cheaper' regions.

Studies have suggested that many manufacturing firms are, in fact, 'footloose', i.e. not critically affected by costs at different locations.[43] If this is so, then government policy is not undertaken at an unacceptable cost to the firms concerned. Government policy may be beneficial in that firms may not always consider the full range of possible sites. The existence of a regional policy may draw the attention of firms to alternative sites and to sites which may well be as, or more, satisfactory than those they would have gone to otherwise.

Undoubtedly for some firms a movement to the high-unemployment regions would mean a significant addition to costs and cash grants can be seen as necessary compensation. Also, a movement to a less-than-ideal location could, if there were not substantial social or external benefits, lead to inefficient use of the nation's resources.

If government policy prevented location in the non-assisted areas (through the Industrial Development Certificate system) then it may be that even the financial incentives could not be enough to attract firms to the assisted areas. No employment would therefore be created anywhere.

A policy that sought to ensure that jobs were created through any form of government assistance could amount to the subsidization of jobs and the perpetuation of inefficient production methods. The search for new, capital-intensive methods of production may be restrained.

Cash grants aid the unprofitable as well as the profitable firm, whereas tax relief schemes are effective only for firms that earn a profit.

There is now an emphasis on selective (rather than automatic) assistance to firms locating in the assisted areas and firms already in the assisted areas no longer qualify for aid for expenditure on replacement machinery and plant.

Overall it is clear that the regional problem persists and at the least it can be claimed that regional policy has stopped it worsening. It is likely from the available studies,[44] however, that policy has played a positive role in reducing unemployment relative to the UK average.

Government and hotels and catering[45]

Industrial and regional policy in particular have been concerned primarily with manufacturing and much less with hotels and catering and the service industries generally. Certainly the same degree of financial support has not been forthcoming for services as for manufacturing.[46] The hotel and catering industry does not, either, receive the favourable treatment given by government in some other countries.[47]

Pleas for government support of this industry (and tourism) have usually been advanced on the basis of its employment-generating and balance of payments effects and its growth potential. As noted earlier in this chapter these are major elements of government macro-economic policy and it would therefore seem sensible for governments to support the hotel and catering industry. Regardless of the merits of hotels and catering, however, government policies have in practice had the effect of favouring manufacturing and discriminating against services.[48]

Regional development grants were mostly confined to manufacturing. Capital allowances were more generous to manufacturing than to services and even when a special case was made for hotels to be eligible for the building allowance it was at a lower rate than that applicable to manufacturing. With the phasing out of initial capital allowances at least the discrimination diminished.

Selective Employment Tax (1966–73) was a tax that explicitly discriminated against services. All firms were subject to the tax per employee but manufacturing industries received a full refund of the tax; services did not. The objective of the tax was to encourage employment in manufacturing at the expense of services in the belief that manufacturing was a more important sector of the economy.

Hoteliers and caterers have also regarded a particular aspect of VAT as being discriminating. Exports of goods and most services are zero-rated for VAT purposes but hotels, catering and other tourist activities are not included in this (apart from some exceptions for block bookings over 4 weeks long). 'This is tantamount to a tax on export sales'[49] which is not imposed on exports of manufactured goods. The attraction of foreign visitors to this country may therefore be made that much more difficult.

Development Land Tax (1976) has also been regarded as discriminatory.[50] This is a tax on the gain in the value of land which results when land is sold or when 'material development' begins on it. Tax liability for manufacturers who build their own factories is deferred until the land or premises are sold and does not arise when development begins. This same concession did not extend to hotels and catering but in the 1981 budget it was announced that the concession would be extended for two years to 'other types of development for the owner's use including commercial and hotel development'. This tax has now been abolished.

There have been a number of positive policies towards the hotel and catering industry, e.g. the 1969 Development of Tourism Act, the establishment of the HCITB, the HCEDC and the Wages Councils. The industry is increasingly being recognized as making a significant contribution to the economy (see Chapter 9) and further government support might be expected. There has undoubtedly been a marked interest in the tourism industry, in particular, by the current UK Government. In line with general industrial policy it has sought to remove obstacles to its development rather than to intervene directly. The nature of this interest is, in part, reflected in the transfer of responsibility for tourism from the Department of Trade and Industry to the Department of Employment in 1985. The movement towards government–industry disengagement suggests that there will not be further financial support for tourism and hotels and catering, but it may, at least, result in parity of treatment for manufacturing and services. Since the prosperity of the UK was founded on manufacturing and trade in the nineteenth century a degree of industrial puritanism has lingered based on the unfounded view that only manufacturing can create wealth and that services are in some sense a collection of 'candy-floss' industries.

If manufacturing is financially supported there may appear to be a *prima facie* case for at least equal support for services if only on the grounds of 'fairness'. The case of equal treatment perhaps becomes stronger when other governments follow such a policy. Unless the UK Government did it, unfair and unequal competition could result.

It may be, however, that manufacturing is in some way 'superior' or 'more important' than other industries.[51] Manufacturing may have greater potential for increasing economic growth rapidly, for creating high-wage employment opportunities and for export sales. A sound manufacturing base may, in itself, be sufficient for the development of a tertiary sector that supplies manufacturing with 'producer services'. Consumer services will be provided in return for the income generated by employment in manufacturing. It may, therefore, be wasteful to give financial encouragement to services. Financial support of services could be interpreted as an 'artificial' stimulation of a sector where development should 'follow on' from that of manufacturing.

Questions for essays and seminar papers

1 Discuss the view that government fiscal and financial support for the UK hotel and catering industry is neither necessary nor desirable.

2 Is there a case for including service industries in government regional policy?

3 How might government policies to reduce inflation affect the hotel and catering industry?

4 Evaluate fiscal and monetary policies as means of managing the UK economy.

5 Consider how far government industrial and competition policies are a reflection of the structure, conduct and performance model.

Practical assignment

What were the details of the last Budget and how is it likely to affect the hotel and catering industry? Find out what government financial assistance is currently available to industry in general and the hotel and catering industry in particular.

CHAPTER 9

Significance

Government policies towards industry in general and the hotel and catering industry in particular, will be a reflection of how far an industry is able to contribute towards the achievement of government economic objectives (see Chapter 8). The consideration in this chapter of the significance of the hotel and catering industry is not prompted solely by the need to present a case for government support but it is within that context that the issues are often discussed.

This chapter will seek to examine how significant the industry is, in economic terms. This will involve a consideration of both its economic strengths and weaknesses. Whether, as a result, the significance is judged to be such as to justify government support must be seen in the context of government economic objectives and of the relative significance of other forms of economic activity.

As with many other aspects of the hotel and catering industry, there is, unfortunately, little research and information about the 'significance'. More work has been carried out on the significance of tourism, however, and reference will be made to this where appropriate. There is a connection between hotels and catering and tourism (see below) but they are separate activities and can be evaluated as such.

Tourism

1 Several definitions of tourism exist but a number of characteristics common to each may be identified:[1]

- It involves the movement of people to destinations.
- It involves a stay at a destination, which is of 'a temporary, short-term character'.
- It is distinguishable from 'normal' travel-to-work activity.
- Visits occur for reasons 'other than taking up permanent residence or employment remunerated from within the places visited'.

Tourism covers more than holidaymakers and includes, for instance, people away from home for business purposes, and those visiting friends and relatives. It is common to exclude day-trippers or 'excursionists' from the definition.

Table 77 *Pattern of tourism spending in the UK 1986*

	Overseas visitors to the UK 1986	*Domestic visitors 1986*
	(% of total expenditure)	
Accommodation	32	31
Eating out	23	25
Travel within UK	9	26
Shopping	27	10
Entertainment	5	4
Other	5	3

Source: Department of Employment, *Employment Gazette* (HMSO August 1988).

Tourists, whether foreign or domestic, are served by a variety of firms including hotels and catering. The importance of the hotel and catering industry within tourism may be assessed by reference to a breakdown of tourist expenditure as shown in Table 77.

Tourist expenditure is spread widely and will include purchases of food, clothing, souvenirs, entertainment and transport services. Expenditure on accommodation and eating out is between 55 and 56 per cent of total expenditure and thus constitutes a large proportion of the total.

With respect to 'accommodation' spending, not all of it will necessarily accrue to the 'hotel' industry however widely defined. About 80 per cent of business and conference trips[2] and 50 per cent of holiday trips taken by British people in GB use the 'hotel' industry, including self-catering (1985). The accommodation industry is also used in nearly eighty per cent of overseas visits to this country.[3] The major alternative for all categories of tourist is staying with friends or relatives.

The provision of hotel and catering facilities will be an important influence on the number of tourists that visits a destination. The most significant influence will be the 'attractions' in the form of scenery, climate, heritage assets, and so on, but the 'amenities' of accommodation and catering must exist if tourism is to happen at all.[4] The amount of accommodation will, in part, set the capacity of a tourist destination and expansion of tourism may require an increase in the accommodation stock. International tourists, in particular, may be influenced in their choice of destinations by the availability and price of suitable hotels and restaurants. This was certainly part of the rationale behind the Hotel Development Incentive Scheme (see Chapter 8) and concern has been expressed on occasion[5] about the image of London hotels as being 'expensive'. Not all tourists seek accommodation within the industry, as noted earlier, but some form of accommodation is essential for significant tourism development. The existence of separate catering facilities may be less critical in influencing

Table 78 *Hotel and catering employment due to tourism*

	Estimate 1 (% of employment in each sector that arises from tourism)	*Estimate 2*
Hotels and other residential establishments	80.0 }	46.3
Restaurants, cafes, etc.	30.5 }	—
Public houses	9.0	—
Clubs	11.0	—
Catering contractors	10.0	

Sources:
1 British Travel News, No. 61 (BTA 1978).
2 J. Morrell, *Employment in Tourism* (BTA 1985).

where tourists go but it is evident from Table 77 that a high proportion of expenditure is on eating out and it will therefore be of some significance in influencing tourist choice of destination.

Given this importance of the hotel and catering industry to tourism the industry will therefore be, in part, responsible for whatever benefits and costs the phenomenon of tourism itself brings. These are issues which are discussed at length elsewhere.[6]

2 Whereas the hotel and catering industry plays an important role in tourism, the industry is not itself wholly identifiable with or dependent upon tourism. There are parts of the hotel and catering industry that may have little, if anything, to do with tourism.

Most of the accommodation sector is likely to be dependent upon tourism but even so, a proportion of income will be derived from people who are not tourists, e.g. local residents using hotel restaurants and bars. Table 78 illustrates the relative influence of tourism demand on employment in the hotel and catering industry.

Generally the catering sectors are much less dependent upon tourism than is the accommodation sector. A further indication of the importance of tourism in catering is given in the national catering survey 'Trends in Catering'.[7] It estimated that 31 per cent of main meals and 21 per cent of snacks eaten out in the commercial catering sector were consumed by British people while on a trip away from home (holiday and business).[8]

National income

The contribution of the hotel and catering industry to the output of the economy as a whole is not particularly easy to determine. The national income

Table 79 *Estimate of contribution of the hotel and catering industry to national income 1985*

	Turnover	£19.3 billion
∴	Output	£ 8.0 billion = 2.6% of GDP

Source of turnover and GDP data: Central Statistical Office, *Annual Abstract of Statistics, 1988* (HMSO 1988).

statistics refer only to the classification 'Distribution, hotels and catering; repairs' (Division 6) and not to this industry separately. Division 6 as a whole has contributed between 12.1 and 14.3 per cent of GDP at factor cost over the period 1972–86.[9] This compares with a contribution from agriculture, forestry and fishing of 1.8 per cent, from manufacturing of 24.8 per cent and education and health services of 9.2 per cent (all 1986).

An estimate of the industry's contribution to national income has been made by the HCEDC and calculated as approximately 2.5 per cent of GDP at factor cost during 1961–71.[10] Similar estimates have not been made for later periods. The same study estimates the separate contribution of 'hotels' as between 0.7 and 0.8 per cent of GDP at factor cost. A later estimation of the hotel contribution, using the same methods, put it at 0.6 per cent in 1975.[11]

It is possible to derive the value of the industry's output from published data of turnover if it is assumed that the relationship between output (or value added, i.e. sales less cost of inputs from other sectors) and turnover is 2.4:1[12] (see Table 79). This output figure can then be related to national income data.

This figure of 2.6 per cent is derived in an indirect and imprecise way but it is similar to that derived from the HCEDC study for 1961–71. The figures are not directly comparable because of the method of calculation and changes in the SIC definition of the industry.

It is clearly difficult to assess changes in the relative importance of the industry over time, though on the same basis as the above estimate, its contribution to national output has remained at 2.6–2.7 per cent between 1978 and 1981. Its rate of growth is difficult to measure in terms that will relate meaningfully to growth of other industries. Between 1980 and 1985, the industry's turnover increased by 55.1 per cent[13] whereas GDP at factor cost rose by 51.4 per cent. This could suggest that the industry is at least growing at a rate similar to that of industry as a whole and is maintaining its share of national output. The output of Division 6 as a whole rose by 62.5 per cent over the same period.

It is possible to determine more readily the importance of the industry with respect to consumer expenditure.

Consumer expenditure

Not all of the industry's output is sold to consumers since some part is sold to 'industry' (see later in this chapter) but Table 80 indicates that 'meals and

Table 80 *Consumers' expenditure on 'catering' (meals and accommodation) 1976–86*

	Expenditure at 1980 prices £m	*As % of total consumers' expenditure*
1976	7758	6.2
1977	7887	6.3
1978	7908	6.0
1979	7934	5.8
1980	7962	5.8
1981	7530	5.5
1982	7299	5.3
1983	7677	5.3
1984	7906	5.4
1985	8197	5.4
1986	8279	5.1

Source: *Annual Abstract of Statistics, 1988* (HMSO 1988).

accommodation' has reduced in importance within total consumer spending over the period 1976–86. Over these years expenditure on 'meals and accommodation' has increased by 7 per cent compared with a growth of 28 per cent in total consumer expenditure.

Despite this falling importance, spending on hotels and catering remains a significant item in household expenditure. Table 81 shows the distribution of consumer spending in 1986; the hotel and catering percentage of 5.1 per cent (from Table 80) is greater than that for the categories 'tobacco' and 'fuel and power'.

The figures in Tables 80 and 81 are derived as part of the 'national income and expenditure' calculations. An additional source of information is the Family Expenditure Survey (see Chapter 1). According to this source, expenditure on 'holidays' and 'meals away from home' amounted to nearly 7 per cent of consumer expenditure.[14]

If alcoholic drink is added to these percentage figures, their relative importance grows significantly; not all expenditure on alcoholic drink will be in public houses and clubs, however.

Employment

The significance of the hotel and catering industry as an employer has been discussed, in part, in Chapter 6. The industry is obviously an important employer.

Table 81 *Consumer expenditure by function 1986*

	% of total
Food	14.1
Alcoholic drink	7.2
Tobacco	3.3
Clothing and footwear	7.2
Housing	15.3
Fuel and power	4.9
Household goods and services	6.7
Transport and communications	16.8
Recreation, entertainment and education	9.6
Other goods and services (including meals and accommodation)	14.9

Source: *Annual Abstract of Statistics, 1988* (HMSO 1988).

Table 82 *Estimated numbers of workers per £1,000 worth of value added*

Agriculture, forestry and fishing	0.29
Manufacturing	0.74
Construction	0.60
Services	0.77
Hotels and catering	0.79

Source: Hotels and Catering EDC, *Hotels and Government Policy* (National Economic Development Office 1974).

Table 82 shows the labour content of £1,000 worth of value added or net output in various industries (1971). The figure of 0.79 for hotels and catering suggests that it is rather more likely to create employment for any rise in output than are many other industries. Table 44 in Chapter 6 illustrates the point that services generally are more labour-intensive than other economic activities. These are all 'point-of-time' figures and do not necessarily indicate what will occur as output changes over time.

The HCEDC study 'Hotels and Government Policy' also gave estimates of 'incremental labour/capital ratios'. These show the *change* in labour content per unit change in value added. The hotel and catering ratios were consistently higher than those for 'all industries'.[15]

The concept of the 'employment multiplier' also relates to 'change'. (For further discussion of the multiplier concept, see later in this chapter.) Spending

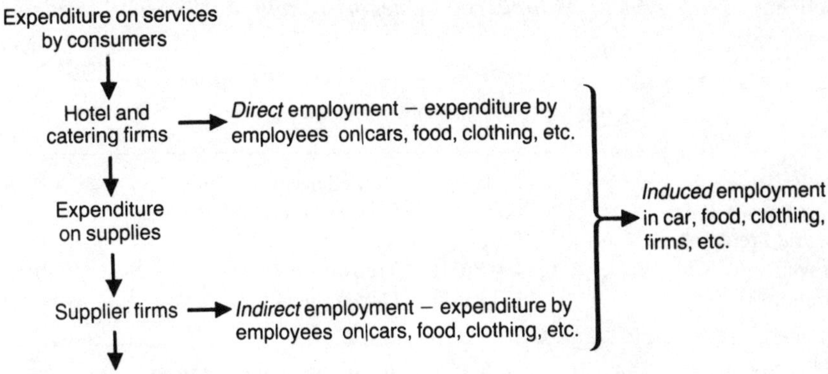

Figure 46 *Employment generated by consumer spending*

on hotels and catering services will create employment in the industry (direct employment effects) but will also be responsible for employment elsewhere in the economy. Some will be in firms supplying the hotel and catering industry (indirect employment effects). Some will be in firms that benefit from the spending that arises from the income generated by the direct and indirect employment, i.e. induced employment effects (see Figure 46).

Tourist employment multipliers are more generally available than for hotels and catering and for the whole of the UK it has been estimated that £1,000 worth of tourist spending created 2.4 jobs.[16] The ratio of direct to indirect and induced jobs was 1:0.46:1.4. At the regional level the value of the multiplier has been estimated at between 0.39 and 0.48 jobs per £1,000 worth of tourist spending compared with 0.23 jobs arising from 'general' spending.[17] At local and regional levels, employment multipliers have distinguished between categories of tourist according to type of accommodation used. From Table 83 it is evident that tourists in the 'serviced' accommodation sector are a more intensive generator of employment than are those in the self-catering and other sectors.

Calculations of employment multipliers for hotels and catering in West Durham and mid-Wales indicate that between 0.87 and 0.98 indirect and induced jobs were created for every one direct job created;[18] clearly a different conclusion from the national figures for tourism noted above. The West Durham and mid-Wales 'multipliers' (actually ratios of indirect and induced employment to direct employment) are high but not the highest in fifteen industries surveyed (food processing and chemicals and pharmaceuticals had the highest values). When the number of jobs per £1,000 worth of expenditure on the product was estimated, the rank position of hotels and catering was much higher, i.e. first in West Durham and second in mid-Wales (see Table 84).

Despite the studies relating to employment multipliers, one study has found

Table 83 *Employment multipliers by category of tourist – Tayside, Scotland 1973*

Employment generated per 1000 tourist nights			
Hotels	1.70	Rented accommodation	0.50
Guest houses	0.89	Friends and relatives	0.39
Bed and breakfast	0.91	Other	0.48
Caravan	0.34–0.36	Transit	0.12
Camping	0.33	Day-trippers	0.09

Source: M. Hanna, *Tourism Multipliers in Britain* (English Tourist Board 1976).

Table 84 *Employment multipliers for a number of industries*

	West Durham	*Mid-Wales*
	total employment per £1,000 expansion of demand	
Agriculture	0.16	0.22
Food processing	0.17	0.21
Chemicals and pharmaceuticals	0.18	0.17
Textiles	0.24	0.24
Clothing and footwear	0.31	0.33
Distributive trades	0.31	0.35
Insurance, banking and finance	0.35	0.43
'Lodging and catering'	0.36	0.38

Source: R. Hopper and L. A. France (eds), *Tourism in Rural Areas* (Northumbrian Tourist Board 1982).

'no direct evidence for turnover increases exerting a proportionate effect on employment'.[19] The study did not recognize that the employment effects of output changes may be discontinuous and time-lagged rather than immediate.

It is generally believed that jobs in hotels and catering can be provided at a lower cost than manufacturing industry because of the relatively limited need for capital investment. Where tourist development, for instance, starts from scratch, it may require very large capital investment, however, especially in roads, water and electricity supply, etc. Estimates of the capital required per employee in some countries have therefore been high.[20] One study for the British Tourist Authority concluded that in the UK 'the capital required per employee in tourist related activities is about half the national average'.[21]

The data in Table 85 suggest that the cost to government of creating jobs may

Table 85 *Cost of employment-creation in various industries*

	Highlands and Islands Development Board financial assistance per job equivalent
Manufacturing	£1438
Tourism	£5281
Fisheries	£5290
Land	£3722
Other	£1604

Source: R. Hopper and L. A. France (eds), *Tourism in Rural Areas* (Northumbrian Tourist Board 1982).

well be higher in the case of tourist activities than for other activities, at least in parts of Scotland.[22]

Also significant in economic terms, however, is the value of output resulting from each pound spent on creating a job or each pound of capital supporting a job. Those job opportunities which give a low return in this sense may be preferable to no jobs at all but this is not necessarily the most economic use of resources. Employment in manufacturing may or may not cost more per job to create or support, but it is likely that the value of output per pound of input will be higher than in hotels and catering.

The hotel and catering industry would appear to have important employment generating effects, regardless of the cost of those jobs, but as previously noted, much of the employment is part-time, casual and seasonal.[23] Some localities experience high seasonal unemployment. Pay is also very low compared with most other occupations. These features are not particularly helpful in achieving a government objective of a high income, and stable and permanently employed labour force in the economy. From the industry's own perspective, these features are likely to attract those on the periphery of the labour force and those who are 'nomadic' and 'non-conforming'.[24] Such employees may not be particularly committed to employment, the hotel and catering industry or to particular firms. These features may give rise to many problems of manpower management.

Regional aspects

The 'regional problem' was noted in Chapter 8. Much of the hotel and catering industry is already located in those regions, away from the main centres of population and industry. In this respect it may be already helping to solve the regional imbalance. Holiday and resort areas are primarily in places where there is little alternative employment and therefore the hotel and catering industry, as part of the whole tourist product, helps in creating jobs that otherwise would not exist. These areas may, by their very nature, be unsuitable

Table 86 *Location factors for the hotel and catering industry 1971*

England	0.98	East Anglia	0.87
North	1.17	South-East	1.01
Yorks and Humberside	0.94	South-West	1.31
North-West	0.93	Wales	0.98
(Fylde)	(2.83)	(North West Wales)	(2.37)
East Midlands	0.80	Scotland	1.10
West Midlands	0.81		

Source: S. Medlik with D. Airey, *Profile of the Hotel and Catering Industry*, 2nd Edition (Heinemann 1978) Chapter 5.

for other forms of industrial development; that, of course may well be an asset for encouraging a holiday industry.

Table 86 indicates the relative importance of the industry in certain parts of Britain. 'Location factors' are determined by relating the percentage of hotel and catering employment in a particular region to the national average. If the regional employment percentage is the same as the national average employed in hotels and catering, then the location factor will be 1: a figure greater than 1 indicates an above-average dependence on hotels and catering.

Northern England, the South East (including London), the South West (including Devon and Cornwall) and Scotland all have an above-average dependence on hotels and catering. Certain subregions such as Fylde (including Blackpool) have a percentage of the labour force engaged in hotels and catering which is nearly three times that of the national average.

In Gwynedd, North Wales, tourism accounts for 15 per cent of direct income compared with 18 per cent from agriculture and 11 per cent from manufacturing. Tourism in Arun (Southern England) generated nearly 6 per cent of total household income in the area and over 12 per cent of the jobs. Between 11 and 12 per cent of employment in Eastbourne and in Woodspring (South-West England) and over 20 per cent of employment in the Isle of Wight is generated by tourism.[25]

The hotel and catering industry, as part of tourism, will contribute to the re-distribution of income within the country (and between countries). Incomes earned in the more industrial (and richer) parts of the country (or world) are partly spent in the regions (or other countries) while on holiday and generate employment and incomes. The net effect of such spending is indicated in part by the multiplier; it may be though that a significant proportion of that spending will 'leak' back to generating areas (see later in this chapter).

Not all of the regions or areas experiencing high unemployment are particularly suitable for tourist development in the same way as seaside or ski resorts have been. Many declining industrial areas are heavily built-up and lack the beaches and scenery that might encourage holidaymakers. Some of these towns and cities are trying to develop different forms of tourism, often based on the 'industrial heritage', exploring old buildings, canals, machinery, as well as promoting holidays based on shopping, sport and theatre-going. The hotel and catering industry may thus contribute towards a regeneration of some 'urban' areas.[26] It is unlikely that the impact is currently substantial, however, given the nature and magnitude of inner-city problems in particular.[27]

Inner-city areas often experience high unemployment and a declining population and that population may experience high levels of poverty and social stress. The physical environment may be unsatisfactory in that it is characterized by empty buildings and poor housing conditions.

It is suggested that many of these problems are inter-linked and an industrial base would not re-establish itself in inner-city areas until physical and social conditions are improved. Tourism can provide jobs that require little training, can improve the environment and can contribute to the 'life and vitality of the city'.[28] In this way it may also, therefore, assist in encouraging industry generally to return to inner-city areas. A complete and objective evaluation of tourism's contribution to this problem has yet to be made, however.

Employment in hotels and catering and other associated tourist activities may not be a particularly attractive proposition for a labour force that has been accustomed to working, for instance, in manufacturing industries. It is arguable, too, that little impact can be made on the problems of regional employment by an industry that is characterized by seasonal and part-time employment. The problem of long-term unemployment especially among males, remains as many of the jobs are for women.[29]

Multiplier effects[30]

1 Spending on hotel and catering services is likely to have wider effects than its direct value would suggest. These wider effects are measured by the multiplier. The multiplier relates changes in output, income or employment to an initial change in spending in some sector of the economy. Multipliers may thus be:

(a) Income multipliers that measure the change in income.
(b) Output multipliers measuring the effect on output or sales.
(c) Employment multipliers.

Spending by consumers on hotel and catering services will result in income for hoteliers and caterers (direct income). Further expenditure by hoteliers and caterers on their supplies will result in further income for these suppliers (indirect income). Suppliers' income will generate further expenditure and so on. The expenditure–income cycle continues.

These continuing rounds of spending will create a further stream of income and expenditure – that of employees in each of the firms receiving the direct and indirect incomes, and this is known as 'induced' income. Figure 46 shows this principle as it relates to employment rather than income.

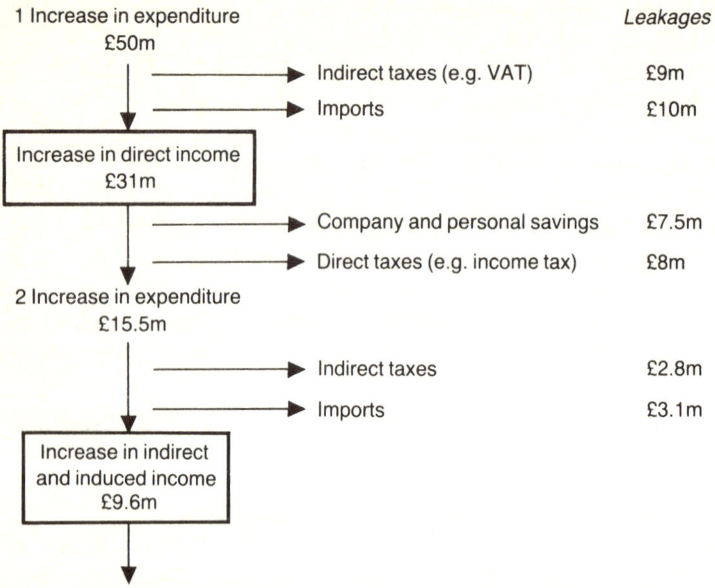

Figure 47 *Schematic representation of multiplier*

Source: Adapted from A. R. Prest and D. J. Coppock, *The UK Economy*, 4th Edition, 9th Edition, (Weidenfeld & Nicolson 1972, 1982).

2 The value of the multiplier effect will depend on several factors especially 'leakages'. These occur in the sense that not all spending will result in incomes being generated for others, as taxes will be paid to government and imports will be paid for. Thus as spending occurs along the chain of production, some is 'lost' through taxes and imports and does not generate further income and spending. In the same way some of the income received by firms and individuals will not be spent because of leakages of tax and saving (see Figure 47).

The greater these leakages are, the less is the eventual impact of any initial increase in spending. In an economy where, for instance, many goods for the hotel and catering industry have to be brought from other countries, the multiplier effects would be lower than in an economy where the hotel and catering industry could be supported from firms within the country.

3 The multiplier effect in a region or country can be given a numerical value; that value may vary according to how it is calculated. First, multiplier values may be estimated using input–output tables or an *ad hoc* model. Without expanding on these two approaches, it is generally agreed that the former approach yields more satisfactory results but the data for such an approach is not always available. The *ad hoc* models are easier to use but give a less comprehensive picture of the effects of increased consumer expenditure and generally give values 20–30 per cent lower than the input–output models.[31]

Table 87 *'Normal' income multipliers for industries in Gwynedd, North Wales 1973*

Ports	1.21
Professional and scientific services	1.08
Rail transport	0.87
Education	0.79
Quarrying	0.74
Agriculture	0.69
Insurance, banking and finance	0.65
Construction	0.56
Local government	0.51
Water	0.42
Hotels, etc.	0.36
Other manufacturing	0.30
Engineering	0.24
Textiles	0.20
Garage trade	0.13

Source: B. H. Archer, *Tourism Multipliers: the State of the Art* (University of Wales Press 1977).

Second, the total income generated may be related either to the direct income generated, i.e. to the figure of £31m in Figure 47; or to the initial increase in expenditure, i.e. to the figure of £50m in Figure 47. If the sequence was followed through in Figure 47 it would eventually result in a rise in income of £44.5m, i.e. the sum of all those amounts in the boxes. If this is related to £50m, a multiplier value of 0.89 results; this may be referred to as the 'normal' multiplier which is 'adopted by most economists'.[32] Relating £44.5m to the £31m would result in a value of 1.45, i.e. a 'ratio' multiplier. Confusion may arise unless it is clear which type of multiplier is being discussed.

4 Multiplier values for tourism, rather than for hotels and catering, have been calculated for several countries and for a number of towns and regions in the UK. Income multiplier values ('normal') for tourism at regional and local levels in the UK have been around 0.3, signifying that for every extra £1 of tourism spending, a total of 30p of income is generated.

The data in Table 87 shows the importance of this industry compared with others in parts of North Wales. Although the multiplier value is not particularly high, it needs to be set alongside the fact that tourism is second only to agriculture as a source of direct income in the region.

National multiplier values can be expected to be higher (e.g. 'normal' income multiplier 1.68–1.78 for UK)[33] because of the larger economic base and proportionately smaller leakages. Regions of economies may be expected to be less economically diverse and self-sufficient than the economy as a whole and they will be more dependent on 'imports' from other parts of the country. In the case of tourism, the employment of labour from other parts of the country may lead to some income leaving the tourist area. If firms in tourism are owned outside the tourist area there may be a further leakage in the form of profits sent to the 'foreign' owners.

Output (rather than income) multipliers have been estimated for 'lodging and catering' in West Durham and mid-Wales and were 1.43 and 1.52 respectively.[34] These values were higher than for those of most other industries considered, e.g. in West Durham, agriculture had a value of 1.20, food processing 1.36 and chemicals and pharmaceuticals 1.26.

5 Multiplier values can be of use in several ways. They indicate the effect on local incomes and employment as a result of an increase in expenditure and can be used to evaluate the amount of spending that actually stays in an area.

It is possible to compare multiplier values for hotels and catering (or more usually tourism) with those for other activities and make some decision about which is the most desirable to encourage. Policy objectives relating to the promotion of industries will not be solely dependent upon multiplier values, of course,[35] and wider issues will need to be considered – employment, productivity, tradeability, implications for other industries, etc.

It is possible to make comparisons within tourism itself by, for instance, estimating multiplier values for different types of tourist. There is no general conclusion to be drawn about the relative merits of each type of tourist in this respect but those staying in hotels often give lower values than those staying in bed and breakfast establishments or guest houses.[36] Those staying in caravans may give relatively low values. Governments and local councils could use such information when considering development of their economies.

The process of calculation of the multiplier can identify the links between hotel and catering activities and the rest of the economy. It will therefore expose the reasons why a multiplier value is low. It may be, for instance, that there is a large leakage to a supplier industry located in another region or country. Governments and local councils could try to encourage the production of that particular good within the country and thus raise the value of the multiplier.

6 Some of the limitations of the multiplier concept need to be recognized, however. One observer[37] has commented that 'the multiplier cannot be used as a reliable indicator of the benefits to be derived from tourism except under very restrictive assumptions which are unlikely to be met in the real world'. In particular, it relies upon an assumption of unemployed resources, so that any increase in expenditure will result in a rise in employment and income. If all resources are fully utilized, there can be little or no short-term increase in these variables and prices and 'imports' may well rise instead.

When it is possible in the longer term to attract resources into hotels and catering or tourism, away from other uses, the multiplier cannot in itself measure the real opportunity-cost of developing this particular activity rather than any other. If there do exist unemployed resources then hotels and catering and tourism cannot be expanded without any real cost to the rest of the economy in the form of opportunities/benefits foregone. Otherwise, a rather more comprehensive evaluation ranging beyond hotels and catering and tourism is called for. The relative worth of all alternative uses of resources needs to be assessed.

Other commentators have remarked that 'since an assumption of the employment of multipliers is that the structure of the economy remains unchanged, their value for long-term prediction is more limited'.[38] Multipliers based on input–output tables may face this problem in particular; as incomes alter, so the way in which consumers spend their money will alter, causing new input–output relationships to emerge. Industries may economize on certain inputs as production increases, some may experience supply 'bottlenecks', and long-term investment in the industry may be stimulated by rising expenditure. These and other factors will cause relationships to alter and affect the value of the multiplier.

It is widely recognized that sometimes appropriate data for multiplier calculation is not available. The problem may be particularly evident at the regional and local levels where appropriate input–output tables are not available or are only obtainable at considerable expense.

Sectoral linkages

The linkages between different parts of the economy may be traced by means of input–output analysis which is, itself, a basis for multiplier studies. Input–output tables for an economy (country or region) will show the value of sales made by each sector (individual industries, consumers, exports, etc.) to each of the other sectors, and the purchases made by each from each of the others.

The extent to which an industry purchases inputs from other industries is measured by its 'backward linkages'. This will indicate how far-reaching is its effects on the rest of the economy. A study of Bermuda estimated that 'hotels, restaurants and nightclubs' had an 'average' backward linkage (fifth highest value out of twelve industries), reflecting its purchases from local industries such as agriculture, food processing, furniture, etc.[39]

In North Wales it was calculated that an increase in demand for the 'hotel, public house, café and restaurant' sector would have the greatest impact on the output of local agriculture, shops and wholesalers, garages and the construction industry.[40] 'Forward linkages' in Bermuda were below average. There is relatively little sale of the product to other industries, unlike transport or wholesalers, for example. Sales are largely direct to the consumer. The hotel and catering industry is, however, sometimes part of the input to other industries, e.g. sales of hotel accommodation through a booking or travel agency, or catering contractors providing meals for clients in industry.

The full range of forward and backward linkages of the hotel and catering industry in the UK has yet to be examined comprehensively.

Balance of payments[41]

1 This topic was introduced in Chapter 8 and it was noted how there had been a tendency for the UK to experience deficits in the 'visible' element of the balance of payments; the value of imports of goods into the UK has tended to exceed the value of exports of goods.

With respect to 'invisibles', the UK has been more likely to experience a surplus; the sale of services, the inflow of interest, profits and dividends, etc., have exceeded the purchase of services and corresponding outflow. The sale of hotel and catering services to foreign purchasers will be largely recorded in this 'invisible' part of the balance of payments account as a 'credit' item, equivalent to an export. There may well be additional effects, however, on other parts of the balance of payments (see later in this chapter).

2 A practical difficulty arises in determining the contribution of hotels and catering to the balance of payments since it is not separately recorded as such. The effects of expenditure by foreign visitors on accommodation, catering, entertainment, shopping and transport within the UK will be recorded within the category 'travel'.

Other aspects of hotel and catering exports, the sale of contract catering services to overseas purchasers, for instance, will be recorded elsewhere in the invisible account, but are not clearly identifiable.

Earlier in this chapter it was noted that 55 per cent of overseas visitors' expenditure (excluding fares to British carriers into and out of the UK) was on accommodation and eating out; i.e. 55 per cent of the inflow of currency recorded in the 'travel' accounts. Given that not all of this accrues to the industry as such, a generous interpretation of the industry's contribution is shown in Table 88.

As an invisible export, hotel and catering earnings were, therefore, 4 per cent of all invisible exports in 1986 and 2.0 per cent of the earnings from all exports (visible and invisible). These are important contributions but it does not appear from data for earlier years that this contribution is currently growing in importance. The contribution of tourism is clearly greater at 7.3 per cent of invisible exports in 1986, and is partly attributable to the hotel and catering industry. In that sense the hotel and catering industry's contribution to the balance of payments may be viewed as considerable.

The rate of growth of hotel and catering earnings has slackened over the period 1976–82. Earnings from all invisible exports have increased by 110 per cent, earnings from all exports by 117 per cent and earnings from hotels and catering by only 79 per cent. The years 1976 and 1977 saw very rapid growth in

Table 88 *Balance of payments and the hotel and catering industry 1985–6*

	1 *Value of hotel and catering earnings from overseas visitors (approx.) £m*	2 *1 as % of invisible earnings*	3 *1 as % of visible and invisible earnings*
1985	2993	3.7	1.9
1986	3053	4.0	2.0

Source: Calculated from data in *Tourism Intelligence Quarterly*, Vol. 10, No. 1 (BTA & ETB 1988) and Central Statistical Office, *Annual Abstract of Statistics, 1988* (HMSO 1988).

hotel and catering earnings[42] – growth that exceeded that of both all export earnings and invisible export earnings.

The period following devaluation of the pound in 1967 also saw a rapid increase in 'tourism' export earnings, in excess of that of export earnings and invisible earnings generally. Growth in tourism's earnings has exceeded, over 1980–6, earnings from the export of manufactures or services.[43]

While tourism is not as important to the UK balance of payments as it is in some other countries such as Spain (21 per cent of export earnings are from 'travel'), Greece (20 per cent) or Austria (17 per cent), it is none the less an important activity.[44] The UK is certainly one of the major tourist destinations in the world; in 1985 the UK had receipts of $7.9b from international tourism compared with $9.8b in Italy, $9.6b in France, $11.9b in Spain and $6.9b in Austria.[45]

3 Given the significant contribution of hotels and catering (as part of tourism) to the balance of payments and its rapid growth during the late 1960s and most of the 1970s, governments have publicly encouraged the industry,[46] though that encouragement has not always taken the form of financial support. One of the UK's economic problems is a balance of payments one. This may be associated with a post-war decline in the UK's share of developed countries' trade in manufactured goods; this share has however, stabilised in recent years.[47] Manufactured goods still account for a large proportion of UK foreign trade, however, and to compensate for slow growth here, a more-than-proportionate growth in other items is necessary. In 1980, for instance, a 1 per cent fall in the exports of manufactured and semi-manufactured goods would have required a 12 per cent rise in the value of 'travel' export earnings to compensate for it (or a 2 per cent rise in the value of invisible export earnings).

Table 89 *UK share of world tourism 1983–7*

	% of world international arrivals	*% of world international tourism receipts*
1983	4.3	5.6
1984	4.3	6.0
1985	4.3	6.5
1986	4.1	6.1
1987 (provisional)	4.4	6.9

Source: *Tourism Intelligence Quarterly*, Vol. 10, No. 1 (BTA and ETB 1988).

It is unfortunate that the UK has been losing its share of world trade in services as well as in manufactures (from 20.9 per cent in 1960 to 12.5 per cent in 1976).[48] The UK share of world tourism arrivals and receipts is being maintained (see Table 89) after a decline between 1977 and 1982.

4 So far the data concerning hotels and catering and the balance of payments has related only to the direct visitor spending. It has been pointed out, however, that there are other less obvious effects that ought to be taken into account.[49] The hotel and catering industry (and other parts of the tourist industry) will import goods and services from overseas, e.g. food, foreign-made souvenirs, etc. Suppliers to hotels and catering will similarly draw in inputs from overseas. If foreign staff are employed and they send part of their pay home there will be an outflow recorded on the balance of payments.

That part of the hotel and catering industry which is not tourist-related will also have an impact through any imports of food, raw materials and equipment they require.

The size and value of these flows are not known with any precision, however. One estimate of the 'import-content' of earnings from overseas visitors is put at 46 per cent compared with 60 per cent for the manufacturing sector's exports.[50]

There are further, even more distant, effects resulting from tourism. Foreigners may be more inclined to buy British goods once they get home. Foreign firms may establish hotel and catering units in the UK because of the demand for hotel and catering services. Both would mean an inflow of foreign currency into the UK.

The full picture of the balance of payments effects of the hotel and catering industry will stretch beyond tourism. The non-tourism part of the industry will 'export' some of its services and will import goods and services from abroad. These effects, in particular, are not easily estimated and are

Table 90 *Travel account balance (UK) 1983–7*

	£m
1983	−87
1984	−49
1985	571
1986	−530
1987 (provisional)	−1018

Source: Department of Trade and Industry, Business Statistics Office, *Overseas Travel and Tourism, Quarter 4, 1987*, Business Monitor MQ6, 1988.

dispersed through several headings of the balance of payments accounts rather than concentrated in one category such as 'travel'.

5 Apart from its 'export-generation' effect, tourism and the hotel and catering industry may have an 'import-substitution' effect. This can arise in the sense that the UK industry may attract UK residents to holiday within this country rather than holidaying abroad. To the extent that the industry is successful in doing this, a potential drain of currency out of the UK is prevented. In a similar way the quality and price of British cars can influence the import of foreign cars; 'good' British cars could lead to 'import-substitution'. It is obviously impossible to measure the number of UK residents who are 'dissuaded' in this way from holidaying abroad but the 'travel account balance' is sometimes referred to as an indicator.

The travel account balance shows the net effect of earnings from overseas visitors to the UK and the expenditure of UK residents on visits to other countries, as shown in the travel accounts. A deficit will arise because exports (earnings from overseas visitors) are less than imports (expenditure abroad by UK residents) and a surplus will arise in the reverse situation. A surplus could be considered to reflect well on the British industry in achieving 'import-substitution' and/or 'export-generation'. The travel account was in surplus from 1968 to 1980 (inclusive) but during 1981 to 1987 it has been in deficit (see Table 90), in six of the seven years.

There may be little significance, however, in the concept of the 'travel balance'.[51] There is a direct connection between the export sales of an industry (overseas visitors) and the imports it requires to meet those sales. There is no such direct link between export sales (overseas visitors) and the import of similar services (UK residents' visits abroad). The two parts of the travel account are not directly influenced by the same economic determinants nor by the same people or companies. The relative success of the UK as a holiday destination is only partially determined by the efforts of the UK holiday industry. For many UK residents the products – a foreign holiday and a domestic holiday – may not even be considered substitutable and it would be difficult to claim that the UK holiday product is succeeding in preventing many people from holidaying abroad. The real restraint on foreign holidays may be more to do with limitations on consumer incomes and so on.

What is important for balance of payment issues is the net effect of all debits and credits and not the individual sub-balances; these are not usually reflections of economic relationships.

Output and income of other sectors

A link with other sectors of the economy has already been established in earlier discussion, especially in respect of the multiplier effect. The output of industry generally might, however, be increased in a number of other, perhaps more indirect, ways because of the existence of the hotel and catering industry.

1 The industry may give an opportunity for rest, relaxation, socializing with others and a change of surroundings – either on holiday, as a meal out or a meal at work. These features should in themselves mean that the labour force is more able, because of renewed physical strength and mental attitude, to work well. Demonstrating the existence of such relationships is by no means easy, however.

2 The provision of industrial catering may lead employees to believe the employer is caring and concerned about their welfare and thus they may have a favourable attitude towards their work and the firm. The existence of a catering service with cheap staff meals may be one reason why staff join a firm and so it acts as an aid to recruitment.

The quality of the industrial catering meal may have a direct effect on attitudes and physical strength of the labour force. Poorly prepared and presented meals can lead to dissatisfaction among the workers which may result in poor work quality and low output rates. There is some connection between food intake and a worker's output; a poor diet can be an important cause of reduced ability to work.

It is arguable that although much can be claimed for industrial catering in these respects, little can be proved.[52] It is possible that workers can gain sufficient nutritional intake from their other meals or by eating home-prepared sandwiches to perform their work adequately. The effects of eating on output may be slight compared with the effects of new technology, new machinery and re-organized work practices. These may have far greater influences on output than whether or not the worker eats a good meal during the working day. Of the workers with industrial catering facilities available less than half use them.

3 School meals may have a particular significance in as much as growing children are especially in need of meals that are nutritionally sound. Diet can

affect future growth and physical development as well as the effort and attention that pupils put into their work while at school. Since 1980 local education authorities have been relieved of the obligation to provide school meals at all (except free school meals) and if they do provide school meals they have more discretion in the prices they charge and need not adhere to nutritional guidelines. Whether this will have an unfavourable effect or not on the health and development of the adults of tomorrow will take some time to determine.

In a rather more indirect way school meals provision may help output by enabling parents to go out to work and not have to worry about providing midday meals for their children.

4 Hospital catering may have a more direct influence on the quality of the labour force. Although it is not always so that nutritionally sound meals are necessary to ensure recovery from illness, patients obviously must eat while away from home. Without an appropriate intake of food and drink, recovery may well be delayed but the importance of food in the recovery of patients may well be of much less significance than the medical care.

There are some patients, however, for whom the 'correct' diet is essential if recovery is to occur. For some illnesses the diet is part of the cure and particular expertise on the part of the hospital caterer may be called for.

5 A separate issue is whether food provided by industrial and welfare catering should be supplied at less than the market price.[53] If food and drink are supplied to consumers at prices below what they would normally expect to pay (including free meals) then the meals are subsidized. The difference between the price actually charged and what the 'normal' market price would be may be made up in the form of a subsidy by the government (in the case of school or hospital catering) or by employers (in the case of industrial catering). Usually subsidies are given in order to encourage consumers to purchase the product. If the advantages of industrial catering, for instance, are felt to be real and substantial then one way of making sure that they actually result is to persuade employees to use the facilities. If there was no subsidized low price employees might not eat 'properly' during their meal break and their output might suffer. Apart from that, low-priced (or free) meals are in themselves a reason for joining or staying with a particular firm. Low prices do not, in practice, attract more than half the staff to use the facilities. Also, it could be that employees should have enough sense of responsibility to ensure their own correct food intake without having to have a financial incentive.

A similar argument can be applied to school and hospital meals. The fact that subsidies on school meals have now been reduced, would seem to suggest that children, or their parents, need no financial encouragement to eat on the premises at midday and can be allowed to exercise their own judgement in the matter. The situation is confused, however, by the relaxing of nutritional standards for meals at the same time, and thus there is no guarantee that those meals that are provided are of the 'appropriate' nutritional standard.

It may be that some charge should be made for meals provided for patients in hospitals. The argument is that patients would have to spend on food if they were not in hospital and perhaps some contribution could therefore be expected from them towards the cost of hospital catering. On the other hand, patients are often experiencing some financial difficulties with reduced incomes during their illnesses. It could be, too, that ill people might be reluctant to seek hospital treatment or they might discharge themselves early if charges were made.

6 With respect to output, it is necessary to point to the contribution the accommodation and catering sectors may make towards 'lubricating the wheels of business'. Many people, in the course of their jobs need to be away from home for periods of time. Sales representatives, in particular, usually require to travel around the country and will rely upon the hotel and catering industry for accommodation and refreshment. Many other businesspeople need to be away from home as a 'normal' part of their occupation or in order to attend meetings, and to consult and discuss with others at conferences and so on.

In 1985 about 15 per cent of all trips (one night or more away from home) undertaken by British residents in Britain were for business or conference purposes; just over 20 per cent of overseas visits to this country was for these purposes.[54] The business and conference market is characterized by a heavier dependence on serviced (hotel, motel, guest- and boardinghouse) accommodation than is the holiday market: above 70 per cent of domestic business and conference trips compared with 19 per cent of domestic holiday trips.[55]

The catering sector may have an important function to perform in providing opportunities for businesspeople to meet and arrange business informally. It is difficult to determine the importance of such business meals to the catering industry but one survey estimated that only between 4 and 6 per cent of all expenditure on meals out in the commercial sector was on 'business/client hospitality'.[56] A recent survey found, however, that two-thirds of company managers and professional people surveyed felt business lunches are a waste of time.[57] Notwithstanding this, meals for clients (actual or prospective) may be seen as a public-relations exercise; industrial catering is increasingly being used for this purpose.

Facilities for people to exchange information at conferences are regarded as important if progress is to be made in advancing human knowledge. Conferences are of many differing sizes and for many differing purposes, ranging from political conferences to educational ones and sales conferences.[58] A large number of conferences (and business meetings and seminars) are held in hotels and even where they are held in specialist conference centres they require catering facilities and rely upon the local hotel industry to provide accommodation. Exhibitions of goods as part of the selling strategy of firms are also often held in hotels.

Without the hotel and catering industry the rest of industry in this country may well find it more difficult to function.

Table 91 *Aspects of relationships between local authorities and tourism*

	Tourist-related local authority *1 expenditure*	*2 income*	*balance*
South-West England	£4.1m	£3m	−£1.1m
Eastbourne	£1.0m	£0.7m	−£0.3m
Isle of Wight	£1.2m	£1.5m	+£0.3m
Woodspring	£0.34m	£0.36m	+£0.02m

Source: H. L. Hughes, 'A Note on Local Authorities and Tourism', *Service Industries Journal*, 3(1) (1983).

7 The income of government, both local and national, may be raised by tourist expenditure. Against whatever extra income might be generated could be set the extra costs incurred because of tourism; if the income exceeds the cost, a net benefit could be claimed.[59]

In the case of UK national government, foreign tourists are believed to contribute £500m in VAT and taxes on liquor, tobacco and petrol.[60] This is equivalent to approximately 3 per cent of all such tax revenue and less than 1 per cent of total national government tax revenue. The contribution of domestic tourists and the extra government expenditure incurred as a result of tourism are not known.

At local government level a number of estimates have been made (see Table 91). The data is such that there is no evidence of a clear and universal net benefit to government. Certainly in many areas, the rate income from tourism-related properties is itself of significance (see Table 92).

Conclusions

The hotel and catering industry is clearly of some significance in the economy. It is a form of economic activity which plays a large part in generating income and employment and contributing to the balance of payments. It would not be realistic to imagine that its significance will increase rapidly, but there is little doubt that it is an industry of the present and the future rather than of yesterday. It is an industry which is of service at one time or another, to most people within this country; eating out and going on holiday are not minority pursuits by any means. The products it offers are those which many people regard as part of the 'good life' and which add considerably to the enjoyment and fulfilment of life. The social and psychological effects of this industry should not be underestimated; in many ways it may be that these non-economic aspects of the industry are of greater significance than the economic aspects. Whatever short-comings the industry may have in making an impact on the

Table 92 *Rateable value of local authorities which is attributable to tourism hereditaments*

	% of total rateable value
Woodspring	2.5%
Arun	2.6%
Eastbourne	7 %
Isle of Wight	9 %

Sources: *Woodspring Tourism Study* (ETB 1979); *Tourism in Arun: a Research Report*, Arun District Council (Corporate Planning Unit 1978); *Eastbourne Tourism Study* (ETB 1977); and *Isle of Wight Tourism Study* (ETB 1981).

economy, it is undoubtedly a large industry and its influence is far-reaching; as such it cannot be lightly dismissed.

Questions for essays and seminar papers

1 Consider the view that a hotel and catering industry is necessary for the effective functioning of the rest of a developed economy.

2 How far is it realistic to claim that expansion of the hotel and catering industry could significantly help solve the UK balance of payments difficulties?

3 Discuss the multiplier technique as applied to studies of tourism and hotels and catering. Assess its contribution to these studies.

4 Discuss the contribution of the hotel and catering industry towards a solution of regional and inner-city problems in the UK.

5 Examine the problems encountered in attempting to discover the economic significance of the hotel and catering industry in the UK.

Practical assignment

By means of a survey, find out how important holidays and eating out are to local residents. Have they ever been on holiday or for a meal out? How often do they go? Where? What priorities do holidays and meals out have in household budgeting? Etc.

References and notes

Chapter 1

1 See R. G. Lipsey, *An Introduction to Positive Economics,* 6th Ed. (Weidenfeld & Nicolson 1983), Chapter 4.

2 See K. Hartley, *Problems of Economic Policy* (George Allen & Unwin 1977), Chapter 3.

3 J. Gershuny, *After Industrial Society?* (Macmillan 1978), Chapter 4, for discussion of the nature of services. Also, J. Gershuny and I. Mills, *The New Service Economy* (Frances Pinter 1983); H. L. Hughes, 'The Service Economy, de-industrialization and the hospitality industry', *International Journal of Hospitality Management,* 1(3) (1982). P. W. Daniels, *Service Industries: growth and location* (Cambridge University Press 1982), Chapters 1 and 2.

4 P. J. Devine, *et al., An Introduction to Industrial Economics,* 3rd Ed. (George Allen & Unwin 1979), Chapter 2.4. See also T. M. Stanback, *Understanding the Service Economy* (Johns Hopkins University Press 1979) and J. Gershuny, *op. cit.*

5 See H. L. Hughes, *op. cit.* and J. Gershuny and I. Miles, *op. cit.*

6 P. W. Daniels, *op. cit.,* Chapter 1.

7 D. Bell, *The Coming of Post-Industrial Society* (Basic Books 1976).

8 P. J. Devine, *et al., op. cit.,* Chapter 2.4.

9 H. L. Hughes, *op. cit.* and *Economic Progress Report,* No. 165 (HM Treasury 1984).

10 This argument is modified by the work of J. Marquand. See P. W. Daniels, *op. cit.,* for summary of her work, Chapter 1.

11 *Economic Progress Report,* No. 165, *op. cit.*

12 F. Blackaby (Ed.), *De-industrialisation* (Heinemann 1979). A. P. Thirlwall, 'De-industrialisation in Britain', *Lloyds Bank Review,* No. 144 (April 1982).

13 R. G. Lipsey, *op. cit.,* Chapters 31 and 42.

14 P. J. Devine, *et al., op. cit.,* Chapter 2.2 and Central Statistical Office, *Standard Industrial Classification – Revised Edition 1980* (HMSO 1979).

15 Central Statistical Office, *op. cit.* M. Sawyer, *The Economics of Industries and Firms* (Croom Helm 1981), Chapter 2.

16 Firms in the electrical and electronic engineering industry produce products

as diverse as light bulbs, meters, gramophone records, alarms, electricity generators, transformers and turbines.

17 P. J. Devine, *et al., op. cit.,* Chapter 2.7.

18 S. Medlik (with D. Airey), *Profile of the Hotel and Catering Industry,* 2nd Ed. (Heinemann 1978), Chapter 1.

19 M. Koudra, 'Industrial and Welfare Catering 1970–80', *HCIMA Review,* No. 1, 1974. *The Hotel and Catering Industry 1982* (Euromonitor Publications Ltd 1982), Section 2.

20 Price Commission, *Trusthouse Forte Hotels Ltd – Charges for Hotel Services in the UK* (HMSO 1978).

21 Price Commission, *Butlin's Ltd – Tariffs of the Main Holiday Centres in the UK* (HMSO 1979).

22 S. Medlik, *op. cit.,* Chapter 1.

Chapter 2

1 R. G. Lipsey, *An Introduction to Positive Economics,* 6th Ed. (Weidenfeld & Nicolson 1983), Chapter 1.

2 See M. Sawyer, *The Economics of Industries and Firms* (Croom Helm 1981), Chapter 10.

3 See P. J. Devine *et al., An Introduction to Industrial Economics,* 3rd Ed. (Allen & Unwin 1979), Chapter 8.3; R. G. Lipsey, *op. cit.,* Chapter 23; W. J. Baumol, *Economic Theory and Operations Analysis,* 2nd Ed. (Prentice-Hall 1965), Chapter 16.

4 R. G. Lipsey, *op. cit.,* Chapter 23; D. Burningham (Ed.), *Understanding Economics,* (Macmillan 1978), Chapters 2 and 8; P. Donaldson, *Economics of the Real World* (BBC & Penguin Books 1973), Chapters 2 and 11; P. A. Samuelson, *Economics,* 6th Ed. (McGraw-Hill 1964), Chapter 3; P. J. Devine, *et al., op. cit.,* Chapter 8; W. J. Baumol and A. S. Blinder, *Economics: Principles and Policy* (Harcourt, Brace & Jovanovich 1979), Chapter 23 and appendix for a full discussion of this and the several facets of allocative efficiency.

5 For further discussion of utility and the theory of demand, see R. G. Lipsey, *op. cit.,* Part 3; Baumol, *op. cit.,* Chapter 9. Further theoretical aspects of demand (including indifference and revealed preference analysis) are discussed in these references but it is not felt that it would be particularly productive to pursue these concepts in this book.

6 R. G. Lipsey, *op. cit.,* page 165.

7 See R. G. Lipsey, *op. cit.,* Chapter 15; W. G. Baumol, *op. cit.,* Chapter 10; and J. L. Pappas, E. Brigham and B. Shipley, *Managerial Economics,* UK Ed. (Holt, Rinehart & Winston 1983), Chapters 5 and 6, where some of the

problems encountered in determining and constructing demand curves are discussed.

8 See the special case of the 'cobweb' which might have some application to the hotel and catering markets as temporary excess demand or supply exist. R. G. Lipsey, *op. cit.*, appendix to Chapter 10.

9 This is a version of arc elasticity. For a more thorough exposition of elasticity formulae, see R. G. Lipsey, *op. cit.*, Chapter 9 and appendix.

10 They include: A. Peaker, 'Holiday Spending by the British at Home and Abroad', *National Westminster Bank Quarterly Review* (August 1973); S. Schulmeister, *Tourism and the Business Cycle* (Austrian Institute for Economic Research 1979); K. Nandola, M. Koshal and R. Koshal, 'Forecasting Restaurant Food Sales', *Cornell Hotel and Restaurant Administration Quarterly* (August 1982); B. Archer, *Demand Forecasting in Tourism* (University of Wales Press 1976); M. Bryn Jones, *Food Services in Britain 1970–80* (New University Education 1970); G. Young, *Accommodation Services in Britain 1970–80* (New University Education 1970). A. Edwards, *International Tourism Development Forecasts to 1990* (Economist Intelligence Unit 1979). A. Arbel, 'High energy cost and the demand for Restaurant Services – a time-series analysis', *International Journal of Hospitality Management*, 2(2) (1983). M. Ellerbrock and G. Wells, 'Tourist and Commercial Demand for Hotel/Motel Services: an empirical investigation', *Review of Regional Studies, XII* (3) (1983). See also *Hotel and Catering Skills – Now and in the Future. Part IV – Meeting Future Needs* (HCITB 1983); and S. Witt, 'A Binary Choice Model of Foreign Holiday Demand', *Journal of Economic Studies,* 10 (1) (1983).

11 G. Bleile, 'Business Cycle and Tourism Demand in Germany', *Tourist Review,* No. 3 (1983). D. Self, 'The Recession and the Hotel Industry in UK, France, Spain and USA', *International Tourism Quarterly,* No. 3 (1981). 'The Effects of the Recession on Tourism', *International Tourism Quarterly,* No. 4 (1980). D. C. Frechtling, 'Tourism trends and the business cycle: tourism in recession', *Tourism Management,* 3 (4) (December 1982).

12 A. Arbel and A. N. Geller, 'Foreign Exchange Sensitivity: How a strong currency weakens hotel revenues', *Cornell Hotel and Restaurant Administration Quarterly,* 24 (3) (November 1983).

13 A. Edwards, *op. cit.*

14 *Ibid.* The price elasticity of demand for air traffic movements into and out of UK has been estimated at an average of 2.1 and income elasticity at 2.3 with variations according to type of traffic and destination (see J. L. Pappas, *et al., op. cit.*, Chapter 6).

15 J. Quayson and J. Var, 'A tourism demand function for the Okanagan, BC', *Tourism Management,* 3 (2) (June 1982).

16 A. Edwards, *op. cit.*

17 S. Schulmeister, *op. cit.*

18 M. Ellerbrock and G. Wells, *op. cit.*

19 See also G. Akehurst, 'Is the Hotel and Catering Industry really Growing?', *Hospitality* (March 1980).

20 A. Arbel, *op. cit.*

21 M. J. Lawless and C. W. Hart, 'Forces that shape Restaurant Demand', *Cornell Hotel and Restaurant Administration Quarterly,* 24 (3) (November 1983).

22 These will include availability, speed and convenience of transport systems, amount and duration of leisure time and paid holidays, occupation, level of education, social pressures and demographic factors such as age, sex and family age and size. See some of the broader discussions such as in 'Leisure Futures', Henley Centre for Forecasting, London; 'Leisure Forecasts', Leisure Consultants, Sudbury, Suffolk; S. Medlik, *Trends in Tourism* (English Tourist Board 1982).

23 S. Medlik (with D. Airey), *Profile of the Hotel and Catering Industry,* 2nd Ed. (Heinemann 1978), Chapter 11.

24 R. G. Lipsey, *op. cit.,* Chapter 32; P. Donaldson, *op. cit.,* Chapter 11; for further discussion.

25 R. G. Lipsey, *op. cit.,* Chapter 23.

26 *Ibid.*

27 A. R. Prest, 'The economic rationale of subsidies to industries' in A. Whiting (Ed.) *The Economics of Industrial Subsidies* (HMSO 1976). H. L. Hughes, 'Is Industrial Catering Worthwhile?', *Hospitality* (March 1981). H. L. Hughes, 'Government Support for Tourism in the UK: a different perspective', *Tourism Management,* 5 (1) (1984). H. L. Hughes, 'A tourism tax – the cases for and against', *International Journal of Tourism Management,* 2 (3) (1981).

28 W. J. Baumol, *op. cit.,* Chapter 16. P. Donaldson, *op. cit.,* Chapter 11.

29 R. G. Lipsey, *op. cit.,* Chapter 33.

Chapter 3

1 *Report of the Committee of Inquiry on Small firms,* Cmnd 4811 (HMSO 1971).

2 Business Statistics Office, *Report on the Census of Production 1985. Summary Volume, Business Monitor PA 1002* (HMSO 1988).

3 P. J. Devine *et al.*, *An Introduction to Industrial Economics*, 3rd Ed. (George Allen & Unwin 1979), Chapter 3; Business Statistics Office (1988), *op. cit.*

4 The Wilson Committee, (*Interim Report of the Committee to Review the*

Functioning of Financial Institutions (HMSO 1979)) could find no evidence to suggest that the decline was continuing. Census of Production figures show an apparent increase in the number and relative importance of small manufacturing firms (1973–85).

5 Business Statistics Office (1988), *op. cit.*

6 *Ibid.*

7 A. Rogers and D. Phipps, *Economics for the Hotel and Catering Industry* (Barrie & Jenkins 1977); Appendices 4B5, 4B6 and 4B7.

8 C. Ryan, *An Introduction to Hotel and Catering Economics* (Stanley Thornes 1980), Chapter 7.

9 *Restaurants and Fast Food Chains,* 2nd Ed. (Keynote Publications 1980).

10 M. J. Lawless and C. W. Hart, 'Forces that Shape Restaurant Demand', *Cornell Hotel and Restaurant Administration Quarterly,* 24 (3) (November 1983).

11 G. P. Akehurst, 'The Measurement of Concentration in the Hospitality Industry', *International Journal of Hospitality Management,* 3 (1) (1984). This article also gives a useful insight into further developments in measuring concentration. S. Horsburgh (Manchester Polytechnic), unpublished data on concentration levels in hotels and catering.

12 Business Statistics Office, *Catering and Allied Trades, Business Monitor SD029* (HMSO 1981). See also Department of Trade and Industry, Business Statistics Office, *Catering Trades 1969 Statistical Inquiry* (HMSO 1972).

13 J. F. Pickering *et al., The Small Firm in the Hotel and Catering Industry – Committee of Inquiry on Small Firms – Research Report No. 14* (HMSO 1971).

14 See J. H. Dunning and M. McQueen, 'Transnational Corporations in International Tourism', ST/CTC/18, Centre on Transnational Corporations, United Nations, New York, 1982, for a related discussion of international hotel groups. Also: U. Davé, 'US Multinational Involvement in the International Hotel Sector – an Analysis', *Service Industries Journal,* 4 (1) (1984).

15 C. Stallibrass, 'Seaside Resorts and the Holiday Accommodation Industry: A Case Study of Scarborough', *Progress in Planning,* 13 (3) (1980).

16 Price Commission, *Trusthouse Forte Hotels Ltd – Charges for Hotel Services in the UK* (HMSO 1978), Chapter 3.

17 *Op. cit.*

18 See Akehurst, *op. cit.,* and S. Horsburgh, *op. cit.*

19 See, for instance, S. Medlik (with D. Airey), *Profile of the Hotel and Catering Industry,* 2nd Ed. (Heinemann 1978), Chapter 13.

20 See *Digest of Tourist Statistics, No. 11,* (British Tourist Authority 1983).

21 J. F. Pickering *et al., op. cit.,* pages 26–7.

22 K. D. George and C. Joll, *op. cit.,* Chapter 6. P. J. Devine *et al., op. cit.,* Chapter 2.

23 J. H. Dunning and M. McQueen, 'Multinational Corporations in the International Hotel Industry', *Annals of Tourism Research,* 9 (1) (1982).

24 Price Commission, *op. cit.*

25 See J. Housden, *Franchising and other Business Relationships in Hotel and Catering Services* (Heinemann 1984).

26 Price Commission, *op. cit.* Price Commission, *Butlins Ltd – Tariffs of the Main Holiday Centres in the UK* (HMSO 1979).

27 For details of firms in the hotel and catering industry see: R. Tiltscher, *The Times 1000, 1987–8* (Times Books 1987); *Hotels and Restaurants International*, 22 (7) (July 1988) and 22 (5) (May 1988); Kleinwort Grieveson Securities *Hotel Companies in the UK, Spring 1987* (1987); *Keynote Market Review: Catering* (Keynote Publications 1986); Jordan's *The British Hotel Industry* (Jordan & Son 1986); Euromonitor, *UK hotels in the 1980s* (Euromonitor Publications 1987); Euromonitor, *Institutional and Contract Catering* (Euromonitor Publications 1986); M. Quest, *A Survey of the British Hotel Industry* (Business Press International 1985); Euromonitor, *The Consumer Catering Report* (Euromonitor Publications 1986); P. Slattery and A. Roper, *UK Hotel Groups Directory 1988* (Cassell 1987); and *Business Ratio Report: The Catering Industry* (ICC Business Ratios 1988).

28 See M. Binks and J. Coyne, *op. cit.,* and G. Bannock, *The Economics of Small Firms* (Basil Blackwell 1981), Chapter 6; D. L. Birch, *The Job Generation Process,* (Massachusetts Institute of Technology, 1979); S. Fothergill and G. Gudgin, *The Job Generation Process in Britain,* Centre for Environmental Studies, Research Series, No. 32, 1979.

29 M. Binks and J. Coyne, *op. cit.,* Chapter 6; Bannock, *op. cit.,* Chapter 7. See also: *Economic Progress Report,* No. 132, April 1981 and No. 98, May 1978, (HM Treasury).

30 J. F. Pickering, *op. cit.*

31 *Ibid.*

32 J. Housden, *op. cit.*

33 See reference 27.

34 W. S. Howe, *op. cit.,* Chapter 3; P. J. Devine *et al., op. cit.,* Chapter 6; K. D. George and C. Joll, *op. cit.,* Chapter 8; P. Donaldson, *Economics of the Real World* (BBC & Penguin Books 1973), Chapter 12.

35 *Ibid.* M. C. Sawyer, *The Economics of Industries and Firms* (Croom Helm 1981), Chapter 7.

36 See Chapter 4 for further discussion of the nature of competition.

37 K. D. George and C. Joll, *op. cit.*, Chapter 3; W. S. Howe, *op. cit.*, Chapter 2; P. J. Devine *et al.*, *op. cit.*, Chapter 3; J. L. Pappas, E. Brigham and B. Shipley, *Managerial Economics,* UK Ed. (Holt, Rinehart & Winston 1983), Chapter 2.

Chapter 4

1 R. G. Lipsey, *An Introduction to Positive Economics,* 6th Ed. (Weidenfeld & Nicolson 1983), Chapters 20 and 21.

2 D. Burningham (Ed.), *Understanding Economics* (Macmillan 1978), Chapter 7. R. G. Lipsey, *op. cit.*, Chapter 21.

3 K. D. George and C. Joll, *Industrial Organisation*, 3rd Ed. (George Allen & Unwin 1981), Chapter 7; M. C. Sawyer, *The Economics of Industries and Firms* (Croom Helm 1981), Chapter 9; P. J. Devine *et al., An Introduction to Industrial Economics*, 3rd Ed. (George Allen & Unwin 1979), Chapter 6; W. S. Howe, *Industrial Economics* (Macmillan 1978), Chapter 8.

4 R. G. Lipsey, *op. cit.*, Chapter 21.

5 See S. Shaw, *Air Transport – A Marketing Perspective* (Pitman 1982), Chapter 4.

6 A. Rogers and D. Phipps, *Economics for the Hotel and Catering Industry* (Barrie & Jenkins 1977), Section 3, Chapter 5; C. Ryan, *An Introduction to Hotel and Catering Economics* (Stanley Thornes 1980), Chapter 9; P. J. Devine, *et al., op. cit.,* Chapter 6; P. Harris and P. Hazzard, *Accounting and Financial Management in the Hotel and Catering Industry,* Vol. 2, 3rd Ed. (Hutchinson 1980), Chapter 9; R. Kinton and V. Ceserani, *The Theory of Catering,* 5th Ed. (Edward Arnold 1984), Chapter 13; H. E. Lane and M. Van Hartesvelt, *Essentials of Hospitality Administration* (Reston Publishing Co. 1983), Chapter 9.

7 *Hotel Pricing Policies* (English Tourist Board 1982).

8 A. Rogers, 'Price Formation in Hotels', *HCIMA Review,* 4, Spring (1976); A. Rogers, 'Pricing in Hotels' in R. Kotas (Ed.), *Managerial Economics for Hotel Operation* (Surrey University Press 1980).

9 Price Commission, *Trusthouse Forte Hotels Ltd – Charges for Hotel Services in the UK* (HMSO 1978).

10 P. J. Devine *et al.*, *op. cit.*, Chapter 6.

11 *Ibid.*

12 F. Livesey, *Pricing* (Macmillan 1976); A. Gabor, *Pricing – Principles and Practice* (Heinemann 1977). For an interesting aspect of pricing see L. M. Kreul, 'Magic Numbers: Psychological Aspects of Menu Pricing', *Cornell Hotel and Restaurant Administration Quarterly* (August 1982).

13 R. G. Lipsey, *op. cit.*, Chapter 20; J. F. Pickering, *Industrial Structure and Market Conduct* (Martin Robertson 1974), Chapter 13.

14 K. George and C. Joll, *op. cit.*, Chapter 10; M. C. Sawyer, *op. cit.*, Chapter 8; P. J. Devine *et al.*, *op. cit.*, Chapter 5.

15 P. J. Devine *et al.*, *op. cit.*, Chapter 5; A. R. Prest and D. J. Coppock, *The UK Economy*, 9th Ed. (Weidenfeld & Nicolson 1982), Chapter 4.

16 C. Hart, G. Spizizen and D. Wyckoff, 'Scale Economies and the Experience Curve: Is Bigger Better for Restaurant Companies?', *Cornell Hotel and Restaurant Administration Quarterly*, 25 (1) (May 1984).

17 *British Business* (9 December 1983).

18 P. J. Devine *et al.*, *op. cit.*, Chapters 4 and 5; M. C. Sawyer, *op. cit.*, Chapters 12 and 13; K. George and C. Joll, *op. cit.*, Chapter 4.

19 P. J. Devine *et al.*, *op. cit.*, Chapter 5.

20 P. Donaldson, *Economics of the Real World* (BBC & Penguin Books 1973), Chapters 11, 12 and 13.

21 See further discussion of this point in R. G. Lipsey, *op. cit.*, Chapter 24.

22 S. Medlik (with D. Airey), *Profile of the Hotel and Catering Industry*, 2nd Ed. (Heinemann 1978), Chapter 8.

23 See G. Davies and J. Davies, 'The Revolution in Monopoly Theory', *Lloyds Bank Review*, No. 153 (July 1984), for discussion of the concept of 'contestable markets'. For 'workable competition', see W. S. Howe, *op. cit.*, Chapter 4; M. C. Sawyer, *op. cit.*, Chapter 15; and P. J. Devine *et al.*, *op. cit.*, Chapter 8.

24 K. George and C. Joll, *op. cit.*, Chapter 11.

25 K. George and C. Joll, *op. cit.*, Chapters 5, 9 and 10; W. S. Howe, *op. cit.*, Chapter 4; P. J. Devine *et al.*, *op. cit.*, Chapters 2 and 8; D. Burningham (Ed.), *op. cit.*, Chapter 8.

Chapter 5

1 Hotels and Catering Economic Development Committee, *Hotel Prospects to 1985: Research Findings* (National Economic Development Office 1976); S. Medlik (with D. Airey), *Profile of the Hotel and Catering Industry*, 2nd Ed. (Heinemann 1978), Chapter 11; Harris, Kerr, Forster and Co., *Trends in the Hotel–Motel Business*, USA Ed. (HKF 1978); Horwath and Horwath International, *Worldwide Lodging Industry, 1983* (Horwath & Horwath 1983).

2 Price Commission, *Butlins Ltd – Tariffs of the Main Holiday Centres in the UK* (HMSO 1979).

3 D. G. Rhys, *The Motor Industry: An Economic Survey* (Butterworths 1972).

4 Price Commission, *Tea Prices; Report No. 32* (HMSO 1978).

5 Price Commission, *Bass Ltd* (HMSO 1979).

6 R. Kotas (Ed.), *Market Orientation in the Hotel and Catering Industry* (Surrey University Press 1975).

7 R. Larmour, 'Some Problems faced by Managers in the Hotel and Catering Industry', *International Journal of Hospitality Management,* 2 (2) (1983).

8 See, for instance, P. Harris and P. Hazzard, *Accounting and Financial Management in the Hotel and Catering Industry,* Vol. 2, 3rd Ed. (Hutchinson 1980), Chapters 5 and 8. See also: R. Kotas, 'Cost Concepts in Hotel Operation' in R. Kotas (Ed.), *Managerial Economics for Hotel Operation* (Surrey University Press 1980).

9 R. G. Lipsey, *An Introduction to Positive Economics,* 6th Ed. (Weidenfeld & Nicolson), Chapter 17.

10 R. G. Lipsey, *op. cit.,* Chapter 21; J. Johnston, *Statistical Cost Analysis* (McGraw-Hill 1960); M. Sawyer, *The Economics of Industries and Firms* (Croom Helm 1981), Chapter 4; G. J. Stigler, *The Theory of Price,* 3rd Ed. (Collier-Macmillan 1966), Chapter 7.

11 R. G. Lipsey, *op. cit.,* Chapter 21.

12 Harris, Kerr, Forster and Co., *op. cit.*

13 W. J. Baumol and A. S. Blinder, *Economics: Principles and Policy* (Harcourt, Brace & Jovanovich 1979), Chapter 20; G. J. Stigler, *op. cit.,* Chapter 8.

14 C. F. Pratten, *Economies of Scale in Manufacturing Industry,* (Cambridge University Press 1971); P. J. Devine *et al., An Introduction to Industrial Economics,* 3rd Ed. (George Allen & Unwin 1979), Chapter 2.

15 C. F. Pratten, *op. cit.*

16 *Ibid;* P. J. Devine *et al., op. cit.,* Chapter 2; D. Needham, *Economics of Industrial Structure, Conduct and Performance* (Holt, Rinehart & Winston 1978), Chapter 2; J. F. Pickering, *Industrial Structure and Market Conduct* (Martin Robertson 1974), Chapter 2.

17 C. Hart, G. Spizizen and D. Wyckoff, 'Scale Economies and the Experience Curve: Is Bigger Better for Restaurant Companies?', *Cornell Hotel and Restaurant Administration Quarterly,* 25 (1) (May 1984).

18 C. F. Pratten, *op. cit.*

19 J. Milross, *et al., The Utilisation of the Cook-Freeze Catering System for School Meals* (University of Leeds 1973).

20 J. F. Pickering, *et al., The Small Firm in the Hotel and Catering Industry – Committee of Inquiry on Small Firms – Research Report No. 14* (HMSO 1971).

21 C. Hart, *et al., op. cit.*

22 *Ibid.*

23 See J. H. Dunning and M. McQueen, *Multinational Corporations in the International Hotel Industry,* Annals of Tourism Research, 9 (1), 1982, for an international perspective on the advantages of large firms.

24 C. Hart, *et al., op. cit.*

25 R. G. Lipsey, *op. cit.*, Chapter 17.

Chapter 6

1 A. R. Prest and D. J. Coppock (Eds.), *The UK Economy: A Manual of Applied Economics*, 9th Ed. (Weidenfeld & Nicolson 1982), Chapter 5.

2 For a thorough examination of service sector employment in the past, and possible future trends see: J. A. S. Robertson, J. M. Briggs and A. Goodchild, 'Structure and Employment Prospects of the Service Industries', *Research Paper No. 30* (Department of Employment 1982).

3 *Economic Progress Report,* No. 165 (February 1984).

4 For further discussion of this view see R. Bacon and W. Eltis, *Britain's Economic Problem: Too Few Producers,* 2nd Ed. (Macmillan 1978).

5 D. F. Harris and F. J. Taylor, *The Service Sector: Its Changing Role as a Source of Employment,* Research Series: 25 (Centre for Environmental Studies 1978). Also A. Rajan, 'Chips with Everything will not mean a Feast of Jobs', *Guardian* (24 October 1984).

6 O. Robinson and J. Wallace, 'Employment Trends in the Hotel and Catering Industry in Great Britain', *Service Industries Journal,* 3 (3) (1983).

7 'Employment Gazette', *Historical Supplement No. 1* (August 1984) *Employment Gazette*, November 1987.

8 *Hotel and Catering Manpower in Britain, 1984* (HCITB 1985).

9 Central Statistical Office, *Social Trends*, No. 18 (HMSO 1988).

10 S. Medlik with D. Airey, *Profile of the Hotel and Catering Industry*, 2nd Ed. (Heinemann 1978), Chapter 15; J. Barker and P. Dunne (Eds.), *The British Economy after oil* (Croom Helm 1988).

11 T. Barker and P. Dunne (Eds.), *op. cit.*

12 Central Statistical Office, *Social Trends*, No. 18 (HMSO 1988).

13 A. R. Prest and D. J. Coppock, *op. cit.*

14 See A. Witz and F. Wilson, 'Women Workers in Service Industries', *Service Industries Review,* 2 (2), 1982 for a discussion of 'occupational segregation'.

15 *Employment Gazette*, November 1987.

16 *Ibid.*

17 See also A. Witz and F. Wilson, *op. cit.*

18 *Manpower Changes in the Hotel and Catering Industry* (HCITB 1983).

19 *Employment Gazette*, November 1987; and D. Parsons, 'Tuning into Trends', *Employment Gazette*, July 1987.

20 See reference 18.

21 O. Robinson and J. Wallace, *op. cit.*

22 J. Creedy and B. Thomas (Eds.), *The Economics of Labour* (Butterworths 1982), Chapter 4.

23 See references 11 and 18.

24 *Hotel and Catering Skills: Now and in the Future. Summary* (HCITB 1983).

25 *Ibid.*

26 See extensive discussion in R. G. Lipsey, *An Introduction to Positive Economics,* 6th Ed. (Weidenfeld & Nicolson 1983), Chapter 17.

27 See reference 11 for discussion of the 'demand' factors that are believed to influence hotel and catering employment.

28 For a useful summary, see P. Donaldson, *Economics of the Real World,* 2nd Ed. (Penguin with BBC 1978), Chapter 14. See also: D. Airey and B. Chopping, 'The Labour Market' in R. Kotas (Ed.), *Managerial Economics for Hotel Operation* (Surrey University Press 1980).

29 See also the data on pay collected by a research team at the University of Surrey and published in *Caterer and Hotelkeeper.* Also: R. Taylor, D. Airey and R. Kotas, 'Rates of Pay in the British Hotel and Catering Industry', *International Journal of Hospitality Management,* 2 (3) (1983).

30 O. Robinson and J. Wallace, 'Earnings in the Hotel and Catering Industry in Great Britain', *Service Industries Journal,* 4 (2) (1984).

31 K. Johnson, 'Payment in Hotels: The Role of Fringe Benefits', *Service Industries Journal,* 3 (2) (1983).

32 See R. G. Lipsey, *op. cit.,* Chapter 26.

33 See D. Begg, S. Fischer and R. Dornbusch, *Economics* (McGraw-Hill 1984), Chapter 11; and J. Creedy and B. Thomas (Eds.), *op. cit.,* Chapter 5.

34 J. Creedy and B. Thomas (Eds.), *op. cit.,* Chapter 6.

35 R. G. Lipsey, *op. cit.,* Chapter 27.

36 D. Begg, S. Fischer and R. Dornbusch, *op. cit.,* Chapter 11.

37 R. G. Lipsey, *op. cit.,* Chapter 27.

38 A. Witz and F. Wilson, *op. cit.* Also: *Statistical Review of the Hotel and Catering Industry* (Catering Intelligence Unit of Consumer Industries Press 1984); *Hospitality*, October 1986. Principal trade unions in hotels and catering include: the General, Municipal, Boilermakers and Allied Trades Union (in the form of the specialist section: Hotels and Catering Workers Union), the Transport and General Workers Union, the Union of Shop, Distributive and Allied Workers and the National Union of Public Employees.

39 *Social Trends*, No. 18 (HMSO 1988).

40 See S. Medlik with D. Airey, *op. cit.*, Chapter 17 for further detail.
41 *Ibid.*, Chapter 19. Also: K. Johnson and T. Whatton, 'A Future for Wages Councils in the Hospitality Industry in the UK', *International Journal of Hospitality Management,* 3 (2) (1984).
42 See an analysis of the effects of abolition in C. Craig, J. Rubery, R. Tarling and F. Wilkinson, *Labour Market Structure, Industrial Organisation and Low Pay,* Department of Economics, University of Cambridge, *Occasional Paper 54* (Cambridge University Press 1982).
43 O. Robinson and J. Wallace, 1984, *op. cit.*
44 *Ibid.*
45 See the views of S. Brittan summarized in C. Craig, *et al.*, *op. cit.*
46 A. Witz and F. Wilson, *op. cit.* J. Creedy and B. Thomas, *op. cit.*, C. Craig, *et al.*, *op. cit.*
47 O. Robinson and J. Wallace, 1984, *op. cit.*
48 A. Witz and F. Wilson, *op. cit.*
49 A. R. Prest and J. Coppock, *op. cit.*
50 R. G. Lipsey, *op. cit.*, Chapter 29.

Chapter 7

1 M. Peston, *The British Economy: An Elementary Macro-Economic Perspective* (Philip Allan 1982), Chapter 3.
2 Central Statistical Office, *Annual Abstract of Statistics, 1988* (HMSO 1988).
3 *UK National Accounts, 1987* (HMSO 1987).
4 *Lloyds Bank Economic Bulletin,* No. 33 (September 1981).
5 D. Burningham (Ed.), P. Bennett, M. Cave and D. Herbert, *Understanding Economics* (Macmillan 1978), Chapter 13.
6 For further details about the 'accelerator' concept see A. R. Prest and J. Coppock (Eds.), *The UK Economy: A Manual of Applied Economics*, 9th Ed. (Weidenfeld & Nicolson 1982), Chapter 1; D. Burningham *et al.*, *op. cit.*, Chapter 13; R. G. Lipsey, *An Introduction to Positive Economics*, 6th Ed. (Weidenfeld & Nicolson 1983), Chapter 42.
7 See R. G. Lipsey, *op. cit.*, Chapter 28.
8 See *Hotel Pricing Policies* (English Tourist Board 1982), Chapter 4.
9 *Ibid.*
10 Economic Development Committee for Hotels and Catering, *Investment in Hotels and Catering* (HMSO 1968).
11 Economic Development Committee for Hotels and Catering, *Hotel Prospects to 1985* (HMSO 1976).
12 Economic Development Committee for Hotels and Catering, 1968, *op. cit.*

13 J. C. Drury and B. Murphy, 'A Study of the Financial Performance of the Hotel Industry', *HCIMA Journal* (September 1979).

14 R. Tiltscher, *An Investment Review of the UK Hotel Industry* (Sector Investments 1983), Chapter 1.

15 *Ibid.* and EDC for Hotels and Catering, 1976, *op. cit.*

16 *Ibid.* See also: D. Mathias, 'Sources and Methods of Finance' in R. Kotas (Ed.), *Managerial Economics for Hotel Operation* (Surrey University Press 1980.

17 *EDC for Hotels and Catering,* 1968, *op. cit.*

18 *Committee to Review the Functioning of Financial Institutions: Appendices,* Cmnd 7937 (HMSO 1980), Appendix 2.

19 *EDC for Hotels and Catering,* 1968, *op. cit.*

20 R. Tiltscher, *op. cit.,* Chapter 6; W. E. Sasser and R. L. Banks, 'Lender Attitudes toward Hotel Financing', *Cornell Hotel and Restaurant Administration Quarterly* (February 1976).

21 *Report of the Committee of Inquiry on Small Firms,* Cmnd 4811 (HMSO 1971). See also the Wilson Committee (reference 18).

22 *The Financing of Small Firms,* Cmnd 7503 (HMSO 1979).

23 W. E. Sasser and R. L. Banks, *op. cit.*

24 M. Binks and J. Coyne, 'The Birth of Enterprise', *Hobart Paper 98* (Institute of Economic Affairs 1983).

25 See R. Tiltscher, *op. cit.,* Chapter 6, for detail of proposed 'Hotel Investment Trust'. See also H. L. Hughes, 'Government Support for Tourism in the UK: A Different Perspective', *Tourism Management,* 5 (1) (1984).

26 R. Tiltscher, *op. cit.,* Chapter 6.

27 *Ibid.*

28 *Annual report 1987–88* (ETB 1988).

29 R. Tiltscher, *op. cit.,* Chapter 3.

30 'Tourism in Action', No. 4 (February 1984). Also: 'Tourism Monitor', *Tourism Management,* 5 (1) (1984) and H. L. Hughes, *op. cit.*

31 R. Tiltscher, *op. cit.,* and H. L. Hughes, *op. cit.*

32 *EDC for Hotels and Catering,* 1968, *op. cit.* Also: J. J. Eyster and A. N. Geller, 'The Capital–Investment Decision: Techniques used in the Hospitality Industry', *Cornell Hotel and Restaurant Administration Quarterly* (May 1981).

33 *EDC for Hotels and Catering,* 1968, *op. cit.*

34 J. J. Eyster and A. N. Geller, *op. cit.*

35 P. J. Devine, N. Lee, R. M. Jones and W. J. Tyson, *An Introduction to Industrial Economics*, 3rd Ed. (George Allen & Unwin 1979), Chapter 7.

36 See C. V. Brown and P. M. Jackson, *Public Sector Economics,* 2nd Ed. (Martin Robertson 1982), Chapter 8 and P. C. Stubbs, W. J. Tyson and M.

Q. Dalvi, *Transport Economics* (George Allen & Unwin 1980), Chapter 6. R. Sugden and A. Williams, *The Principles of Practical Cost–Benefit Analysis* (Oxford University Press 1978). T. Newton, *Cost–Benefit Analysis in Administration* (George Allen & Unwin 1972).

37 A. C. Simmonds, 'The Recreational use and value of Norfolk Beaches' in M. J. Moseley (Ed.), *Social Issues in Rural Norfolk* (University of East Anglia 1978).

Chapter 8

1 For a full discussion of macro-economics and macro-economic policies see R. G. Lipsey, *An Introduction to Positive Economics,* 6th Ed. (Weidenfeld & Nicolson 1983), Parts 8–11 (inclusive). J. Black, *The Economics of Modern Britain,* 3rd Ed. (Martin Robertson 1982). W. Godley and F. Cripps, *Macro-Economics* (Fontana 1983). R. Backhouse, *Macro-Economics and the British Economy* (Martin Robertson 1983). R. Shane, *Issues in Macro-Economics* (Martin Robertson 1984). S. Sayer, *An Introduction to Macro-Economic Policy* (Butterworth 1982).

2 See the following for discussion of the nature and effects of growth and whether growth can be equated with the standard of living. P. Donaldson, *Economics of the Real World*, 2nd Ed. (Penguin 1978), Chapters 8–10. W. J. Baumol and A. S. Blinder, *Economics: Principles and Policy*, 2nd Ed. (Harcourt, Brace, Jovanovich 1982), Chapter 35. D. Begg, S. Fischer and R. Dornbusch, *Economics* (McGraw-Hill 1984), Chapter 9. J. Harvey, *Intermediate Economics,* 4th Ed. (Macmillan 1983), Chapter 16.

3 J. M. Keynes, *The General Theory of Employment, Interest and Money* (Macmillan 1936).

4 *Economic Progress Report,* No. 169 (July 1984).

5 *Economic Progress Report*, No. 197 (August 1988).

6 R. G. Lipsey, *op. cit.*, Chapter 43.

7 F. Livesey, *A Textbook of Economics*, 2nd Ed. (Polytech Publishers 1982), Chapter 13.

8 M. H. Peston, *The British Economy* (Philip Allen 1982), Chapters 5 and 7.

9 R. G. Lipsey, *op. cit.*, Chapter 44.

10 R. G. Lipsey, *op. cit.*, Chapter 39. M. H. Peston, *op. cit.*, Chapter 7. Lloyds Bank Economic Bulletins, No. 13 (January 1980), No. 44 (August 1982).

11 R. G. Lipsey, *op. cit.*, Chapter 48.

12 R. G. Lipsey, *op. cit.*, Chapters 38 and 44. F. Livesey, *op. cit.*, Chapter 12.

13 For a review of the strategy and its effects, see *Lloyds Bank Economic Bulletins,* No. 17 (May 1980), No. 29 (May 1981), No. 34 (October 1981), No. 40 (April 1982), No. 68 (August 1984). D. T. Llewellyn and C.

Kearney, 'The British Monetarist Experiment: a preliminary assessment', *Economics XX* (1) (Spring 1984).

14 R. G. Lipsey, *op. cit.*, Chapter 44.

15 A. R. Prest and D. J. Coppock, *The UK Economy*, 9th Ed. (Weidenfeld & Nicolson 1982), Chapter 3.

16 See *The Next Ten Years: Public Expenditure and Taxation into the 1990s,* Cmnd 9189 (HMSO 1984).

17 D. Cowell, 'Service Markets: the Effects of Competition Policy and Consumer Protection', *Service Industries Journal,* 4 (3) (1984). A. R. Prest and D. J. Coppock, *op. cit.*, Chapter 4. P. J. Devine, R. M. Jones, N. Lee and W. J. Tyson, *An Introduction to Industrial Economics,* 3rd Ed. (George Allen & Unwin 1979), Chapter 11.

18 M. C. Sawyer, *The Economics of Industries and Firms* (Croom Helm 1981), Chapter 16.

19 See A. R. Prest and D.J. Coppock, *op. cit.*

20 For example, Monopolies Commission, *Beer: a report on the supply of beer* (HMSO 1969).

21 Monopolies and Mergers Commission, *Pleasurama plc and Trident Television plc and Grand Metropolitan plc*, Cmnd 9108 (HMSO 1983). MMC, *Elders IXL Ltd and Allied-Lyons plc*, Cmnd 9892 (HMSO 1986); MMC, *Foreign Package Holidays*, Cmnd 9879 (HMSO 1986); and MMC, *Trusthouse Forte plc and Enterprises Belonging to Hanson Trust plc*, Cm 96 (HMSO 1987).

22 T. T. Jones, 'Restrictive Practices in the Supply of Inclusive Tours', *National Westminster Bank Quarterly Review* (February 1984).

23 See Chapters 1, 3 and 4.

24 For example, Price Commission, *Bass Ltd* (HMSO 1979). Price Commission, *Whitbread & Co Ltd* (HMSO 1979), and the earlier: National Board for Prices and Incomes, *Beer Prices,* Report No. 136 (HMSO 1969).

25 A. R. Prest and D. J. Coppock, *op. cit.*, Chapter 4. P. J. devine *et al.*, *op. cit.*, Chapter 9. D. Morris (Ed.), *The Economic System in the UK*, 2nd Ed. (Oxford University Press 1979), Chapter 19. F. Livesey, *op. cit.*, Chapters 19–20.

26 A. R. Prest and D. J. Coppock, *op. cit.*, p. 236.

27 M. C. Sawyer, *op. cit.*, Chapter 15.

28 Quoted in: D. L. Hodgson, 'Government Industrial Policy', *National Westminster Bank Quarterly Review* (August 1977). M. C. Sawyer, *op. cit.*, Chapter 15.

29 See A. Peacock, 'Privatisation in Perspective', *Three Banks Review,* No. 144 (December 1984). M. Beesley and S. Littlechild, 'Privatisation: Principles, Problems and Priorities, *Lloyds Bank Review,* No. 149 (July 1983). A. Maynard, 'Privatising the NHS', *Lloyds Bank Review,* No. 148

(April 1983). Also, *Lloyds Bank Economic Bulletin*, No. 60 (December 1983), 'Privatisation in Progress'.

30 See A. J. Burkart and S. Medlik, *Tourism: Past, Present and Future*, 2nd Ed. (Heinemann 1981).

31 See *Tourism in Action*, No. 2, December 1983.

32 English Tourist Board, *The Hotel Development Incentive Scheme in England* (London 1976). D. Goymour, 'Now, Where's the Bedroom Glut?', *Catering Times* (September 1983).

33 For example, Cunard International, Sheraton Park Tower, London Metropole, London Tara.

34 *Annual report 1987–8* (ETB 1988).

35 'Guide to Industrial Support, No. 2, January 1984, in *British Business* (20 January 1984). See the following for an aspect of USA policy: R. M. Cantwell, 'Taking Advantage of the SBA's Programs', *Cornell HRA Quarterly*, 21 (3) (1980). For aspects of the BES in UK see *Hospitality*, July/August 1986, and *Economic Progress Report*, No. 183, March/April 1986.

36 M. Binks and J. Coyne, 'The Birth of Enterprise', *Hobart Paper 98*, Institute of Economic Affairs (London 1983), Chapter 6.

37 A. Cairncross, P. Henderson and Z. A. Silbertson, 'Problems of Industrial Recovery', *Midland Bank Review* (Spring 1982).

38 A. R. Prest and D. Coppock, *op. cit.*, p. 244.

39 P. J. Devine *et al.*, *op. cit.*, Chapter 11. A. R. Prest and D. J. Coppock, *op. cit.*, Chapter 4. 'Survey: Regional Development', *The Financial Times* (25 January 1985).

40 *The Guardian* (29 November 1984), report of speech in Parliament by Minister of State for Trade and Industry.

41 *British Business* (30 September 1983).

42 R. Botham and G. Lloyd, 'The Political Economy of Enterprise Zones', *National Westminster Bank Quarterly Review* (May 1983).

43 A. R. Prest and D. J. Coppock, *op. cit.*, Chapter 4.

44 *Ibid.*

45 See D. W. Airey and B. Chopping, 'Government Intervention' in R. Kotas (Ed.), *Managerial Economics for Hotel Operations* (Surrey University Press 1980).

46 See Horwath and Horwath (UK) Ltd, *Fiscal and Incentive Treatment of the Hotel Industry in England* (English Tourist Board 1979). Economic Development Committee for Hotels and Catering, *Hotels and Government Policy* (National Economic Development Office 1974).

47 See the related discussion in D. W. Airey, 'European Government Approaches to Tourism', *Tourism Management*, Vol. 4, No. 4 (1983).

48 For a view on the desirability of cash grant support see H. L. Hughes, 'Government Support for Tourism in the UK: a different perspective', *Tourism Management,* Vol. 5, No. 1 (1984).

49 D. W. Airey and B. Chopping, *op. cit.*

50 *Legislation Affecting Tourism in the UK* (British Tourist Authority 1982).

51 A. P. Thirlwall, 'De-industrialisation in Britain', *Lloyds Bank Review,* No. 144 (April 1982). F. Blackaby (Ed.), *De-industrialisation* (Heinemann 1979). H. L. Hughes, 'The Service Economy, de-industrialisation and the hospitality industry', *International Journal of Hospitality Management,* 1 (3) (1982).

Chapter 9

1 A. J. Burkart and S. Medlik, *Tourism: Past, Present and Future,* 2nd Ed. (Heinemann 1981), Chapter 4.

2 *British Tourism Survey* (ETB 1985). A tourist trip is defined as a stay of one or more nights away from home for holidays, visits to friends and relatives, business, conferences or any other purposes except such things as boarding education or semi-permanent employment.

3 Euromonitor, *The UK Travel and Tourism Industry 1986.*

4 See further discussion in A. J. Burkart and S. Medlik, *op. cit.,* Chapter 4.

5 For example, *Good Hotel Guide* (Consumers Association 1980).

6 See, for instance, the excellent summary in A. Mathieson and G. Wall, *Tourism: Economic, Physical and Social Impacts* (Longman 1982).

7 Ceased general publication in 1977.

8 *Trends in Catering. A Study of Eating-Out. Annual Report, April 1974–March 1975* (National Economic Development Office 1975).

9 *Annual Abstract of Statistics, 1988* (HMSO 1988).

10 Hotels and Catering Economic Development Committee, *Hotels and Government Policy* (National Economic Development Office 1974), Appendix 4/9.

11 D. W. Airey, 'Hotels and the National Economy' in R. Kotas, *Managerial Economics for Hotel Operation* (Surrey University Press 1980).

12 See reference 10.

13 See reference 9.

14 *Social Trends*, No. 18 (HMSO 1988); Department of Employment, *Family Expenditure Survey 1986* (revised) (HMSO 1988).

15 Value of 1.70 for hotels and catering and 0.45 for all industries over the period 1966–71.

16 See D. W. Airey, *op. cit.*

17 B. Archer, 'The Impact of Domestic Tourism, *Bangor Occasional Papers in Economics No. 2* (University of Wales 1973), Chapter 5.

18 R. Hopper and L. A. France (Eds.), *Tourism in Rural Areas* (Northumbrian Tourist Board 1982).

19 C. G. Hughes, *Estimating Employment in Hotels and Guest Houses – A Case Study of Pitlochry,* Tourism Planning Study, Occasional Paper 1 Department of Urban Design and Regional Planning, (University of Edinburgh 1980).

20 See A. Mathieson and G. Wall, *op. cit.,* Chapter 3.

21 J. Morrell, *Employment in Tourism* (British Tourist Authority 1982).

22 A study of grant-assisted tourist projects in Wales concluded that £8,813 of capital investment was required to create the equivalent of one full-time job in the tourism sector. No comparison was made with the cost in other industries. See B. Archer and S. Shea, *Grant-Assisted Tourism Projects in Wales: An Evaluation* (Wales Tourist Board 1980).

23 For example, a 179 per cent increase in the number of staff employed in the hotel and guest house sector in Pitlochry (Scotland) between February and August, see reference 19. Unemployment in Arun (South England) was 26.4 per cent higher in February 1977 than the preceding August and persons previously employed in tourism were 16 per cent of total unemployment, compared with 11 per cent in previous August: see *Tourism in Arun – A Research Report* (Arun District Council (Corporate Planning Unit) 1978).

24 Hotels and Catering EDC, *Staff Turnover* (HMSO 1969), p. 8.

25 B. Archer, S. Shea and R. de Vane, *Tourism in Gwynedd – An Economic Study* (Wales Tourist Board 1974); *Woodspring Tourism Study* (ETB 1979); *Eastbourne Tourism Study 1976* (ETB 1977); *Tourism in Arun: A Research Report* (Arun District Council (Corporate Planning Unit) 1978).

26 See *Tourism and the Inner City* (ETB 1980) and *Tourism and Urban Regeneration: Some Lessons from American Cities* (ETB 1981).

27 For an introduction to inner city problems see G. Hallett, *Urban Land Economics* (Macmillan 1979) and P. N. Balchin and J. L. Kieve, *Urban Land Economics,* 2nd Ed. (Macmillan 1982).

28 *Tourism and Urban Regeneration, op. cit.*

29 See M. Brownrigg and M. A. Greig, *Tourism and Regional Development,* Speculative Papers, No. 5 (Fraser of Allander Institute 1976).

30 For a thorough treatment of this topic see B. H. Archer, *Tourism Multipliers: the State of the Art,* Bangor Occasional Papers in Economics No. 11 (University of Wales Press 1977) and M. Hanna, *Tourism Multipliers in Britain* (ETB 1976).

31 S. R. Wanhill, 'Measuring the Economic Impact of Tourism', *Service Industries Journal,* 3 (1) (1983).

32 B. H. Archer, *op. cit.*

33 D. W. Airey, *op. cit.*

34 R. Hopper and L. A. France (Eds.), *op. cit.*

35 S. R. C. Wanhill, *op. cit.*

36 See, for instance, examples quoted in M. Hanna, *op. cit.*, and in A. Mathieson and G. Wall, *op. cit.*

37 J. M. Bryden, *Tourism and Development* (Cambridge University Press 1973). Much of the remaining section on the multiplier relies on this work.

38 A. Mathieson and G. Wall, *op. cit.*

39 S. R. C. Wanhill, *op. cit.*

40 P. Sadler, B. Archer and C. Owen, *Regional Income Multipliers,* Bangor Occasional Papers in Economics, No. 1 (University of Wales Press 1973).

41 For a good survey of some of the issues raised here and the problems associated with measuring tourism's contribution to the balance of payments, see: D. Airey, 'Tourism and the Balance of Payments', *Tourism International Research: Europe* (3rd Quarter 1978). See also: 'Tourism as an Export Industry in the UK', *Midland Bank Review* (Spring 1981).

42 Overseas visitors' expenditure on hotels and catering increased by 45 per cent in 1976 (on 1975) and by 33.0 per cent in 1977 (on 1976) compared with growth of invisible export earnings of 31 per cent and 12 per cent respectively and growth of all export earnings of 30 per cent and 21 per cent respectively. Source: as Table 88.

43 *Tourism Intelligence Quarterly*, 10 (1) (BTA and ETB 1988).

44 Figures for 1986 in *Tourism Policy and International Tourism in OECD Member Countries* (Organisation for Economic Co-operation and Development 1987).

45 *Ibid.*

46 See letter from Mrs M. Thatcher, Prime Minister of UK, reproduced in *Tourism in Action,* No. 1 (November 1983), part of which reads 'Tourism is already one of our biggest industries. Its overseas earnings, in excess of £3 billion, are equivalent to our total exports of road vehicles'.

47 A. R. Prest and D. J. Coppock, *The UK Economy*, 9th Ed. (Weidenfeld and Nicolson 1982), Chapter 3. In 1983 the UK experienced a deficit (of £2b) on its 'manufacturing' trade account for the first time, i.e. it imported more manufactures than it exported; see *The Guardian* (20 December 1984) (article by C. Huhne). *Economic Progress Report*, No. 193, December 1987 (HM Treasury).

48 A. R. Prest and D. J. Coppock, *op. cit.*, Chapter 3.

49 D. Airey, *op. cit.*

50 *Ibid.*

51 *Ibid.*

52 H. L. Hughes, 'Is Industrial Catering Worthwhile?', *Hospitality* (March 1981) and 'Industrial Catering – The Equal of Other Catering Activity?', *Hospitality* (October 1981).

53 *Ibid.* and see discussion in Chapter 2 of this book, section on 'Intervention in the price mechanism'.

54 *British Tourism Survey – Monthly* (ETB 1985); Business Statistics Office, *Overseas Travel and Tourism, quarter 3, 1987*, (Business Monitor MQ6 1988).

55 *British Tourism Survey – Monthly* (ETB 1985).

56 *Trends in Catering, Quarterly Report 12, January–March 1977* (National Economic Development Office 1977).

57 Reported in the *The Guardian* (7 January 1985).

58 For further information about conferences see, for instance, *The Conference and Exhibition Market in Brighton and Hove, 1976–80* (British Tourist Authority 1982). F. Lawson, *Conference, Convention and Exhibition Facilities* (Architectural Press 1981), and *The UK Conference Market 1977* (BTA 1978).

59 For a view on the validity of this and similar comparisons, see H. L. Hughes, 'A Note on Local Authorities and Tourism', *Service Industries Journal*, 3 (1) (1983).

60 *Tourism in the UK – The Broad Perspective* (British Tourist Authority and the national tourist boards 1981).

Index